BETTER CALL

LOUIS

Louis Charalambous

Hardback published November 2025
This paperback published May 2026
ISBN 978-1-917447-38-6
Text © Louis Charalambous
Typography © Bath Publishing Ltd

Published by Cinto Press (an imprint of Bath Publishing Limited)
27 Charmouth Road, Bath, BA1 3LJ
Tel: 01225 577810; email: info@bathpublishing.co.uk
www.bathpublishing.com
Bath Publishing is a company registered in England: 5209173
Registered Office: As above

EU RP (for authorities only)
eucomply OÜ
Pärnu mnt 139b-14, 11317 Tallinn, Estonia
Email: hello@eucompliancepartner.com; Tel: +3375690241

To Debbie and daughters Anna, Eva and Nina

About the author

© Jennifer Moyes Photography

LOUIS CHARALAMBOUS is a leading media lawyer who advises in major libel and privacy cases. Since the 90s he has worked with newspapers, journalists, broadcasters, politicians, editors and creatives as well as representing some of the most high-profile victims of media malpractice. He has been a partner at Simons Muirhead Burton since 2004 and is a trustee of the Kiln Theatre in London. He is also the author of two novels.

Praise for *Better Call Louis*

'An engrossing and revealing insider's cooks tour of a range of infamous media cases in all of which one of the two sides did 'call Louis'. After this you would too!' *Will Hutton, Journalist and formerly editor-in-chief of The Observer*

'It's written with great pace and clarity and – never mind the lawyering – it's really an excellent book about journalism. *Better Call Louis* offers Access All Areas credentials into some of the most high-profile media crises of our age, showing you how to respond and who to trust." *Ed Howker, Award-winning investigative producer and author*

'Louis is that rarest of beasts; a lawyer who can write crisply, insightfully and entertainingly of these clashes between the media and an array of politicians, Hollywood stars and ordinary people caught up in extraordinary events.' *Clive Coleman, Former BBC news legal correspondent*

'Charalambous is as good a writer as advocate, offering unique behind-the-scenes perspectives with real verve. A natural storyteller.' *Peter Morgan, Playwright and Screenwriter*

'Louis has dug me out of the shit on many occasions; in fact the only time I didn't call him I ended up in prison. His book is packed with juicy anecdotes of celebrity skulduggery.' *Chris Atkins, Filmmaker*

'A riveting account of why the rule of law matters and why no one, however powerful or famous, should be above it.' *Baroness Deborah Mattinson, Former Director of Labour Strategy*

'A breathtaking romp through some of the most sensational and fascinating media cases of this generation'. *John Critchley*

'Finally, we get his thrilling exposé memoir and it's jaw-dropping! Reads like a movie already! Again.' *Graham Brough*

Editor's note

Queen's Counsel and King's Counsel: the acronym QC has been retained throughout the book to reflect Counsels' status at that time.

Judgment and judgement: court judgments which have been referred to are spelt 'judgment'; all other uses of the word have been spelt 'judgement'.

Newspaper titles: these have been rendered in italics and the following titles maintained: *Daily Express, Daily Mail, Daily Mirror, Daily Record, Daily Star, Evening Standard, The Guardian, The Independent, Mail on Sunday, News of the World, The Observer, The Scotsman, Sunday Mirror, Sunday Sport, Sunday Times, Sun on Sunday, The Sun, The Daily Telegraph, The Times, The Washington Post.*

First names and surnames: first names have been used for people where the author has a personal connection to them. Surnames have been used otherwise and the author means no disrespect towards those individuals. Occasionally, people are referred to interchangeably by both first name and surname, for example Johnny Depp has been referred to as Johnny and Depp.

Contents

Preface

July 2020

L itigation is a drug and many of us are addicts.

This was going to be the best high of them all and, better still, it was the only show in town.

Literally.

Cinemas and theatres were all shut. Masks were *de rigeur*. Social distancing a must. The Covid pandemic was only just starting to lift. Trials anywhere in the land had not yet begun after lockdown earlier in March. All, that is, except this one. And not just in one court. We had to have five courts to comply with the strictures of staying several feet apart and to satisfy global curiosity. Unused for weeks, the courts smelt of beeswax as someone had been polishing whilst they stood empty. And disinfectant.

The Times called our case the "trial of the century" and the crowds outside were rooting for my opponent. I took my seat in Court 13, better known to media lawyers as the principal libel court, located in the Royal Courts of Justice on The Strand in London. It's the place where reputations are won or lost.

Our opponent stepped into court quietly. He looked both fabulous, in his immaculately tailored three-piece suit, but also faintly stupid wearing his impenetrable sunshades in the gloomy, panelled courtroom.

The eyes tell you a lot.

Perched on the same wooden bench as him, I made a sidewards glance to my left and there he was, just a few feet away from me. His is one of the best-known faces in the world and a hero to millions. And there was I, a lawyer tasked with one job these past couple of years: to prove he was a wife beater.

For once he was *sans* minders. No room for them in court. In front of him was my opponent, Jenny Afia, a partner from the go-to firm for many celebrities, Schillings, with their eye-popping hourly rate. What a gig. She appeared to placate him every few minutes when he scowled before passing her a note. It reminded me of a truculent teenager not getting his own way. He sat there alone to win back his reputation after my client, *The Sun* newspaper, called him a wife beater in no uncertain terms. Stony faced, armed only with pen and pad, Johnny Depp looked the part. Hollywood fabulous.

What was he writing on the art pad in front of him? I sneaked another look. To my surprise it was a line drawing of a skeletal face looking shocked, like Edvard Munch's *The Scream*. Nice, I thought. Hope he's screaming mad by the end of the case.

The artwork looked surprisingly good. I had to take my hat off to him, he was the epitome of cool. He was about to be taken apart in the witness box by our Queen's Counsel, Sasha Wass. Was he confident despite the evidence? Did they have a hidden witness or document that would blow our case out of the water? Or was the PR and social media war he had launched against Amber Heard, his ex-wife, enough for him? We would soon find out. At that precise moment I remember looking back over the past 27 months of this astonishing case and smiling at the line from David Byrne's song *Once in a Lifetime*: "And you may ask yourself, 'Well, how did I get here?'"

London is known by American media lawyers as a town called Sue, a haven for claimants looking to sue for libel. And they really don't like the growth in privacy law over here. The cases in this book illustrate the ups and downs of media cases from both sides. And what it is like from the inside. And life as a media lawyer. When you are in the thick of it, and news reports and features are mis-reporting your case, you just grit your teeth and get on with it, aware that it would be unwise to say anything and add more to the story, especially if it is a feeding frenzy.

This book tells the stories of what it's like acting for newspapers, TV channels and their journalists as well as victims of media malpractice who want to kill their stories or, post-publication, get redress. Some might call this a contradiction, hypocrisy or even poacher turned gamekeeper. Such a binary outlook doesn't cut it for me. I prefer to say it is more consistent to work for victims/journalism on *either* side of the divide, the 'good' guys against the 'bad' ones. In media law, there is no automatic good side versus bad side despite the efforts of many evangelists in both camps trying to persuade the public this is the case.

The stories in this book range from celebrity hysteria and histrionics, monstered or scapegoated little guys to newspapers defending free speech and high principles. It is an attempt to bring new perspectives on well-known cases. Most of them are scandalous, one way or the other.

The work of a media lawyer is never the same from one day to the next. Like criminal lawyers (which I used to be) anything can be thrown your way at any time. Back in the nineties I was described by an erudite colleague as "exuding brooding machismo and tough authority, balanced by calm support for my client" who was facing ruin and jail time. Less sure about the machismo description, I would say that staying calm, giving clients confidence and acting strategically are all pre-requisites for a good lawyer. Less bombast is always a good thing. When the proverbial was hitting the fan, as one broadcast lawyer told me, the shout would go up: "Better call Louis!" Or, as another told me when I was seen signing in at their reception, they knew the station was in trouble.

This is a look into my world after my transformation into a media lawyer and takes in the mid-nineties to the present day. Peering behind the scenes and revealing some of the secrets of what goes on and how a case is built and delivered isn't normal or the done thing. But it is necessary, especially after years of tongue biting whilst everyone else but you speculate on what is really behind the headlines.

As Jerome K. Jerome put it in his preface to *Three Men In A Boat*:

"Its pages form the record of events that really happened. All that has been done is to colour them; and, for this, no extra charge has been made."

Chapter 1

Roots, rock, reggae

"If you know your history, then you would know where you're coming from, then you wouldn't have to ask me, who the heck do I think I am."
(Bob Marley, *Buffalo Soldier*)

G rowing up a second-generation Cypriot in the terraced houses of Hackney, I never imagined I would be a lawyer. It wasn't in the mix. Five of us shared two bedrooms in my early years and the dining kitchen was also the sitting room whilst the top of the house was let out to lodgers. Heating was from a paraffin fire with weekly deliveries by the Esso Blue van with its giant hose at the back. Most of the street would queue up to fill their five-gallon containers. Earliest memories were of me trying to tune into a pirate radio station, Radio Luxembourg, on the ancient walnut and beige fabric radiogram to hear the early sixties hits.

Dad, Peter, was a barber and mum, Despina, when she could spare the time from bringing up three children, a machinist in the rag trade. She was initially a homeworker but then graduated to a small factory around the corner.

Europe was a mess, with millions of displaced refugees. Colonial neglect meant that the subjects of the British Crown, be they from Cyprus, India or Jamaica, could at least make their way to these shores and fill the labour gaps in post-World War Two Britain. Those Cypriot pioneers who came over on their very own *Windrush* boat took a circuitous route. From Famagusta they sailed first the wrong way to Alexandria in Egypt on the *SS Messapia*, before heading to the Greek port of Piraeus. From there the ship squeezed through the Corinth canal and on to Italy, disembarking at the port of Genoa. Sharing cabins with other couples to save costs, the immigrants then disembarked and made their way by train via Paris to Calais. The last leg of the seven-day marathon was a ferry to Dover and a train to Victoria.

What brought my parents here was the chance to get out of poverty. Colonial Cyprus was dirt poor for the vast majority of Cypriots back in the forties. The adventurous made it their life's ambition to come to England where they were welcomed as colonial subjects.

Mum was from a tiny village, Ardana, perched just under a half ruined medieval castle called Kantara. She had five brothers and one sister, Barbara, whom she adored. Two brothers died from malnutrition and two others, George and Chris, were in the very first wave of Cypriots to arrive here in the thirties. Chris fought for the British Army in Malaysia against the Japanese in World War Two. The fifth brother Spyros stayed in Cyprus and became a stevedore at Famagusta docks. Barbara was the only one of the seven to stay in the village. Seven days a week she milked the family goat herd and with it, made the most fabulous halloumi cheese, Cyprus' most famous export.

Mum's greatest regret was never having the opportunity to learn to read or write. There was no school in the village and at the age of eight she was sent into service, as a maid, for the rest of her childhood. She became the resident servant to a middle-class family in Famagusta. Although illiterate, her ability to wittily recount stories was unparalleled.

Dad's family were all agricultural workers. He left school at 12 to become a barber, opening a tiny shop in his mid-teens. His village was closer to Famagusta, and you could stare at the sea from the village square a couple of miles away. I recall telling one of my cousins of the same age (11) on my first visit to Cyprus how great it must be to be able to go to the seaside all summer long. He turned to me and admitted he had never made it to the coast. It brought home to me the luck I had in having parents who made the great journey across Europe and started life in London, despite having to sleep on the floor of my Uncle George's rental in Ladbroke Grove, until they had saved enough for their own place.

Back then, places like Stoke Newington (the north London bit of Hackney) and Ladbroke Grove were home to a fantastic mix of Londoners: cockneys, West Indians, Irish, Italians, Nigerians, Jews and us lot – the Greek Cypriots. For some reason I never fathomed, the Turkish Cypriots mirrored the island's separateness and gathered around Newington Green. Above all, Hackney was working class. When one of my sisters moved to suburban Kingsbury I was shocked to see semi-detached houses with drives.

Until the age of 10, I was one of three at home. Athena, the eldest, was 10 years older than me. Bright and ambitious, she didn't make it into sixth form let alone university because the old-fashioned Cypriot way was that girls wouldn't have a career as they would soon be settling down and having babies. And that's exactly what happened. She was married and a mum by the age of 19. Sheer determination and talent meant she still managed to pursue an office-based career with international travel once her children were old enough. My other sister, Mary, was also married before she was 20 and a daughter soon followed. Things didn't turn out so well for her, but she now leads a steady life on her own in an English coastal resort.

Despite these modest circumstances, mine was a happy childhood, at first with my two sisters being around and then, essentially, being the only child at home from around the time I went from my local primary school to the grammar school. By then I had got my own bedroom.

One teacher stood out at primary school: the gangly Mr Jenkins with his tall forehead and broad shoulders. As well as teaching me the power of narrative and descriptive prose, including the directive never ever to use 'nice' to describe anything ("too bland, conveys nothing") he was also the closest thing to show business I knew back then. As well as being my English teacher, he was a Black and White Minstrel, the song and dance show broadcast live by the BBC every Saturday night. In the mid-sixties, this is what passed for light entertainment. Nowadays, white men in blackface make-up, like Justin Trudeau, cause themselves lasting reputational damage.

But to us 10-year-olds, Mr Jenkins was a superstar.

By the age of 11, I was all set to go to the local secondary modern – where you did CSE's at 16 and 'O' levels in the sixth form – until Dad said no, that he'd put me in for tests at the grammar school round the corner from his shop in Marylebone where he cut the hair of the caretaker and some of the teachers.

It was a lucky break. Perhaps my luckiest.

The children, all boys, were bright and an interesting mix. Although stuffy and clinging on to its original name (the Philological School) when it suited, St Marylebone Grammar School produced some illustrious former students. The historian E. J. Hobsbawm, the writers Jerome K. Jerome and Len Deighton, as well as jazz musician, Benny Green, were all old boys.

In my time there, we had Adam Ant, a pop star who shined in the early eighties, and John Barnes, one of the greatest footballers of the era. The thing my school best taught me was the headmaster's mantra: the world is your oyster. "You can do anything" was his favourite phrase in his weekly talks to sixth formers. It bred confidence in me, a vital and necessary ingredient for life which I try to pass on to young people from disadvantaged backgrounds. Drama and chess were the two things I enjoyed most at school together with English Literature and History.

My escapes from family life and grammar school were mostly cultural: libraries for reading (hoovering up the novels of Ian Fleming and Arthur Conan Doyle as well as escaping into science fiction), the local cinemas including the flea pits for films, my record player and those of my music obsessed friends for the latest sounds, and, of course, Highbury for football.

I also had to work in Dad's shop, taking the money and asking customers if they wanted "anything for the weekend". I graduated onto shampooing the ladies in the rear of the shop which could accommodate three customers at the most. They were kind to their jug-eared shampooist, giving me half a crown tip despite damp backs from my amateur technique.

By the age of 15, I was working in a record shop in Chapel Market in Islington every weekend. My music tastes began to broaden around that time, no longer four white blokes including three with guitars. Bowie had come on the scene, and by the time I got to university it was mostly Black American and, of course, reggae. Sweet reggae music.

I had a parallel life at something called 'Greek school'. This was the Saturday morning schlepp to a North London church school where the sons and daughters of the migrants learnt to read and write Greek. My dad had been a member of a barbers' trade union in a communist trade union federation back in British ruled Cyprus, but he was also very traditional, insisting on sending me through this formal education process for several years. I learnt little, instead preferring to focus on meeting girls, an opportunity sorely lacking at St Marylebone.

And I also suffered at the hands of the teachers, sometimes literally. Some of them were pro-junta nationalists which gave me the excuse to ignore them and feel alienated. I vividly recall getting a slap to the face for mis-pronouncing a little jacket ("sakkaki") to the howls of laughter from my classmates and instead calling it a little turd ("skakkaki").

Five years earlier, in 1967, Greece, the so-called homeland for nationalist Greek Cypriots, was ruled by a military junta. Known as the Colonels, these ultra nationalist tyrants imprisoned and tortured their enemies. Giants such as Mikis Theodorakis, the singer, composer and poet loved throughout the Greek speaking world, was thrown into prison and tortured for his leftist views.

The Colonels banned Beatles records and made long hair an offence (in the early seventies we all tried to wear our hair long and I sported an unruly Afro). They also plotted to take over Cyprus with support from Cypriot ultra-nationalists.

In 1974, the elected President Makarios, known as 'Castro in the Med' by hostile US politicians for his promotion of non-aligned countries, was overthrown by their proxies. They failed to kill him despite announcing they had done so. Instead, he flew to London where communist party members, dressed all in black from top (berets) to toe (Doc Martins), formed an honour guard in the grounds of the biggest Greek Orthodox church in Camden Town, then an epicentre of the Greek Cypriot community. It was an extraordinary occasion with thousands of families crammed in every corner of the church and its grounds to see the return of Makarios, revered by the majority in the community. Even an atheist like me stood and applauded, remembering the shooting dead of my uncle's shepherd dog the previous year because he would not join the village's ultra-nationalists in condemning the chain-smoking President.

1974 was the year I grew up. I was 17 and knew from then that politics would always be a huge part of my life.

The next two or three years saw me immersed in politics, acting on the fringe in agitprop productions which carried through to university where I soon became involved in student journalism and anti-fascism. To this day, I am implacably opposed to ultra-nationalism which invariably leads to fascism of one form or another.

The things which grabbed me in my youth – fiction, music, film and football – have sustained me ever since and are, together with family and friends, my escape from the carnival and chaos which forms the bedrock of life as a busy media lawyer. My 48-hour long playlist is always with me and includes childhood favourites shared with my Stoke Newington friends: The Beatles, Jethro Tull, Small Faces to my 'most played', Gil Scott Heron, Bob Marley and Nina Simone.

* * *

University was a blast – both academically and socially.

Bradford, back in the mid-seventies, was mind blowing. Students lived in the inner city, among the stone terraces and textile mills. This was a very different working-class community. Half of the inner city was from Kashmir, the hotly disputed region claimed by both India and Pakistan. I was reading Peace Studies, a unique course founded by Quakers which had non-violent theory for social change at its heart. Other academic disciplines tried to scoff at us. But we had the last laugh. Lecturers came from South Africa, Israel, Palestine and Russia. Courses on Women's Studies, Middle Eastern conflict, Southern Africa and political theory floated my boat. We even had Joan Baez come and give us a talk. And, studying at university was much more fun than

'A' levels. I came out with a good degree wanting to write, agitate and further my academic career. These were the days of punk, the Anti-Nazi League and Red Wedge, the cultural front against Thatcherism.

In my twenties I became a DJ, mixing sounds (but never speaking) for the latest fund-raising benefit gig. Getting people onto the dance floor was a joy, up there with your team scoring a goal.

After a year working with children in care, I took a Master's degree course in Political Sociology at the Politics Department of Leeds University. I knew it affectionately as a Cook's tour of Marxist theory. I immersed myself in esoteric subjects such as correspondence between Marx and Engels on the question of Ireland. But, as well as bringing up baby, having become a dad at 24, I became preoccupied with a case called the Bradford 12.

'The 12', as we called them, were in a newly formed radical black group made up of local youth, students and wannabe intellectuals. Racist thuggery was rife in those days, often carried out by outsiders, and there were rumours of an impending invasion of National Front supporters into a predominantly Asian area of the city. These 12 young men decided to prepare for it by making petrol bombs in milk bottles and then leaving them hidden in grounds in case 'the Front', as they were known, came into the area looking for trouble. It was to form a wall of fire *!no pasarán!* barricade, they claimed.

The discovery of these Molotov cocktails led to arrests and a defence campaign quickly formed under the slogan 'Self-defence is no offence'. My role, as campaign organiser, was to act as a kind of secretariat for the campaign and the various bodies up and down the country lending support.

The campaign had to co-exist alongside the legal case which brought me into contact with two remarkable lawyers who, between them, represented the 12. Gareth Peirce and Ruth Bundey, both solicitors, gave me my first insight into how the law can be used for social change. The case became nationally famous, and I managed to watch most of it, admiring the arguments of the defence barristers who included the likes of Helena Kennedy and Geoffrey Robertson, then junior counsel. It was watching Robertson's spellbinding speech to the jury – "12 reasons why you should acquit my client" was his attention-grabbing opening line – which made me decide, there and then, to become a lawyer.

All 12 were acquitted on a self-defence basis, opening the way for more nuanced, political defences. The post-acquittal celebration was raucous. The buzz it gave me made me realise this was how I wanted to live my life.

Several of the jury joined us in the pub over the road from Leeds Town Hall after delivering their 11-1 verdict. Defeated by us jovially arguing our case and filled with beer, the juror who held out fell off his bar stool and declared that after all, he was wrong, and they were not guilty. We slapped his back and helped him back up.

I then entered two years of intensive law school with my head in law books, intent on passing the 13 exams which lay ahead. I studied hard. I was driven. The rights of others were the main thing which compelled me forwards.

However, there was a price to be paid. My relationship with my eldest daughter's mother, Sarah, came to an end. Perhaps, I reflected, I had studied too damned hard.

What was I to do with getting 'articles', the compulsory two-year apprenticeship to become a solicitor? I wrote to several criminal law practices, but training contracts were hard to come by. And then I got a lucky break.

Another Peace Studies graduate, Fred Hasson, was now working for a solicitor called John Pickering. I had seen John three years earlier in 1982 in a heartbreaking *First Tuesday* ITV documentary called *Alice A Fight For Life*. It was about Alice Jefferson, a single parent mill worker who had worked at Acre Mill, an asbestos factory in Hebden Bridge – now a bougie market town known for its *Happy Valley* connections. Alice was dying of the terrible lung cancer mesothelioma when the film was made. She was filmed in her final weeks trying to teach her children, then aged 15 and five, how to live without her. The killer disease she died from was about to become a big part of my life. And the *Alice* documentary was to become pivotal in a major case I was to take on a few years later.

John was a brilliant and fearless lawyer who gave everything for his personal injury clients, especially victims of work-induced lung diseases. He still lives in Hebden Bridge, and he had taken on Fred, a near neighbour, to be a witness tracer and statement taker despite his lack of legal training.

John agreed to interview me. Until then, it was just a two lawyer practice. To my immense joy, he said he would take me on as his first ever trainee solicitor. He liked the fact that I was political and had not gone straight into law (a fact that had harmed my other applications). He was a lifelong communist and, whilst I was never tempted to walk the Moscow or later Eurocommunist road, we had a mutual respect for each other's political standpoints.

So it was that on 1 September 1985 I walked into John's office in Oldham in my best and only suit, fresh off an early morning National Express coach over the Pennines, to start my legal career. I was quickly immersed into cases, even running some of my own. The next 15 months passed by in a whirlwind and I quickly learned my trade as a civil litigator.

But I never forgot my love of criminal law.

One night, at a university gig, raising funds for yet another threatened deportee, I bumped into Ruth Bundey who told me, amidst the music, smoking and clinking of beer glasses, that she was starting a new law firm in Leeds. She needed a trainee solicitor and asked me if I was interested in joining her.

I was so happy to be asked. And utterly torn.

John had given me my big break, and I loved working for victims of industrial disease and accidents. It gave me a huge insight into British manufacturing practices and the treatment of workers. But I couldn't resist Ruth's offer. She had fantastic cases and was the go-to lawyer if you were in trouble for political activities. And it was crime, with a political angle, which brought me into the law.

John was very good about me transferring to Ruth and I started straight away with several cases on the go. I quickly earned my spurs. Ruth was an advocate in the magistrates' courts of West Yorkshire which meant that most days I had to cover all the police station interviews. I soon realised that giving advice before an interview under arrest conditions is among the most difficult things you are called on to do as a lawyer; you are taking huge and often risky decisions in the heat of the moment and often knowing only part of the jigsaw.

Soon I was advising on major drugs cases, undercover stings by cops and murder cases. Most of all Ruth taught me to care for my clients and I don't just mean their cases. The stress of a case takes an immense toll on clients. She got that and instilled it in me.

I qualified in 1987 and became a duty solicitor, being on call for anyone needing legal advice at the cop shop or advocacy in the magistrate's court. I decided I wanted to be a criminal lawyer based in Bradford, the city where I had settled into living. I then spent a year at a rather strait-laced mixed practice law firm in Bradford, learning the art of advocacy and spending most of my time in court. But I kept in touch with John and his business partner, Anthony Coombs, another supremely talented lawyer who had studied PPE at Oxford. They were chalk and cheese in many ways but together they forged a brilliant law practice doing one thing really well: getting compensation for victims, especially victims of asbestos poisoning.

John and Anthony agreed to let me open an office in Bradford to accommodate their Yorkshire clients. The next few years saw me take on and win cases. But there was one case which really stayed with me and taught me never to take no for an answer when your opponent says they have no documents to give you that are relevant to your client's case.

It was the case of Arthur Margereson, who developed mesothelioma in late 1990. On being instructed, I rushed to see him at his home. He was a quiet, dignified man who gave me his life story despite the pain caused by the cancer. He still lived in Armley, Leeds having grown up 200 yards from where an asbestos processing factory, JW Roberts, was located. It spewed out dust and had no adequate measures to contain the fibres. Back in the 1930s Arthur, like other children, played in its grounds which provided the only open space in the otherwise packed terraced streets and it was where the tiny fibres entered his teenage lungs.

The cancer took hold when Arthur was in his sixties and he survived for just over a year. Environmental cases against companies for asbestos inhalation were unknown back then. We quickly issued the case and made an application for disclosure against JW Roberts which, whilst long closed down, was still a registered company. Why was it still registered? So that anyone suing it would be met with an empty list of documents because the company had kept none since closure. Simples.

Frustrated, I remembered back to Alice Jefferson who died aged just 48. The documentary had featured the same parent company, Turner & Newall (T&N), and how a case brought by a US bank, Chase Manhattan, had resulted in success for the building damage caused by the discovery of asbestos in its buildings and the need to strip it out. The case in the US hinged on when T&N knew about the dangers of dust inhalation and the bank was successful in proving their date of knowledge was much earlier than the asbestos manufacturer claimed.

I decided to get in touch with Yorkshire TV who had made the *Alice* documentary in case they had kept their research material and luckily their producer was able to hand me some boxes of their US research from the case. I read through it night after night, looking for an early date of knowledge which we might be able to pin on JW Roberts for environmental harm.

The documents included minutes of Board meetings of the parent company which suggested they had not made public their knowledge of how harmful the dust could be. As JW Roberts had become part of T&N I decided to issue an application against T&N for relevant documents in their possession, to pierce what is called the 'corporate veil': to seek documents held by a parent company when the employing company had retained no records.

At the first hearing in the local county court, T&N sent a big gun QC to oppose us. The local judge decided this was a major enough issue to be heard by a superior judge of the High Court and the application was adjourned.

Knowing this was now a massive fight we had on our hands, we instructed counsel and eventually the case came before Mr Justice Laws in London. I sat in court and enjoyed every minute of the hearing as Laws demolished the other side's contentions about why the parent company should not be made to give discovery of their documents to us. Even though Laws ruled in our favour, T&N continued resisting disclosure until they eventually had to concede.

The case was tried in 1995 after I left Pickerings. By then a number of other cases were waiting on this decision and at trial, Mr Justice Holland ruled decisively in his widow Evelyn's favour as she had become the plaintiff after Arthur died. In his judgment, the judge talked about T&N's conduct of the case "reflecting a wish to contest these claims by any means possible, legitimate or otherwise, so as to wear [Evelyn] down by attrition. Thus it has not just been by respect to discovery that the defendants have remorselessly persisted in taking bad points...". He described the eventual release of documents as being in "superabundance" despite their case starting with an affidavit claiming there were none.

Once the win was secured, others were able to successfully sue for environmental harm caused by cancer as far afield as South Africa. And the lesson learnt has remained: obfuscation about documents which smells wrong probably is wrong so don't take it at face value.

By the mid-nineties, however, I felt the pull of home and the capital. Together with my wife, Debbie, and our two young daughters, we decided to move to London, and I started heading south for interviews.

I'd had enough of tense police interviews, interminable delays in courts, protracted Crown Court trials and I also felt drained by the asbestos cases. The victims were either dying or terribly ill. If they had died, then you had to help pick up the pieces with the grieving family. And, I admit, I wanted something more. Something exciting.

The practice which really attracted me was a small, headline grabbing outfit called Stephens Innocent headed by a charismatic lawyer called Mark Stephens. Ros Innocent had moved to France by the time I joined but her surname was a gift to anyone with a criminal practice. In 1992, it was best known for its media and art world connections and its profile received a massive boost by acting for the National Union of Mineworkers in its successful judicial review of the pits closure policy being pushed through by the Secretary of State for the Environment, Michael Heseltine. Thatcher was on the rampage. This tiny practice had taken on and beaten the ideological Conservative administration.

Stephens Innocent's other union client, the National Union of Journalists, was sending instructions to the firm and as well as helping with the personal injury cases, I could lend my criminal expertise to members who had become embroiled with the police. They snapped me up, especially as I had a lot of union experience from the days when I worked for John. I had also taken on the National Union of Teachers as a client to defend their members facing assault allegations by pupils. All bar one of the allegations I advised on over several years were unfounded.

The NUJ members, especially the freelance branch, were screaming for help from the union for members who were arrested or having their material seized. Soon enough, I was working in the world of the media, and I never looked back.

Chapter 2

Media law: through the looking glass

My induction into media law beginning in 1995 was chiefly through three rather strange cases.

Representing filmmaker Ray Brady was an eye opener. His film, *Boy Meets Girl*, was up before the Video Appeals Committee having been refused a video certificate by the censors. Filmmakers are granted a video release certificate in the same way as films get their cinema classifications and the committee hears appeals from dissatisfied filmmakers who have been refused a certificate. Ray's horror film is entirely set in a basement where the female slowly tortures the male whilst strapped to a dental chair. James Ferman, the then chief censor, told the young filmmaker in a two-page letter, "This video focuses unrelentingly on the process of torture, mental as well as physical, including mutilation, sexual violation and evisceration, all in full view of the camera." It was a highly subjective view given most of the torture is off camera, a point we unsuccessfully made to the committee. I didn't manage to get it unbanned, calling the likes of critic Mark Cousins to give evidence and opine about its value to the horror flick genre.

Another unusual client was Savoy Books.

Savoy Books was a collective of writers and artists based in Manchester who were obsessed with Lord Haw Haw, Britain's own wartime Nazi, and the actions of the then Chief Constable of Manchester, James Anderton. Their adult comics depicted him as an authoritarian cop running Manchester on moral grounds including shutting down Savoy's bookshop, which showcased their own publications, in the northwestern metropolis. And lo and behold, with truth following fiction, Anderton sent his officers to the shop to seize the magazines under obscure obscenity legislation. Our role was to defend the comic on free speech grounds. We lost the case because we failed to persuade the magistrate it wasn't obscene. Whilst the comic was objectionable, the main point which the court just didn't get was that it was a biting satire. But in fighting the case, even though we lost, we managed to expose the actions of Britain's most political and best-known cop who would brook no criticism. It was also the last prosecution of an adult comic in Britain.

Perhaps the strangest of my introductions to media law was acting for the first ever Kurdish TV station, Med TV.

Med TV's satellite station had just set up in London's Regent Street. At the helm was Hikmet Tabak, an extraordinary character who I was to get to know extremely well. He had been a political prisoner in Turkey for many years. He was a lifer, found guilty by a military tribunal on trumped up murder charges. He decided to use his jail time productively by learning English despite the most severe restrictions. Using a much-thumbed dictionary he read every word of the only books he was allowed: LP Hartley's *The Go-Between* and *The Moon is Down* by John Steinbeck. There was no other way to learn, he told me. Even today he can recite whole passages from both books.

Hikmet was released in an unexpected amnesty and arrived in England soon afterwards, determined to make a go at working in the media. He quickly got himself onto a filmmaking course and not long afterwards, with other Kurds, set up the new TV channel from scratch. It had obtained a UK broadcasting regulation licence from Ofcom's predecessor, the Independent Television Commission (ITC) so had to adhere to their rules on such things as impartiality.

The Channel soon ran into problems with the ITC. Their first set of lawyers were not geared up to regulatory advice especially where the context was so often the conflict between Turkey and the PKK rebels. To this day Turkey brands them as terrorists and imposes a fierce rule in the southeast of Turkey where most Kurds in the country live.

So they sought out Stephens Innocent to keep them on the right side of the regulator's code and help with the attacks and criticisms being levelled at them by opponents. I was the obvious choice, becoming known for handling esoteric cases including the banned *Boy Meets Girl* and Savoy's impounded comics. My origins from the eastern end of the Mediterranean were also a bonus.

I spent much of the next few years trying, with Hikmet's help, to drill the rules into the programme makers and journalists most of whom were located in production studios in Denderleeuw, an out of the way location in the Flemish part of Belgium next to a smelly glue factory. The ITC code became my bible in the sense that I was always preaching adherence to it if they wanted to keep their licence. For several months I flew to Brussels once a week to impart my wisdom, supported by Hikmet as the Managing Director, and giving lectures on the rules and how to best meet them, which were gradually being complied with.

Their biggest problem was their reverence for the PKK leader, Abdullah Öcalan, fondly known as Apo ('uncle') and the inability of their journalists to challenge him whenever he came on air. Öcalan resembled a tanned version of Joe Stalin with high cheekbones, a bushy moustache and deep eyebrows, At the time the Kurds were prevented from any expression of their culture or language in Turkey despite forming 20% of the population. My mantra was that Med TV had to interrupt Öcalan's long monologues, put difficult questions to him and not give the appearance of bias.

The presenters and reporters were getting better each week at remaining within the ITC guidelines and the pressure from the regulator was easing. That was until the day Öcalan lost his status in Syria, where he was based with a rebel army, and was forced to find a new home. His epic journey around various countries was followed by millions and he was the main item on all Med TV's news bulletins.

The story of Öcalan is taken up in a later chapter, when I came to be part of his European Court of Human Rights legal team.

By 1998 Hikmet relied on me so much I may as well have been his in-house lawyer. The joke around the firm was that I was spending so much time with Med TV that colleagues had forgotten what I looked like, and a rumour spread that I must have joined the European Commission given the frequency of my trips to Brussels.

I was once lucky enough to be asked to go to the United States with Hikmet for some lobbying in Washington and to attend a major television conference hosted by the United Nations. In the lobby of the UN building hosting the jamboree, Med TV and other stations representing nations from all over the world had been invited to display a five minute reel of their output. Med TV's offering was brilliantly put together by Hikmet and his team and I had checked it to make sure there were no ITC bloopers. It showed the varied output of the Channel, the only one which broadcast in the main Kurdish language, Kurmanji, which has 17 million native speakers.

We checked every monitor. The reel was missing. What the hell?

I approached the organisers from Italy's RAI TV.

"It was considered too…political. Controversial. So we removed it."

"What gives you that right?" I asked, angrily. A shrug of the shoulders and a cold smile told me they had the power and well aware that the film would upset another delegation: Turkey.

"Fuck this," we all agreed. "We will not take it lying down." The next day, finding an ally among the US delegation who was due to speak in a conference session, we plotted. The delegate spoke about censorship and the importance of emerging nations being allowed to express themselves. He then introduced Hikmet to speak on the subject and within seconds he was on his feet with a speech we had written together the night before. Another delegate, red faced and furious, noisily got to his feet and stormed out. It was the delegate from Turkey.

The rest of the audience stayed to listen and gave Hikmet a loud round of applause. They say revenge is a dish best served cold but here it was served warm. Hikmet soon made friends and contacts far beyond expectations after this crass act of censorship.

To let off steam, the following evening I treated Hikmet to a night at the Rainbow Room, then the most desirable bar in which to be seen, up on the 65th floor of Rockefeller Center. Not long after arriving we were approached by an unlikely couple. The man was in his late sixties, white, suave and silver haired with a silver tongue to match. The woman was black, no more than 30 and stunning. She also had a plunging neckline. They were dressed up and looked like they were ready to go to a black-tie affair.

"Howdy," the man began. "We heard you folks were at our television conference." My eyes expressed surprise. They sure didn't look like delegates.

"We're from the CIA, thought we'd say hello." Yes, they were that brazen. We fell into conversation for a few minutes standing around a bar table. They invited us to breakfast in the morning on their yacht in the harbour.

"Why not?" Hikmet responded.

I had to step in. "Sorry we've got lots of meetings lined up."

Afterwards Hikmet chided me. He confessed he and the woman were getting on so well they were stroking each other's hands under the table.

"That, my friend, is what is known as a honey trap."

My client sighed and stared at the stars outside. He had a lot of catching up to do. 11 years in a prison had made him vulnerable and hungry for new experiences, a factor the spooks from Langley must have reckoned on.

* * *

Seizure of journalistic material by the police became a speciality of mine pretty quickly. One of my cases was for *The Observer* newspaper in November 2004. I was having a fairly humdrum morning in the office when a call came in from Siobhain Butterworth who used to work alongside me at Stephens Innocent. Siobhain had joined Guardian Media seven years previously as their first in-house lawyer where she had a huge job advising on all media law matters for their two titles, *The Guardian* and *The Observer*. Both were compulsory reads in our household.

"The cops have raided Tony Thompson's house. He's under arrest," a concerned Siobhain was telling me. "And what if they arrive here and come for his computer in the newsroom?"

It was a fair question. Police love any opportunity to look at the material journalists build up as a prelude to publication or transmission. I knew Tony as he had been a boyfriend of another Stephens Innocent colleague. Even back then, Tony was something of a legend. He was and remains the foremost writer on crime gangs, dividing his time between writing books about gangs and being *The Observer*'s crime correspondent. More pertinently he was a youthful looking Afro Caribbean journalist.

I told Siobhain I was grabbing a cab, and we would talk on the way. First, I had to get my head around Tony's arrest. As later reported, 30 cops had smashed his door down and flooded his home.

Just then, my attention was diverted by the news on the cabbie's radio. A nationwide dawn raid on homes had taken place to seize the import of weapons and ammunition which had been obtained by mail delivery from France. My ears pricked up. All I had been told was that Tony had been arrested as part of an investigation into possession of illegal arms which had been found in the early morning raid on his flat. Luckily, Tony had stayed with a friend the previous night, but the police had found his mobile number and rang him. Tony was immediately arrested and called the newspaper with his one and only call. (It is still the case that if you're arrested, you can make one call to family/friend and one to your solicitor.)

I rang Siobhain back before arriving at Wembley Police Station and suggested she wrap up the computer and put a sticker on it, indicating the contents were journalistic material exempted from the normal seizure rules.

"I'll get to it," she replied, thanking me for coming up with a practical solution.

I arrived at the police station anxious to explain everything to the police.

"Good thing he wasn't home when the specialist unit got there," the cop running his arrest told me.

"Why?" I asked.

The cop then explained that the raid was led by armed police from a specialist squad who would have first rolled Tony up in a carpet and chucked him out of the window to make sure he could not use any of the weapons they went on to find in his wardrobe.

A few minutes later I was led to Tony in his cell.

"What's all this about firearms in your wardrobe, Tony?" I asked.

He looked concerned and was right to be. A new law had recently been introduced carrying a minimum of five years imprisonment. He didn't need to be told as he had written about it. He had been dwelling on this and whether his career was over for the past two hours in the cell.

"I did a story a few months back – 'Criminals dodge laws by buying stun guns on the net' – which exposed this French outfit guns2.com who would send you over all sorts of banned weapons in the post. So, to stand up the story, I had them sent to me at my home – I couldn't use the paper's address as that would be giving the game away – and then wrote up my story as an exclusive, with photos of the stuff."

"But how come you then didn't get rid?" I asked.

"My latest book was going into paperback, and I wanted to keep them to use as photos for an updated edition and then get rid."

I exclaimed loudly and said, "Right, make sure you give them all the details when they interview you." This wasn't going to be a 'no comment' job, we both agreed.

I went and spoke to the officer in charge, and asked for advance disclosure – the gist of the case against Tony which the cops now have to give as a *quid pro quo* for suspects losing the unqualified right to silence in interviews under caution – but really what I wanted was to win the officer over early, getting the explanation into his head before the interview started. The only game in town was changing the police's perceptions of him.

The officer explained that the raids and arrests had been coordinated on a national basis to stop the offending website. They were liaising with the French authorities who had passed to the British police all the names and addresses of the French company's clients.

I explained that the only reason Tony's name was on the list was because he was the one who, in buying the weapons from the firm supplying arms, exposed the illegal trade and that was why he had come to the police's attention. And how come he wasn't exempted from the dawn raid list given that guns2.com was mentioned in Tony's article? At the very least some investigation should have been carried out?

The penny dropped with the affable officer.

"Oh dear, not exactly intelligence-led policing, is it?" he quipped. We both fell about laughing. He then introduced us to the custody sergeant merrily announcing Tony was *The Observer*'s crime correspondent and I was his highly paid solicitor.

In his interview, Tony patiently explained the detail of his investigation and why he had kept the imported weapons – photos for the paperback edition about to come out. The police agreed to free him without charge. It had been a long day especially for cops who would have been in from 4am for a pre-dawn briefing. By now it was 6pm.

As he was collecting his keys and wallet from the custody officer after being bailed, Tony turned to one of the investigating officers and asked if he could please have back the crossbow they had taken from his dining room wall. He explained he had hand carved this at school and it was a proud memento.

The reply? "Yes, you can have it back Mr Thompson but the moment you step outside this police station we'd have to arrest you for possessing an offensive weapon in a public place."

I laughed the loudest at that moment. Fair enough, I told Tony. The cops had seen the funny side of this farrago, they had treated him well and done the right thing. And he should put the officer on his Christmas card list for life. Tony was no further actioned (or NFA'd as it's known in the trade) and has gone on to write several more books on crime.

Chapter 3

Paula, Michael and Bob: the unholy trinity

Stephens Innocent was once described in *The Guardian* as "the nearest thing to *LA Law* in London". That comparison between the US television series about glamorous lawyers and their often star-studded clients fitted this small, dynamic law firm. It was widely acknowledged we punched well above our weight and celebrities were not an uncommon sight in the firm.

My favourite was Paula Yates. She became a client of the firm when her marriage to Bob Geldof imploded not long after Paula made out with INXS mega rock star, Michael Hutchence, on the TV show *The Big Breakfast*. She'd already become a household name presenting *The Tube* with Jools Holland in the eighties.

By this time, Bob Geldof was warmly known as Saint Bob, the scourge of world leaders trying to dodge their responsibilities to third world poverty. Live Aid had been a phenomenal success.

At the heart of Paula and Bob's divorce dispute, which first erupted in 1996, were their three young children. One of my then partners, Stuart Lockyear, was handling the divorce for Paula. I became embroiled in this messy breakup when, a few months after an initial arrangement was reached at the High Court over accommodation, Paula was on a visit to Australia to see Michael's family with her fourth child, Tiger Lily, then only a few months old. She was Michael's first child. Back home in the UK, the other children were left with Anita, their nanny. While Paula was away Anita discovered something she thought was an illegal drug. The resinous lump she found in a smarties tube was opium.

Accounts differ with Anita claiming she was looking for the instruction manual to turn off a car alarm whereas Paula believed – with no basis – that she had been snooping. Anita reported it to the police, an unusual thing to do against your own employer, and all hell broke loose.

A warrant for Paula's arrest was issued whilst she and Michael were in Australia and leaked to the media. Suddenly, as the firm's only criminal specialist, I became Paula's solicitor as she flew in to face the music followed days later by Michael, Tiger Lily and a new nanny. I had met Paula in the office a few times when she dropped in to see Mark and Stuart about her protracted divorce case.

I admit that it felt cool hanging out with her gang and getting my mug on the front pages next to the glamorous Paula, but the flip side – the private anxieties, the excesses, the mood swings of everyone involved – was much less cool. On top form, Paula was the funniest person in the room, lifting the mood even in the midst of a crisis. At other times, the legal team and her close friends had to help her emerge from doom and gloom.

Before going further with this story, a bit of history is required. Bob and Paula were a well-known, A-list couple back in the day. They were together for the best part of 20 years. Their Las Vegas wedding in 1986 was attended by David Bowie, George Michael and a stack of rock stars from bands like Spandau Ballet and Duran Duran.

Paula was a TV natural, totally at ease in front of the cameras. Bob was the Boomtown Rats singer whose pop chart fame (*I Don't Like Mondays* became a massive No 1 hit) was then eclipsed by him becoming the driving force behind 1984's Band Aid single *Do They Know It's Christmas?*. He followed this up with Live Aid, raising millions to combat famine in Africa. They were the ultimate pop power couple with three children, Pixie, Fifi and Peaches. Even the children were household names – Paula was not one known to scream for privacy. Far from it.

For Paula's first book of photography, she persuaded rock stars to be snapped in their underpants. Described as one of the world's biggest flirts, I experienced it first-hand whenever she wanted to say thanks or just tease me.

Then, in 1994, Michael Hutchence, the lead singer of INXS, a world-famous rock band from Australia, walked into Paula's life. Not only did she fall for the rock star's charms, she did it all on live TV, interviewing him in her regular slot 'on the bed' for the morning show. As can still be seen on YouTube, she draped her naked thighs over him and shamelessly flirted throughout the interview. Michael, regarded as a handsome lothario, fell for her undoubted charms.

It wasn't long before Bob and Paula's marriage fell apart, very publicly. Paula and Michael were besotted with each other and didn't much care who knew it. At first, Bob was cool with it. Michael took up residence in Bob and Paula's London terraced home in Chelsea while Bob occupied Michael's flat in London when he wasn't in the rural Kent residence where he spent most of his time. The tabloid media depicted Bob as heartbroken over Paula's romance with Michael, although by the time I got to meet her he was already with a new partner, Jeanne Marine (now his wife).

Paula was also said to have had other affairs with famous people, notably the actor Rupert Everett and eighties pop star Terence Trent D'Arby. An author in her own right, it should never be forgotten that Paula hungered for celebrity.

Once we learnt that Paula and Michael were wanted for questioning, we recognised that this was an irrevocable step. It would mean total war between Paula and Bob. She had a hard fight on her hands being up against a legend.

I soon found it was one thing acting for a celebrity and quite another acting for two: Paula and Michael. And Michael came with baggage in the form of two Aussies, a manager and a lawyer who also acted as a kind of financial advisor. They seemed to be in charge of most aspects of Michael's life including managing his wealth. Up close, I decided the life of a rock superstar wasn't that much fun.

The first decision to make was how we were going to handle Paula and Michael coming back to face the police. The story of their imminent return and arrest filled pages and pages of tabloid newspapers every day. We decided in discussions with them and the managers that Paula should come back first, without the baby, to face the music.

I negotiated with the police at Chelsea Police Station that her return should be managed in such a way as to avoid her humiliation and unnecessary drama. They agreed. So long as we kept to an appointment a few days after her return, she and I could turn up at her local police station for her to be interviewed under caution. All well and good on that score, or so I thought.

But first, we had to get her into the country without a huge phalanx of media trying to interview her and take photos. We came up with a cunning plan. We let it be known that she was coming in on a long-haul flight early one morning at one of the terminals at Heathrow whilst, in fact, she was travelling via Paris rather than direct from Oz, arriving at a different terminal and *incognito* into my waiting arms (metaphorically speaking).

All was going to plan. I was picked up at 4.30am from home in a large limo with smoked glass windows en route for Heathrow. I would be the only one meeting Paula at arrivals in a couple of hours if nothing went wrong.

I was waiting at arrivals in Terminal 2 and got word that Paula was about to come through when suddenly there was a rush of bodies behind me. A group of photographers and reporters had surrounded me and it was clear they knew Paula was about to emerge. Whilst I wore a perplexed frown, Paula came through and did not look at all surprised. In fact, she looked pleased. She stopped to talk to the journalists and pose for the photographers with me looking on, still scratching my head as to how they had found out about her secret arrangements.

She announced to the media that she would fight the interim order which allowed Bob to have temporary custody of their children. She protested her innocence about any class A drug allegations. She came up with an immortal line which the tabloids and broadsheets gobbled up:

"You've all heard of Live Aid, well this is now Lie Aid."

She turned and winked at me; it was time to go, and we headed off for the limo. Even in this most stressful of moments, she was relentlessly cheerful

30

and funny. Indeed, Paula would tell the story about how Princess Diana once said to her how much she liked Paula being on the front page of the tabloids because it meant she got the day off.

I managed to call Mark who had arrived at the office to tell him the media was somehow tipped off about our plans.

"Oh yeah, that was me. We decided to have an impromptu press conference and spin them a few lines to seize the narrative rather than hide away."

I kicked myself for not factoring in Mark's amazing ability to give the media what they wanted. Yep, I had to concede, we sure would be grabbing the headlines with Lie Aid but it might have been a good idea to let me in on it. But knowing him well, I suspect he was too busy briefing journalists and knew I could handle the surprise. "Typical, Mark!" was a common reaction back at the office.

Within a few hours I was on the front page of at least one tabloid standing next to Paula at Heathrow with the caption: 'Paula Yates returns to Heathrow with her security guard alongside her'. There were guffaws all round the office at my new job title.

Back at the office we held a long meeting with Paula to plan the next few days, especially management of the media. Photographers were loitering outside our New Fetter Lane office but luckily, we were 12 floors up and the desk security was carefully monitoring who was coming in.

The immediate crisis was to sort out where Paula should stay. Press photographers and assorted paparazzi were camped outside her terraced home in Chelsea. On top of that Paula, in her scramble to get home, had lost her front door key, so we suggested she stay with a close friend until they left, by which time we could sort out access.

Trouble was, Paula had to get something out of the house first which, she feared, might be found by the more unscrupulous members of the pack outside the house and used against her.

"What is it?" I asked.

"Photos, very intimate photos, of me and Michael, naked. Having sex."

The photos were in a drawer in her living room. She was insistent I went and retrieved them, and she could not rest until they were safely in her hands. We couldn't ask the children's nanny, Anita, who also had a key, because she was now firmly in the enemy camp.

Luckily, she remembered that Banhams, the posh lock company, had installed her locks. I got on the phone and had to negotiate with them about how they would be satisfied I had Paula's authority to break her own front door lock and replace it with another expensive set. After authorisations were faxed through to their office and a promise of the original for the locksmith I jumped into another limo – I was getting used to the high life – and headed to Chelsea.

There were about 15 or so press outside, waiting just in case Paula turned up. They were disappointed when it was just me and the Banhams technician who was already on the scene. They were intrigued as to why the front door was being drilled open and the technician had taken a signed document off me.

They snapped away at me, the car I came in, the technician and even the form of authority which he had unwisely shoved into his front window with the writing showing. I stayed silent as they asked me in 20 different ways: where was Paula, what's going on, is she under arrest and what was I doing?

My mouth stayed firmly zipped up.

After about 15 minutes, the technician got the door open and let me in. I drew the curtains and went to the drawer, apprehensive about whether the photos were still there. In an envelope I found a thick set of snaps. They were deeply intimate and once satisfied I had them all I stuffed them back in the envelope. I was about to get ready to check on the newly installed locks when I heard a quiet tapping at the door. I peered out of the window as something told me it wasn't the press and opened the door a few inches. There was a little elderly Italian lady on the doorstep.

"Hello, I am Mrs Paula's neighbour. She's a lovely lady. She give me her front door key to look after so who are you and why you change the locks?"

I let her in, explaining I was Paula's lawyer and that she must have forgotten she held a key and thanked her for looking after it. I apologised for the hassle going on outside.

When I got back to the office and told Paula, she slapped herself on the forehead for forgetting. I told her not to beat herself up, she had a lot on her plate. She was hugely grateful I had retrieved the photographs.

All part of the service, I muttered.

But now the serious legal bit was looming. Our date at Chelsea Police Station a couple of days hence.

Normally, police station interview strategy and advice is undertaken between you, the solicitor, and your client.

Not with A-list celebrities.

Everyone wanted a piece of the action. It wasn't just other partners at my firm – which was fair enough as anything at the police station would have consequences in the divorce case and the custody battle – but also the barristers who had been brought in on both the family and potential criminal side plus Michael's representatives. What Paula said or didn't say became a conference of many people all wanting to advise her. Too many chefs, I thought to myself.

In the end there was agreement, so I then conveyed the advice to Paula, explaining she was free to accept or reject it.

I rang the police officer again because I wanted his cast iron assurance there would be no leaks to the media about her upcoming appointment at the police station. Yes, it was totally confidential, he assured me.

Paula was her usual chatty, ebullient self en route, in the back of another limousine. By now, she had got to know me better and, I'm sure to pass the time and amuse herself, did a bit of her customary flirting, calling me a Greek Sex God. Ha, I thought to myself, no wonder she persuaded rock stars to undress to their underwear for her. Underneath it all, however, there was no doubt in my mind this was a very worried woman with a custody battle on her hands and possible class A drugs charges ahead.

We got to the police station, made it inside quietly via a garage entrance as agreed and got on with the formalities of the tape-recorded interview. Paula was a dream client. She did not stray from what we agreed once and, full denials now on the record, it was soon over. She was bailed to return to the police station by a custody sergeant at a future date.

Getting out of the police station, however, was a different matter. The press lay waiting. One of the tabloids had been tipped off about our presence and snapped away as we left. It was well known that back then an officer, breaching all the rules, could earn 'a few bob' for a tip like this to a tabloid. It was annoying but nothing could be done about it except to get in the car and leave as soon as possible.

The next significant moment was Michael's return. He was due back with baby Tiger Lily. Thankfully, after a few days, the press pack had moved on elsewhere and Paula could return home and get ready for their arrival. It meant another early morning trip to Heathrow was needed to make sure the police weren't going to make a song and dance and try and arrest him. Again, we had secured an interview by appointment with the police so Michael could give his side of the story. Back then, such arrangements were rare, but a VIP could secure one by calling ahead, mentioning the mutual need to avoid a media scrum and negotiating an arrival with the officer who would conduct the interview.

This time, the flight in from Oz went smoothly. There were no snappers or reporters. The baby was quiet and had been good on the long flight. A new nanny, to replace Anita, had travelled over with Michael. Paula told me with a straight face she always picked nannies that were not Michael's type "so he won't be fucking her".

Michael was a gentle, reflective soul who was very courteous to people around him despite being a 'Rock Giant' and all the baggage that comes with that. We got back to the house in Chelsea at about 7am and, displaying typical Australian manners, Michael asked me if I wanted a tinny. I settled for a cup of tea. He was one of the most handsome men I have ever met although he also had a habit of constantly changing spectacles, many of which were dotted around the house. I remember thinking to myself this was a sign of a restless soul, never settling on anything. We talked through things together and with Paula happily reunited with Tiger Lily, we went out for lunch at a nearby pub.

Heads turned everywhere we went, and you could see people asking their companions: "Isn't that…?"

Whilst we waited for the family case to resume, we decided to make representations to the Crown Prosecution Service as to why Paula should not be prosecuted. We all agreed Michael was best served by having his own separate solicitor because of the potential for a conflict of interests. I recommended Anthony Burton to Michael and his representatives. Anthony was then my current firm's senior partner and a highly respected criminal practitioner.

For the next few weeks, Paula's cases dominated our lives. It felt like she was always in the office, and she would regularly use the office shower. One time she was so bored with the latest report she came and sat on my lap during a meeting. I'm not easily embarrassed but this was a first in keeping close with your client.

There were many twists and turns in the two cases, but the most significant decisions were those of the CPS and the family judge.

The CPS announced there wasn't going to be a prosecution as there was insufficient evidence against Paula or Michael to prove possession. This meant there would be no further action.

Whoop for joy. We could now announce it to the media. But that was only half the battle.

Paula was then immersed in an internecine warfare of a custody battle which loomed ahead. It involved demands for drug testing and all sorts of other invasive personal demands. I helped out with this as it was a big task and I remembered how draining family law could be. The dissection of personal relationships and the spilling out of often long festering emotions makes this a tough area of law to practice in. An all or nothing trial loomed. It was to last several days but one saving grace was that it was to be heard in private.

Fortunately for Paula, the judge allocated to hear the case was a then not very well-known judge of the High Court, Mrs Justice Brenda Hale, who later became renowned as the Supreme Court's first woman President. Famously, she delivered the lead judgment against Boris Johnson's attempt to prorogue Parliament. She also plays a significant role later on in this book.

I sat through the whole of the family case with Paula. She wasn't feeling confident given the battles of the past few months. During one of the breaks, she got so bored, as did Bob, that the two were seen to walk into a side room together. It was anathema. Our team was horrified – talking to the enemy. I didn't think it was so terrible as they would have to find a way of getting on post-divorce anyway. I shrugged my shoulders but did as I was asked by counsel to prise her away from Bob. I gently tapped on the door and walked in.

"Hi, Louis." Paula cheerfully introduced me to Bob (as if I needed an intro) and we shook hands. "We were just having a chat as it's sooo boring in there," she said, referring to the courtroom. We chatted a bit longer, just small talk. Bob was reading *The Independent* which he called his second favourite newspaper and wasn't it everyone's, I agreed. I made an excuse that we needed a chat with Paula, and she followed me out.

A day later, with us feeling confident at how it had gone and getting a good reception from the judge that the case should be firmly and solely based on the children's best interests, we sat and waited whilst the judge delivered her decision.

Mark and Stuart sat alongside me, with Paula in front of me, just behind our counsel. When Hale J spoke the crucial words – that Paula was to resume being the primary carer for her three daughters against Bob's wishes, who continued to maintain she was an unfit parent – she turned to us with a wide grin and, *sotto voce*, delivered another classic Paula one liner:

"You were right after all – I've won. Blow jobs all round, boys!"

Tragedy was to follow which makes me wonder if this was the right outcome for the children. Michael's death the following year and Paula's inevitable descent into depression followed by a fatal heroin overdose in 2000 was terrible enough. But 14 years later, the death of Peaches, who launched herself into a similar career trajectory as her mother, was utterly tragic. In 2014 Bob told *Saga* magazine: "[I blame the] entire family court system for so much of their [his children's] subsequent pain…I wanted to keep my kids away from this decadent world Paula had fallen into."

Although the lawyers came out well in this case, no one else did, especially the children. Compulsory mediation, particularly where children are involved, is now a given; it is a shame that it wasn't back in the nineties.

The deaths of Michael, Paula and Peaches demonstrated to me that fame is, for so many, a curse and addiction so often follows. After this episode I told myself to try and avoid working closely with any celebrity who wasn't utterly grounded and secure. Otherwise, you were at the whim of someone who was often irrational or changed course without good reason. I was happy to leave the task to others who love to be 'starfuckers' as it's known in the trade.

Chapter 4

Going solo down in Old Street

They say all good things come to an end and it sure did with Stephens Innocent on Millennium Eve. The firm had lost the NUJ as a client and a few of us decided to quit at the same time which made the firm's future as a standalone practice untenable. After toying with a couple of practices Stephens Innocent merged with a larger firm in the West End. By then I had secured a berth with an East London outfit which saw me handling a wide range of criminal cases as well as keeping my media clients. I was cooling my heels, figuring out what to do next.

One late afternoon, in the long, hot summer of 2000, I went to the pub after work to watch one of the games in the Euros. It was a boring game and my mind drifted. Something had been building up for a while which I hadn't let surface. But suddenly it did. Start my own firm, especially as the Human Rights Act (HRA) was about to kick in, in October 2000.

Back then the regulatory jungle and admin involved in starting your own practice was less dense than it is now. I could start it with a modest bank loan, a couple of computers and a small staff. I invited a former colleague, Sarah Culshaw, a like-minded soul to join, and she agreed. We shared a secretary and three rooms in Old Street, which bordered the City of London. For the next few years, we grew the firm and became something of a noise among media lawyers.

Being small meant we could be nimble and take on cases without more staid partners looming over us, wondering if the latest no win, no fee case was ever going to bear fruit. The firm, which we called CCL, was adventurous and whilst working long hours to also handle the very boring admin which came with having very little back-office support, I decided to read the main libel and privacy textbooks. It was a back-to-basics approach which was to pay dividends.

One of the cases I took with me from Stephens Innocent was against the London Borough of Newham. Back in 2000 privacy law was in its infancy. Very few cases had gone to trial. The HRA had only just passed into law. I arranged for our firm's dispute lawyers to attend a lecture from a rapidly rising star at the Bar, Keir Starmer, who had just authored a 900-page manual on the Human Rights Act. By then, Keir had become a friend as well as counsel on many of my cases.

A couple of weeks later a lovely Nigerian couple came to see me. They explained that their daughter, who I will call Cynthia, was at a special needs school due to her various disabilities and one day they received a booklet from the local authority featuring Cynthia on the front cover. The subject matter of the booklet was children with HIV and AIDS. Cynthia's parents explained how their 10-year-old girl was distressed because she would now be considered, both at school and in the local community, as having a condition which might result in her being shunned.

They showed me the letters between them and Newham Council. Newham, instead of fessing up to their mistake, doubled down. They insisted the parents had given permission for Cynthia to be featured. They claimed the photographer who had visited the school had got their consent. The parents insisted otherwise. They were stuck. All they wanted was an apology which they could then show anyone shunning Cynthia and her family.

I explained that we now had a new weapon, section 8 of the Human Rights Act, which protects the right to respect for private and family life, and we would use it in making a claim. With the assistance of a media barrister I knew well, John Critchley, we sent a letter before action, but Newham continued with the same stance they had adopted with the parents.

We then issued a writ and served it. Still nothing doing. Their defence was even more belligerent than their correspondence. As fast as we could go, we got the case ready for trial and avoided interim hearings. Their witnesses insisted there was consent. Our repeated response was: where is it then? If they had come up with evidence of consent, albeit belatedly, our case would have been torpedoed. But I was 100% confident in Cynthia's parents.

The case was listed for trial in October 2001, just 12 months after taking on the case. We got the jury bundle together, showing the evidence of both sides. On the very eve of the trial, we then got a letter from Newham Council's law firm. Full capitulation. Please let us pay you damages. John explained to the judge, Mr Justice Garland, that as this was one of the first cases to come to trial under the HRA, damages were hard to work out; no scale had yet been developed based on precedent.

We had won, and in record time, and victory tasted sweet. The judge approved the settlement, as required due to Cynthia's age, and the damages went into a trust fund for when she became 18.

* * *

Privacy was the new kid on the block, and a place to make your name.

Another haunting case soon came my way. As the only criminal solicitor practitioner also working in media, I pushed the line that unlike other libel and privacy lawyers, I knew my way around crime and criminal courts.

The notorious Essex Boys murder in 1995 brought me right back into that world. Three men were executed in what was considered to be a gangland shooting. They were drug dealers who were lured to some woods in Rettendon, a quiet village in Essex, under the pretext of a deal, only to be executed. Films, documentaries and books about the murders have since followed.

The youngest victim, 26-year-old Craig Rolfe, was found in the Range Rover in which all three men died. His mother came to see me, devastated that a newspaper had got its hands on the mortuary photographs of the body, including a close up of Craig with a bullet hole in the middle of his forehead.

I was staggered. Even by the wild west standards of the tabloids prevailing back in the early 2000s, this was utterly beyond the pale. Craig's mother had avoided looking at anything which might upset her in all the years since her son was murdered only to be shown this by outraged friends who, whilst meaning well, should have protected her from it. Not surprisingly, it led to a deterioration of her mental health.

I looked into how it had come about, and it soon became apparent that a true crime blogger had somehow got hold of inquest photographs which should only have been in the control of the prosecution team, the defence team of the three men convicted of the murders and the police.

I had come across the blogger before and wasn't impressed with his publicity seeking antics then. Here, the same photographs were on his website, and I felt sure he had sold them to Sport Newspapers for a tidy sum.

I had to explain the law to his devastated mother. I told her there is no privacy claim for the deceased. But I thought it would be worth mounting a claim based on the private and family life rights contained in the new HRA.

Despite the lack of a strict right, the newspaper capitulated. They agreed to ban further use of the photographs and destroy their copies of the images. And we got an apology.

Chapter 5

Breaking into libel

Much more high profile were my two cases against Time Life Entertainment, the publishers of Duwayne Brooks' book, *Steve and Me: My friendship with Stephen Lawrence and the search for justice*. The murder of Stephen Lawrence was the most famous racist murder in Britain. It became a cause celebré when the fall out of the subsequent police investigation led to changes of attitude on racism and the police with, eventually, two perpetrators convicted of his murder in 2012. A judge led inquiry, a charity in Stephen's name and a highly regarded play as well as thousands of publications worldwide followed as a result.

Duwayne Brooks wrote the book in the aftermath of his disastrous appearance at the Old Bailey as the key witness to the savage murder of his friend. Elvin Oduro, widely acknowledged as Stephen's best friend, had come out badly in the book. Elvin was accused of exaggerating the closeness of his friendship with Stephen. It was Duwayne who wanted the 'best friend' title, and he claimed that Stephen could not truly rely on Elvin. These comments were not the most serious of libels, but it was hugely important to Elvin. More seriously, Duwayne accused Elvin of being hostile to white people.

There was evident bitterness between the two. One passage in the book describes Elvin threatening Duwayne just before giving evidence in the ill-fated private prosecution of the five suspects to the murder. Elvin described the exchange differently to Duwayne; he hadn't threatened him.

Elvin was understandably enraged at the descriptions of him in the book. The Lawrence family's solicitor, Imran Khan (now a KC), who was later to become a friend I played tennis with on Sunday mornings, got in touch with me. He asked me to read the book. I said that whilst it would not be easy to fight a publisher with huge resources and which undoubtedly had the book cleared by a libel lawyer, I would take it on. It was clear to me that Duwayne's take on the events and his friendship with Stephen were controversial. I met Doreen Lawrence, Stephen's mother, to discuss the book and the true state of affairs between Elvin and Duwayne. She supported Elvin's version of events. She also explained to me she was hopping mad about the way she was characterised.

I hired Lucy Moorman, a young star at the Bar, to come on board. She was at Doughty Street Chambers which was headed up by Geoffrey Robertson who I knew from the Bradford 12 days.

As expected, we met with stiff resistance. The publisher's case was run by the then best-known defendant firm of solicitors, RPC, and a barrister called David Sherborne who we will come across in later chapters. It was the only time I was opposite him where he was acting for a publisher defendant.

The publisher's tactic was to go for broke. They sought a ruling that our case be struck out because the book wasn't defamatory. This meant an all-day fight in front of Mr Justice Tugendhat (who incidentally is MP Tom Tugendhat's father).

I recall a tense day with Lucy sticking to her guns despite the usual extravagant claims by Sherborne which I would later come to know as his litigation style. Some media lawyers prefer to go over the top in an attempt to get something better than they might otherwise have got if their case had been sensibly pitched in the first place. I was always in the 'sensible pitch' camp, partly because it suits my personality but also to avoid the important legal maxim: never piss off the judge. The book, we said, strayed beyond acceptable opinion and into territory – the best friend claims, the hostile to white people allegation – which a jury could find were defamatory of Elvin.

Just under four weeks later, in late July 2003, we got the result. Tugendhat (or Tugs as he was fondly known) ruled mostly in our favour. He directed the complained about passages were, for the most part, capable of being defamatory of Elvin, which a jury should decide on at trial rather than be struck out by him, and a defence would need to be produced by the publisher. They soon settled.

Next up was Doreen, a remarkable woman in so many ways. Plunged into the limelight in a way no one would envy, she has fought and won many battles.

Doreen, later made a Baroness for her heroic struggles to get justice for Stephen, weighed in with a claim, this time complaining about criticisms levelled at her by Duwayne. Claims that her authoritarian style of parenting contributed to her son's death and that the pair were rushing home to beat a curfew were particularly hurtful. Imran gave me access to all the evidence – a large room load – to check there were no problems with her account of their family life and what the police had been told. I interviewed family members and got witness statements and made sure all my tackle was in good order before sending the letter before action.

Again, the publishers caved in, this time without putting up a fight. They paid damages and the book was withdrawn from sale although Duwayne still tries to sell it through other means. I hate any book being effectively banned like this, but it is an inevitable consequence of libel being found or admitted.

I keep in touch with Elvin who is a visual communication director. Also, I still see Stephen's younger brother, Stuart, who I got to know as a potential witness in the two cases. Despite being a south Londoner, he too is a fervent follower of Arsenal and we occasionally 'worship' together. Stuart is now a public speaker and author.

Chapter 6

The unreachable Comrade Öcalan

International politics was always my thing. At university I gravitated towards studying global conflicts.

How I came to act for the foremost leader of the Kurds and founder of the Kurdish Workers Party (the PKK), Abdullah Öcalan, is told elsewhere in this book (see Chapter 2).

So what was Abdullah Öcalan's case all about? Öcalan had spent many years in the Syrian mountains, establishing and building up his guerrilla army, the PKK, and developing the party's political wing. Directing the rebels' manoeuvres as the military and political head, and issuing his directives through various media, he had been safe in Syria. Yet growing pressure from Turkey forced the Syrians to move him out and he became a hot potato nobody wanted to handle. Anxiously, I watched the news of him trying to make a base in several places, including Greece and Italy, and how it was being covered by the TV station, Med TV. Then, in 1999, came news of his dramatic abduction.

Unexpectedly, he had flown to Kenya and was hosted by the Greek Ambassador in a country residence. At that time there was a lot of sympathy in Greece for the fate of the Kurds. Not long after, Öcalan was due to fly to yet another location – this time, Holland, which had agreed to accept him – when there was a sudden switch of arrangements. The Greek Ambassador, who had arrived to escort his guest, was told by Kenyan police that he was not allowed to travel in the same car as Öcalan (as a guarantee of his safety) and instead Öcalan was forced to go in a car alone with just a Kenyan official at the wheel. His advisors and bodyguards were required to follow in another vehicle just behind. As they tailed Öcalan, they feared something was wrong.

They were right. Öcalan's car suddenly left the convoy and went to a security area at the airport. There he was grabbed by officials and bundled onto a plane waiting on the tarmac. His abductors were masked members of Turkish MIT (their SAS) waiting to whisk him into Turkish custody.

Öcalan was handcuffed, blindfolded for the whole flight and, he claimed, given tranquillisers at some point. After landing, he was taken to Imrali island, in the middle of an inland sea called Marmara, with a hood over his head.

Turkey's most wanted had been captured.

Öcalan's abduction grabbed headlines around the world. Kurds everywhere were outraged both at his capture and the treachery involved in his abduction and protests followed. In London, the Greek Embassy was besieged by his supporters claiming Greek involvement in the abduction. At Med TV's broadcast studios in Belgium the more radical elements in the station, scathing about the regulator's impartiality mantra, took over. Instead of continuing with the now well established and multilingual daily diet of children's programmes, women's health discussions, news, religious programmes and old movies, only one thing was being shown: Öcalan and his PKK fighters.

I was then plunged into a battle with the ITC who suspended the Channel pending a hearing to determine whether its licence should be revoked for a gross breach of ITC rules. We presented our case over a long day at the ITC headquarters but to no avail. To the sounds of protesters in the streets outside, where many had been camped for weeks, the regulatory panel upheld the original decision making the ban permanent. Med TV now had to find a new regulator on mainland Europe which it managed to do. It was the first ever revocation of a TV station for broadcasts "likely to encourage or incite to crime or lead to disorder" which is against UK law.

I was gutted. But not surprised.

The indictment laid against Öcalan included all 37,000 deaths from the conflict which had raged since the early eighties. The old Marxist-Leninist had been brought to heel. By June 1999, a mere four months since his capture, a State Security Court came to his one-man prison to try him.

His trial lasted a month, and his defence team complained of multiple obstacles put in their way, including the most limited access to their client. An unfair trial on top of an illegal arrest – the abduction had shades of Nazi Adolf Eichmann's capture in Argentina, his removal to Israel and subsequent execution – was ripe for legal challenge in the European Court of Human Rights (ECtHR).

The case against Turkey began in earnest soon after Öcalan's arrival. The initial application was lodged in the same month – February 1999 – and an international team of lawyers was put together, acting *pro bono* (that is without being paid) to present his case at Strasbourg.

What, it should be asked, did we think we could achieve by taking his case to Strasbourg when we must have known full well that Turkey, a member of the Council of Europe, would never accede to any rulings of the ECtHR relating to Öcalan? The answer is simple enough: upholding the rule of law is fundamental. Allowing Turkey to escape censure from the ECtHR would be shameful. Turkey has more cases against it than any other ECtHR member – more than a third of all applications. As of December 2024, there were over 21,600 pending applications against it; a staggering number. It has been severely criticised for failing to comply with rulings over the years. Critics cite any compliance is largely procedural and does not result in any meaningful changes for the applicants.

The English-speaking part of the team was to be led by one of the most prominent lawyers in the world, Sir Sydney Kentridge, who focused on the death penalty sentence Öcalan had received. He had been one of Nelson Mandela's lawyers in the 1964 Rivonia Treason trial which saw the ANC leader branded a terrorist and imprisoned for the next 18 years on Robben Island just off the Cape Town coast, before being transferred to mainland prison and eventually released in 1990. Then in his early eighties, Kentridge would always address me very properly as Mr Charalambous despite my pleas to just call me Louis.

Others in the team included a high-flying human rights lawyer, Mark Muller, who had done tons of work for Kurdish organisations and individuals, and the eminent Gareth Peirce, the only other solicitor in the team. Gareth was famous for her work defending five of the Birmingham Six, the Guildford Four and the family of Jean Charles de Menezes. Her role for the Four was even the subject of a major film, *In the Name of the Father*, where she was played by Emma Thompson. I was among legal royalty. Whilst Gareth was handling the criminal side as the other solicitor in the team, I was there to handle the matters media-related.

In my work for Med TV, I had managed to soak up a huge amount of knowledge and empathy for the plight of the Kurds which, together with my media expertise, was considered important and relevant to the brief for Öcalan. But I have been asked whether I had any qualms acting for this controversial leader and his organisation which has been proscribed in the UK as a terror organisation since 2001.

My answer has always been the same. The Kurds deserve their own country, just like the Jews demanded and managed to found the state of Israel. The Kurds have similar problems in that the four countries where the majority are based – Turkey, Syria, Iran and Iraq – share a disdain for Kurdish rights and have their own repressive regimes.

It is no wonder the most common saying I heard from many Kurdish friends was that they had "no friends but the mountains". So, acting for the leader in respect of the multiple breaches of his human rights did not cause me any philosophical problems. It did not mean that I had to agree with his and the organisation's politics, which is never the role of an independent lawyer in defending their clients on criminal charges. The role is to uphold their rights, especially when the process is unfair.

None of the team got to meet Öcalan which was a source of huge frustration. One of his criminal defence lawyers who tried got herself deported soon after landing in Turkey. Access to lawyers was one of several breaches which we laid before the court.

In March 2003 I turned up, unusually early for me, at the departure gate for the flight to Strasbourg. Sydney Kentridge was already there and had been for the past hour. "I like to be punctual, Mr Charalambous," he said. I got the clear impression that none of us should ever be late for any meeting with the great man.

At our hotel in Strasbourg, we got down to the business of final preparations for the hearing the next day. We had to agree who would say what. We also had several lawyers from Turkey in the team and dividing the allocated time between us required some diplomatic skills as the apportioning was negotiated. The ECtHR doesn't allow anyone to drone on as we were soon to find out. We were 10 in total. Our opponents, the state of Turkey, outdid us with 16.

The hearing turned out to be extraordinary. The court was more like the Colosseum and the surrounding streets were packed. Officials met us at the doors and escorted us to our private room.

We were then escorted to the courtroom itself. It was huge. The case had been referred to the highest tier of the court, the Grand Chamber, which meant it would be heard by human rights judges from 17 Council of Europe member states. It took several minutes for them all to file in and settle into their seats. The two legal teams fitted into the legal representatives' seats. Fortunately, we were far apart from each other as there was no love lost between us. Each regarded the other as the work of the devil.

There was room for several hundred people in the public areas and every space was taken. Behind us were Öcalan and PKK supporters. Behind the Turkish side of the court were rows and rows of Turkish civilians. I asked the chief lawyer of the Kurdish Human Rights Project, Kerim Yildiz, who they were. He explained that Turkey had brought along families of soldiers killed in the conflict to keep up the emotional pressure on the court. "Let's hope they and our supporters don't all leave by the same door afterwards," I replied.

But our client was not with us in court. He could not even watch remotely from his one-man prison.

Once we had settled down with our papers, we were all individually and collectively photographed by media photographers for the record. No doubt we would be on the front of Turkish newspapers the following day.

Once we got going and everyone had put on their headphones, we listened as each side, in turn, presented its arguments. The translators sat in glass boxes doing simultaneous translations for the participants. Only two advocates spoke for Turkey, which was a good thing because one of them overran his time slot, ignoring the traffic light warning the court had in place. Rather hilariously, his microphone was cut off when the amber light turned red and despite this, he still kept talking even though no one except the team nearby could hear him. He soon sat down, looking rather foolish.

When Kentridge got to his feet, the judges appeared to me to sit bolt upright. They listened very hard to his submissions. He addressed the court on the issue of the death penalty which had originally been imposed on Öcalan by the Turkish court.

The hearing was over by lunchtime. Judgment, as usual, was reserved. We could all let our hair down. The PKK supporters in court were just the tip of the iceberg. There were thousands more in the city, many from neighbouring countries. They had gathered close by, and a festival was in full swing by the time we got there. We were treated like celebrities but soon came away after the initial meet and greets because Sir Sydney had invited us all to a Grand Salon for a late lunch. It was my first Michelin three-star restaurant.

I chose a modest salad and some fish. Next to me Gareth ordered the most expensive fillet steak I had seen on any menu.

It was to take more than two years, in 2005, before a decision came from the court. We had won. The court ruled Öcalan's trial had been unfair – it was neither independent nor impartial. But if ever an individual had won a Pyrrhic victory, this was it. Despite the public reaction by Turkey claiming it would address flaws found by the court, it did nothing of the sort. Like so many responses by public and corporate authorities held to have acted wrongfully, the statement used to explain away the ruling by Turkey was pure PR spin. Some commentators, taken in by the wording, became so optimistic they even thought he might be permitted a re-trial. This hope was soon scotched when, as *The Guardian* reported the foreign minister, Abdullah Gül, "Even if [Öcalan] were re-tried a hundred times, he would get the same sentence."

However, very little changed for Öcalan. He challenged his conditions again in 2014 and again the same court ruled in his favour.

In 2011 over 40 lawyers who were connected to Öcalan's representation in Turkey were arrested and their homes were raided. They were all imprisoned in Istanbul. Their 'crime' was that in acting for Öcalan, they were a vehicle for his ideas and the PKK. Perhaps the PR spin about "addressing the [2005] ruling" did just simply mean revenge: that any lawyer concerned with Öcalan would now be harassed and criminalised. These colleagues were utterly brave and fearless in upholding fundamental rights at their personal expense.

A quarter of a century on and the Kurdish leader remains in his island prison, in isolation, much like Nelson Mandela's incarceration on Robben Island. Soon he will have been there longer than the 27 years the South African leader spent in custody. Even in 2025 Öcalan is grabbing the head-lines with his announcement of the end of the armed struggle. The ban on visitors, including lawyers, which lasted for several years, has since eased up.

Like Sydney Kentridge's other client, also labelled a terrorist leader, I remain hopeful he will one day be freed and able to realise his dream of Kurdish self-determination.

Chapter 7

A nightmare on Elm Street: the SFO reverse

Advising whistle-blowers is a privilege because you get to see so
much that's under the skin of large organisations. I have immense
respect for any whistle-blower because they take a long and lonely
road which few are willing to travel.

This was especially the case with Peter Gardiner. It takes guts and dedication to become a whistle-blower and my new client had both as well as a determination to do the right thing despite it causing the loss of his business and entire livelihood.

I have always wanted someone to write a book called 'How Britain *really* works'. If they did, then Peter Gardiner's extraordinary story would have to be included as a chapter. It reeked of bribery, government interference, cut out characters worthy of a John le Carré novel and financial malpractice on a massive scale.

But before I recount Peter's tale, let me introduce you to David Leigh, *The Guardian*'s legendary investigative reporter. David had been running a series of stories about one of the biggest corporate scandals of the age involving British Aerospace (BAe), the semi-public giant corporation and the UK's largest manufacturer. Back then, with Alan Rusbridger at the helm and investing in investigative reporting, *The Guardian* broke important stories. Now, not so much.

David had long suspected there was something smelly about the Al-Yamamah rearmament of the Saudi air force by BAe and said as much in early articles although he had no proof. The process had been running for 20 years and was up for renewal each year. David explained to me that BAe was so enmeshed in it that the aerospace company virtually ran the Saudi air force. He wrote that over the past two decades the contract was worth $100 billion of revenue.

Peter Gardiner had spotted David's articles and called him, claiming to know something about the story. David knew of my work for the newspaper, so I was asked to meet and help Peter navigate the various agencies who wanted to investigate his story. I rapidly read the stories David had already written before Peter walked into CCL's small but cosy suite in Old Street, about a mile away from the newspaper's then headquarters on Farringdon Road.

Peter sat down and told me about how he and his company, Travellers World, a small executive travel company specialising in high end business travel, had become entangled with the Saudi arms deal and BAe. He would fix flights, cars and hotels typically for company executives. One of his clients, whose account was growing each month, was a corporate client who he had no direct dealings with. Everything was done through an individual who commissioned Peter's services from his tiny Mayfair office.

The man in Mayfair was Tony Winship. He sounded like a Terry Thomas character, "Hello old boy" sort of thing. He was a retired RAF Wing Commander. It turned out he was the keeper of the BAe slush fund and Peter, who had no direct relationship with the aerospace company, was to be its cut out. Peter was very efficiently servicing Tony's demands for travel and accommodation. But there was a catch. Peter explained to me that once Tony's client had become his biggest customer, the retired airman called Peter and said he needed to let go of all his other clients so that he could work exclusively for Tony.

Peter felt unable to agree – he'd like to keep his other clients too. Initially, he succeeded in servicing them as well as Tony, but he was fighting a losing battle. Tony was keeping him so busy, increasing the orders, that it got to the point where he couldn't afford to lose Tony's account and eventually, he was forced to jettison his other clients to service just this one. It was, Tony had explained, the way BAe worked when doing business with the Saudis.

Tony was operating the massive slush fund to pay bribes to Saudi officials by arranging, through Peter, all manner of services. It wasn't illegal as it was all overseas but, Peter explained to me, he didn't feel entirely comfortable with it either.

The contract's biggest beneficiary was a Saudi Prince called Turki bin Mohammed bin Nasser bin Abdulaziz Al Saud (hereafter bin Nasser) who was a member of the ruling Royal family. Peter regularly mentioned him and in time I got to realise why when the full story emerged. One summer, bin Nasser's family enjoyed £2m of BAe's 'hospitality', such were the demands on the company. Peter used to turn up at a tearoom in the Carlton Tower adjacent to Tony's home office once a month with all the receipts – for things like grand pianos and Rolls Royce cars – and Tony, once satisfied with the paperwork, would then reduce it down to a single page with the most generic description e.g. £1.25m on "travel and accommodation services" for whoever it was in BAe he reported to.

As the extravagance increased year by year, Peter, then in his fifties and being an upright and moral individual, become worried about this largesse and his role in it. He always prided himself on acting properly and lawfully. And then came 9/11 and the massive surge in tightening security. A new law, the Anti-Terrorism, Crime and Security Act 2001, was about to come into force which, for the first time, criminalised overseas bribes by making it an offence which could be prosecuted here.

Before the law came into force Peter took advice from two leading lawyers who said the same thing: if you carry on after this becomes law then you could be prosecuted for payments which amount to bribes.

He went to see Tony with the advice who poo-poohed it. The response was to the effect of 'nothing to worry about old boy, this is all government business and hush hush' and that BAe were looking for ways to get round the new restrictions. Peter was assured the programme of bribery payments would continue after the law change in February 2002. Tony also told Peter he would never be prosecuted whilst (literally) tapping the side of his nose to demonstrate secret approval of their set up. In other words, Peter was effectively instructed to carry on regardless of the law change and he would be immune from prosecution. What they were doing was in the public interest, Tony insisted. Pressed further, Tony told Peter a new system would have to come into operation due to the law change, as he later told BBC2.

Peter's next step was to change his life. He stopped working for Tony and BAe. His ethics and determination not to break the law meant everything to him. With no other existing clients, he was forced to wind up Travellers World. It was crushing. Everything he had worked for went down the drain because he was not prepared to go along with Tony and carry on servicing the Saudi officials with their exorbitant requests which 'oiled the wheels' of the annual Al-Yamamah contract renewal.

With Peter's documents, David could now press BAe to explain what these payments were all about. The paperwork described Tony as a customer relations executive. David met with a blank denial of wrongdoing and an absolute refusal to explain away the paperwork. Bravely, Peter agreed to be named and photographed. He was now no longer a confidential source for David. He was out in the open and exposed. He needed a lawyer to help him navigate what was becoming a major scandal. That's where we came in. I was to be Peter's independent lawyer, advising him on both his whistle-blowing to the criminal enforcement agencies and media advisor.

Our first step, once I got the whole story from Peter, was to follow up David's initial contact with the Serious Fraud Office (SFO) to tell them I would be happy to attend with Peter for him to become their witness in any investigation against the giant defence contractor.

Other media outlets were now picking up the story. The BBC interviewed Peter for *The Money Programme,* a special on the scandal called *Bribing for Britain?* which promised to lift the lid on the secret slush fund operated for bin Nasser.

Peter went on air and explained how the client payments went from a few hundred pounds in 1989 to hundreds of thousands and then up towards seven figures a year. He explained how he would lay on endless streams of five-star hotels, luxury limousines, personal security and chartered aircraft. Shopping expeditions were not only paid for but also the booty then carted back on a specially chartered Jumbo costing a quarter of a million dollars: all this on the back of the slush fund. He told the programme that bin Nasser's son had been provided with a £99,000 honeymoon. Perhaps most damaging of all was the revelation that bank transfers would be arranged to pay off credit card bills averaging $100,000. The video suite constructed in the desert just to record the wedding of the Prince's daughter costing almost £200,000 also got a mention. Entries for bin Nasser were written in code: T1 for him and N1 for his wife, Nora.

The programme also spoke to another whistle-blower who had his payments authorised by a senior BAe official reporting directly to the man at the top: Chief Executive, Sir Richard Evans. Sir Richard had told a Parliamentary Select Committee a few months previously that they "are not in the business of making payments to members of any government". The use of "are" and absence of "have never been" was telling and one member of the Committee loudly grumbled about it. Rightly so. Cover ups often begin with a careful use of the present tense.

Meanwhile, the gears were grinding into place to prosecute the company. After spending several hours with Peter at the Elm Street headquarters of the SFO, giving them a very long witness statement against BAe, the case was referred to Ministry of Defence police to take forward as a joint investigation; this was because of a connected payment to an MoD official which appeared to breach domestic bribery restrictions. I arranged for the transfer of Peter's huge hoard of documents to be safely conveyed to the authorities. Luckily for the SFO and the MoD he was a meticulous record keeper.

We also engaged counsel and agreed a strategy in a meeting with Peter about how we would balance the confidentiality requirements of the investigating authorities with the need to keep the story in the public eye.

For the next couple of years, we worked closely with the prosecution authorities whilst at the same time negotiating and navigating the media rapids, trying to make sure nothing Peter said or did would compromise him as a witness.

In 2004 *The Guardian* published a major article about Peter alongside various documents which showed the payment system. One single month's file listed 23 payments in August 1995 totalling almost £1m. Peter had also got a signed off bill, approved as "OK to pay". The person approving the payment at BAe's headquarters was Steve Mogford, who was one of their most senior officials.

We were hearing positive noises from the SFO about the case getting the green light to go ahead. One day Peter and I were called in to see the SFO case officers who were immensely proud to show me their case management system which would allow them access to Peter's trove of papers instantly. They were most definitely up for prosecution of BAe.

But the power of BAe was not to be under-estimated. The former Labour Foreign Secretary, Robin Cook, later recalled in his memoirs, *The Point of Departure*, that the Blair government would never make any decision which would "incommode" BAe. He joked that in his time Sir Dick Evans even seemed to have a key to No. 10's garden door.

In October 2006, the Attorney General, Lord Goldsmith, rejected representations by government departments who feared pressure on the Saudis would lose the government business. The Law Chief's response was to resist the warnings saying it would "send a bad message about the credibility of the law in this area, and look like giving in to threats". But then something changed.

Two months later, caving in to Saudi pressure is precisely what the British government did in a massive *volte-face*.

Not long after Lord Goldsmith's statement, pressure from the Saudis increased. Rumours emerged that the Saudis were threatening to pull out of a deal to buy 72 Eurofighter jets from BAe and deal with France instead. This was the Saudis exercising their considerable leverage.

Suddenly, in December 2006, the decision to prosecute BAe was reversed. And the decision came from the very top: the Prime Minister. Tony Blair had apparently stepped in and told the AG to stop the case as it was not in Britain's best interests. Goldsmith told the BBC the decision was his, in his role as AG, and the decision was made on the merits. He claimed there were some very big problems with the case "and my judgement was that it [a prosecution] wouldn't succeed". Pull the other one, it's got bells on it, I muttered through gritted teeth.

It was hogwash and the Attorney General was trying, poorly, to cover his tracks given his previously stated position.

Peter was aghast. And deflated. When we next met, he was more upset than at any time in the past three years. I was more shocked by this than anything I had seen the government do. The Executive, in the form of the Prime Minister (and a Labour one at that), had made a political decision and interfered with the prosecution authorities in a manner which undermined the principle of separation of powers.

It was utterly shameful.

The threats had worked. Blair had leant on his Attorney General, making him eat his October 2006 words. The AG in turn leant on the then Director of the SFO, Robert Wardle, who announced in December the discontinuance of the three-year investigation which had already cost a huge sum, paid out of public funds. Wardle's explanation was that the decision was taken after representations made to him and the Attorney General concerning the need to safeguard national and international security. The rule of law had to be "balanced against the wider public interest".

Goldsmith told the House of Lords that a further 18 months of enquiries would be needed, and, in these circumstances, such a delay would potentially damage the public interest and so the SFO's inquiry would be halted.

In 2007, two NGOs, The Corner House and the Campaign Against the Arms Trade, started a judicial review of the decision. Early on in the proceedings they managed to get some heavily redacted documents which revealed that Blair had sent Goldsmith a personal minute about the "real and immediate risk of a collapse in UK/Saudi security, intelligence and defence cooperation". He also mentioned the risk of losing the unsigned 72 Eurofighters deal.

The following year, the High Court ruled in favour of the judicial review brought by the NGOs. The SFO had acted unlawfully in dropping the investigation. The case forced the SFO to open up and argue that it was powerless to resist the Saudi threats to not co-operate with intelligence sharing on terrorism and further lucrative deals. In other words, it admitted to caving in to Saudi blackmail.

This was how Britain worked. And still works.

Lord Justice Moses and Mr Justice Sullivan said, using unusual immoderate language, that "so bleak a picture of the impotence of the law invites at least dismay, if not outrage". They went on to say that if an individual operating in this country had made such a threat as the Saudis had made, "he would risk being charged with an attempt to pervert the course of justice".

It was a damning indictment of the government and the SFO. Not only did this huge semi-public company spend millions on bribing the Saudi officials with just about anything they wanted, but they were also powerful enough to stop a prosecution by the mere issuing of threats.

The House of Lords later overturned the High Court ruling, stating that Wardle had acted lawfully in abandoning its investigation in face of the "ugly and obviously unwelcome threat" as Lord Bingham termed it. The famous judge concluded, "The issue in these proceedings is not whether his decision was right or wrong, nor whether the Divisional Court or the House agrees with it, but whether it was a decision which the Director was lawfully entitled to make."

The rule of law took a heavy beating. It was disgusting. Justice, the human rights group, called it a sad day.

When I heard about the murder of dissident Saudi journalist Jamal Khashoggi more than a decade later in 2018 my mind raced back to the impunity the Saudi regime and its ruling family felt it could operate under. The journalist did not think that he could be harmed on Turkish soil when he went to collect papers from the Saudi Embassy. He was murdered and his body then chopped up. Initially the Saudis claimed the journalist had left the Embassy; then they claimed he died in "a fight"; later they admitted he died in a "chokehold" by a Saudi official.

The official story kept changing except in one respect: that it was not authorised from the Kingdom's ruler. The truth, like Khashoggi's body, remains to be found.

As for Peter, he became a witness for the FBI and the Department of Justice in the United States in another extraordinary turn of events. The Foreign Corrupt Practices Act (FCPA) makes it illegal for non-US companies to arrange overseas bribes and operate in the US at the same time. The paperwork which has to be completed declaring compliance said so. BAe has a huge volume of business in the US and prosecutors in the US started to look into and demand, through court processes, the massive archive which the SFO had collated. Peter became an important witness for the FBI special agents who were investigating. Of course, there were US commercial interests at stake there as well, with its US rival, Lockheed Martin, vying for the same aerospace business as BAe so a cynical view is that it suited US business interests to pursue BAe so aggressively. It turned out the SFO had found other corrupt practices which they kept under wraps. Thankfully, with other whistle-blowers following Peter's example, we were able to find out some more about how they greased the Saudi wheels.

On 1 March 2010 BAe pleaded guilty in court to conspiring to defraud the United States by making false statements about its FCPA compliance programme. The sentence was a colossal $400m fine together with an agreement to undertake remediation measures. The breach was all about competition law. Reading the very long document which remains online for all to see, the manner of the prosecution reminded me of the way Al Capone was eventually convicted: for taxation breaches rather than harder to prove gangsterism practices.

The detail was extraordinary: with the SFO's help, which they gratefully acknowledged, details emerged that the Travellers World payments were just the tip of an iceberg. The offshore operations run by BAe were exposed, showing that a re-cycling back of a chunk of the contracts (one estimate put it at close to 20%) was used to pay the ruling family in hard cash, exorbitant gifts and expenses.

BAe held its hands up to everything the US investigation uncovered. By making false FCPA statements confirming that it hadn't operated corruptly, which it is required to do each year, the British company had exposed itself and had nowhere to hide if it still wanted to do business in the United States. The most egregious example was BAe's British Virgin Island's operation in which, from May 2001 onwards, BAe admitted it contracted with and encouraged "advisors" to receive payments of £135m to ensure it was "favoured" in foreign government decisions. In many instances there were no legitimate activities to justify the payments. Although unrelated to Peter's revelations, BAe also paid a UK fine of £30m for false accounting. The Crown Court judge referred to one secret payment of £7.7m as a "bribe" to win a £28m contract.

But for Peter opening the can of worms, would this have emerged? Perhaps, but without the first one to stand up and be counted and take the flak, nothing gets going. And it was that first call to David Leigh which did it.

Did anyone at BAe suffer for this colossal bribery exercise? I think the answer is not as far as I am aware. BAe is 'too big to fail' so it paid up and moved on. The fact it had declared the allegations as "ill-informed and wrong" adding they could "categorically state that there is not now and there has never been in existence…a slush fund" and that BAe "operates in accordance with the laws of the United Kingdom and all other countries in which it operates" was an outright lie. Just take a look online at the indictment the company pleaded guilty to, together with the accompanying Department of Justice press release. Not long afterwards, Sir Dick Evans left BAe in the same month as the company pleaded guilty and accepted the whopping fine in the US.

But something did happen to Peter which I was pleased about. The US has a very different attitude to witnesses. If warranted, they will pay a witness for the help afforded to them by individual whistle-blowers. One day Peter called me and said, "Guess what, a substantial sum has just arrived in my account from someone called 'A. Plumber'." He explained that he was told by his FBI contacts the reward payment would happen at the appropriate time but not how.

Whilst not professing any knowledge of witness reward payments, I speculated that things are done very differently by the FBI and the US generally. But, of course, their target was a massive British multinational – a much easier target than Saudi Arabia.

Tony Winship, who has never admitted wrongdoing, was arrested by Ministry of Defence police acting for the SFO, but no charges were brought.

Peter died recently after a long illness, and he should never be forgotten as a hero whistle-blower. And the SFO, hiding behind the Department of Justice skirts, finally made use of the evidence it had spent three years accumulating.

Chapter 8

Mark Covell's double whammy

J ournalists come in all shapes and sizes. I have represented some of the most right-wing journalists in Britain – step forward Kelvin Mac-Kenzie, Katie Hopkins, Trevor Kavanagh and Dan Wootton – and also the most left-wing, including the editor of *Socialist Worker* and Indymedia journalist, Mark Covell.

If I had taken the path of becoming a journalist, which was my plan B, I might have been Mark, covering protests like the G8 Summit. I had great affinity with Mark and the independent media he was part of. Instead, I was to become his media lawyer, taking on the *Daily Mail* for him.

It was Mark's fate to be the victim of Italian police brutality in July 2001 whilst covering the G8 Summit which was being held in the port town of Genoa. The most powerful western alliance countries were meeting. Their host was the notorious right-winger, Silvio Berlusconi, then Italian Prime Minister. The Genoa protest against the G8 gathering of leaders was the most significant of the anti-capitalist, anti-globalisation movement's protests, which peaked at the turn of the century in this northern Italian port town and, to a lesser extent, in the G8's gatherings in Seattle and Edinburgh. Two decades on it now looks like protests from a different era.

200,000 people had gathered in the town to protest against what they saw as illegitimate attempts to set the rules for the planet at large. A blockade was planned. The police were on high alert, tear gas and batons at the ready. The day before, one demonstrator, Carlo Giuliani, a 23-year-old Genoan, had been killed by a Carabinieri police officer. He was shot and his body run over by a police vehicle. Tensions were running very high.

The Armando Diaz school and adjacent Pertini building had been made available by the local authority to accommodate the Genoa Social Forum and its supporters, including the alternative media. Mark had spent the day there, filing reports for Indymedia – he didn't go anywhere near the protests.

On July 21 2001 shortly before midnight, the cops attacked the buildings. Mark had the terrible misfortune to get in the path of advancing police whilst crossing the road between the school's buildings. The first wave of cops smashed into him as the first person to get in their way, batons raised and intent on raiding the temporary residents in the school, mostly by this time in their sleeping bags. 92 protesters were arrested. Mark was placed under armed guard, with police waiting to make him arrestee number 93.

Shockingly, the attack on the building resulted in 63 protesters being taken to hospital because of the seriousness of their injuries. Only 19 were well enough to go into custody. Worse was to come for many of the injured. The ambulances were followed by police, and several protesters were then taken away to a transit military facility called the Bolzaneto. 24 applied to the ECtHR for compensation after their Bolzaneto experiences. Mark counts himself "lucky" that his injuries were so serious he could not be moved.

Nick Davies, another of our firm's brilliant journalist clients, wrote pithily about Mark's fate in his *Guardian* report:

> *It was just before midnight when the first police officer hit Mark Covell, swiping his truncheon down on his left shoulder. Covell did his best to yell out in Italian that he was a journalist but, within seconds, he was surrounded by riot-squad officers thrashing him with their sticks. For a while, he managed to stay on his feet.*

But then, as Mark told me, after falling to the ground another officer came over and kicked him in the chest with such force it punctured his left lung. His last thought before he lost consciousness was that he was not going to make it. His other injuries included a fractured hand and a damaged spine. He lost 16 teeth in the attack. It was a minor miracle this slight man, weighing just eight stone, survived.

Mark was taken to hospital, under arrest, his room guarded by an armed riot cop.

When I met him a couple of years later his broken bones had healed but the trauma was still very evident. He had hired Italian lawyers to take on the police and seek damages for his wrongful arrest and assault, but he also wanted to pursue the *Daily Mail*. He had become the victim of the tabloid's deceitful interview of him and his family in one of the most disgraceful episodes in modern newspaper history. Were the broken bones from the truncheons of riot cops worse than the mugging Mark and his family got from the *Mail*? Certainly, Mark saw them as being on a par.

While Mark lay in hospital, heavily bandaged, sedated and with tubes sticking out of him, a personable British woman sat by his bedside. Taking her to be a British Embassy official, he answered her questions as best he could. She must be official to have got past the cop outside his room, he thought. Another man was with her, who had stayed silent. Part way through the interview he pulled out a camera, asking if he could take Mark's photograph. It was only at this point that the woman announced she was from the *Daily Mail* and that her name was Lucie Morris. Disgusted by this ruse, Mark ordered them to get out.

The hospital visit was only part of a pincer movement against Mark. That same day Morris rang Mark's mother, Janet, breaking to her the news of his serious condition and that she had been to see him. The newspaper then pounced, choosing to see Janet when she was at her most vulnerable, having just heard about Mark's fate.

Janet described to me in excruciating detail how the sting unfolded. Unaware of the details of how her son had been almost clubbed to death, the newspaper sent a two-person team to her straight after their call to tell her what had happened to Mark. Sitting in her immaculate home counties front room, the pair had introduced themselves as sympathetic journalists who wanted to write about Mark.

"How did they do this?" I asked when I went to call on Janet in the same front room they had sat in. She explained how they expressed their sympathy for him and how some information about his family, his upbringing and ideally a photo of him from better days would help them write a positive piece. Unaware of the newspaper's antipathy to anyone like Mark – a proud radical devoted to reporting the news through alternative media – Janet opened up and told them about him. Despite her shock, she refused their repeated invitations to badmouth her own son. She posed for a photo, showing her unhappiness at his fate.

Mark's sister quickly arrived at the house after being called by Janet. She was immediately suspicious about the journalists' claim to be sympathetic to his plight. She went upstairs and called the number of the British Consul in Genoa. Her worse fears were realised. The official told her that Mark had already been "interviewed" in his hospital bed despite the armed guard outside his room and the order that only authorised people could enter his room. This gave rise to a suspicion that Morris had gained entry to Mark's room by somehow persuading the police she was "authorised". The consul, Alan Reuter, later told me that even he wasn't permitted to see Mark despite his consular status, so he was very surprised when he heard about Morris' success, especially with a photographer in tow.

Back in the newsroom in Kensington, the editorial team was busy planning their big 'exclusive' in which the headline screamed Mark was the Briton who led the rioters with a photo of him propped up in his hospital bed. It was to be the front-page splash. The angle was unambiguous; Covell had led a riot, linking him to the notorious 'Black Bloc' anarchists who were, in the tabloid's eyes, public enemy number one. Mark was the *Mail*'s personification of the scary, violent man plotting to overthrow capitalism.

The message to *Mail* readers was clear enough: he got what was coming to him.

I was asked to take over the case from another law firm which had let Mark's case get stale. They had not progressed his case very far, for reasons which were unclear to me. The strict 12-month rule within which you can bring libel proceedings had already passed by the time the case came to me so Mark could only proceed with a privacy action.

The first thing was to get a detailed account first from Mark and then his mother. I also interviewed Mark's sister. There was no doubt that a privacy claim should be winnable. The right to privacy was a relatively new area where damages could be recovered.

The hospital intrusion had remarkable parallels with another notorious case, that of *'Allo 'Allo* TV star, Gorden Kaye, who sued a tabloid newspaper in 1990. He had suffered brain damage when he was injured in a car accident. Two *Sunday Sport* journalists, posing as doctors, took photographs of him lying in his hospital bed. He tried to obtain an injunction to stop the photographs being published which was initially granted but the Court of Appeal ruled against him because there was no right to privacy at that time. The court expressed a strong view that there should be, and by the time Mark sued through me we stood a much stronger chance.

Unsurprisingly, the *Mail* put up a fight and said they would not accept any wrongdoing on their part or pay Mark any damages. It was the exact same response I was used to getting from other organisations fighting individuals who they took a dislike to.

With Lucy Moorman, we got going on the claim, describing the *Mail*'s actions as grotesque and outrageous. Mark was already consumed with the case, especially against the police officers who had beaten him to a pulp. I wanted to get him a quick win to get his bigger case off to a good start. He needed the fillip of an early victory in his many battles to come.

Even though the *Mail*'s lawyers did put up an initial fight they knew the claim, grounded in privacy law and data rights, was ultimately likely to go against them. Medical confidentiality rightly attracts high levels of protection. Mark agreed with me that the priority was to get the *Mail* claim quickly won and, importantly, to get their recognition that there was no truth in the extremely damaging headline alleging that he was not only a rioter but a leader of the riot.

This was crucial. Details were emerging of how the Italian police, to cover up their brutal beatings of protesters in their sleeping bags, had planted Molotov cocktails as well as knives and tools in the school that night. One officer even went so far as to claim he was stabbed and saved only by his bulletproof vest which he showed off complete with a slash to the lining. The truth was he had slashed his own vest; no one had attacked him. He was later convicted of defamation and forgery.

Our claim settled relatively quickly with Mark winning damages, costs and the *Mail's* acceptance that he had not led any riot. They resisted publicly apologising to him but agreed to provide a private letter which he was able to deploy in his Italian litigation. Their false story was thereby neutralised.

Mark spent the next few years, along with the other victims of the police brutality, pursuing his damages claim in Italy. The turning point was the trial of a large number of police officers charged with maltreatment.

Mark came to see me and asked if I would go with him to Genoa for the verdict. Unlike in this country, the tribunal of fact was not a jury but, in this case, a panel of judges. I landed in Genoa and met Mark at the Indymedia facility where, true to form, he was covering the event as a journalist, keen eyed with a roll up in hand. He was totally in his element.

We then went to meet his Italian lawyer, Massimo Pastore, who explained the importance of the trial about to be decided. With guilty verdicts, the victims could then progress their cases which had been held up awaiting this outcome. This 'stay' (postponement) was normal – we have a similar set up in this country. "And what if they are acquitted?" I asked. "Impossible," the lawyer pronounced. I smiled and thought to myself: I bloody well hope so.

The weirdest thing about the decision of the judges was the timing. The listing was not, as we know it over here, the usual civilised post-breakfast 10am slot or after lunch at 2pm but "by the end of the day". It was explained to me the verdict had to be delivered no later than midnight.

Genoa is an ancient port town which is also quite edgy. Beautiful, colourful with a medieval town centre. It is a maze of alleys and grand buildings. I had little time to take in the architectural significance of the Ligurian capital as we were immersed in discussions with Mark, his co-claimants and their lawyers. Thankfully, the lawyers spoke excellent English.

The evening wait at the courthouse after a hurried pizza wore on. One of the lawyers predicted the judges would not emerge until the last possible moment given the number of defendants and charges. He was spot on. I wandered over to the other side of the vast waiting area and looked at the splendid uniforms of the police officer defendants, complete with tricorn hats.

Just before midnight, we got word that the judges were about to come into court. Everyone hurried into the huge courtroom. I sat next to a nervous Mark and Massimo. As the loud bongs from the town clock began their countdown to midnight the judges in their colourful garb walked in and took their seats. Immediately their judgment was read by the president of the panel.

When the judge had read out their decision some of the defence lawyers got up from their places in the front of the court and made their way out. One of them even had his mobile phone out and was loudly talking into it. Massimo whispered to me that many of the police officers had been found guilty. I turned to Mark who had tears of joy running down his cheeks. Outside the victims enjoyed a mass huddle of victory. The convicted officers walked past us with an air of indignation. Surly does not begin to describe it. 15 out of 45 had been convicted. I wondered if it would be enough to continue the fight for the victims to win their damages claim.

We then went to a cobbled medieval square to celebrate with some good Italian vino. At last, I managed to get Massimo to explain what would happen now to the convicted officers. "This is Italy, my friend. These bastards will not spend even a single day in jail," he told me in no uncertain terms. He explained that for most offences, including these, defendants do not go to jail until all appeals have been exhausted. If you keep appealing, time will eventually run out (because of the statute of limitations which imposes strict limits on concluding cases) meaning the conviction is erased. The jail sentences just handed down, ranging from five months to five years for the 15 officers, would be wiped off the record. So, if you play it right and have the necessary financial resources to keep your lawyers busy with filing appeals, playing the system to the maximum, you effectively get off Scot-free despite being convicted.

I was still shaking my head at this ridiculous state of affairs when something caught the corner of my eye. It was brown and furry. A kitten perhaps?

It was moving fast between tables. No, it was a gigantic rat. I nodded my head and thought to myself this must be a sign. I turned back to Massimo and asked what the point of all this was.

The lawyer explained the only real effect of the verdict was to allow victims like Mark to finally receive compensation.

Mark's civil claim against the state could proceed at last. Not long after, in September of the same year, the Italian Interior Ministry awarded Mark €350,000 for the injuries he sustained. It had taken him more than a decade to get to this point, shuttling between the two countries and pursuing justice. His resources were so drained from his legal battles that he was facing eviction from his council flat for unpaid rent but, he told *The Guardian*, he now hoped to buy it.

What happened to Lucie Morris and her counterpart who went to Janet Covell's home? Nothing, so far as we know. She told one journalist she had done nothing wrong, claiming she had taken personal risks to get to Mark so he could put his side across. The notion of the article telling his side was a nonsense especially as the front-page article 'ARMED GUARD ON BRITON WHO LED RIOTERS' had been brandished by lawyers representing the police who were seeking to undermine his compensation claim in later proceedings. Morris later claimed to have been "duped" by Italian police about the facts of what happened.

I went on record describing the paper's coverage of Mark as "the worst example of its kind I've ever come across". The newspaper's response was feeble. "If there was a hurt, it was completely inadvertent."

What you might call a non-apology apology.

Since then, Mark has tried to re-build his life and recover from that night in Genoa. Happily, he's now working as a professional bike courier and participating with a forthcoming Netflix documentary to coincide with the 25th anniversary of the Genoa raid in 2026 which will feature what happened to him on the night the Italian police nearly killed him.

Chapter 9

The straight coppers

The experience of losing after winning and knowing it's the wrong result really hurts, especially for my client.

When my phone pinged on that fateful day, seven months after a hotly contested Court of Appeal hearing, I read the first line of my barrister's message, attaching a draft judgment.

It began, "I'm afraid...". I didn't need to read any more. I knew we had lost. I let out a curse and my Blackberry fell to the floor, bouncing a couple of times before clattering on the tiled surface. A secretary standing nearby asked if I was alright. She could see I wasn't. I made a hurried excuse, reassuring her and rushed off to print out the very long 100-plus page decision. These days lawyers are forbidden to print unnecessary documents in order to save the environment unless, like me, you are old school and for certain things only paper will do.

For the next two hours I read the reasoning of the three appeal judges in a cloud of gloom. Jeffrey Smele, then my trainee, didn't dare speak to me. When I finished, I told him to grab his jacket; we were heading for the closest pub on Berwick Street, Soho. I needed to drown my sorrows. Once allowed by the usual embargo, I would have to tell my client the bad news that despite winning we had now lost and, worse still, there was no way back.

I still maintain that what happened in the case of former Detective Constable Michael Charman was a travesty from start to finish. Nothing ever suggested to me that this cop was bent; quite the opposite – he was not just clean but brave and utterly decent.

Together with his Inspector, John Redgrave, they had the rawest of times with a record breaking seven-year suspension from the Metropolitan Police despite plaudits and commendations in their careers.

And it was all based solely on the word of a double-dealing grass called Geoffrey Brennan, a loud character straight out of Bermondsey, complete with a facial tick which got more pronounced when agitated.

My involvement began in 2003 when Michael Charman, a tall and balding ex-Flying Squad officer, came to see me in my Old Street office to tell me his story. It took a long time for him to explain why he had been suspended for so many years. He looked haunted, scarred by his experiences.

It was eye popping.

Brennan had been Michael's informant for many years; he would give information to Michael which would then be passed up the chain for others to assess. Brennan's father was an old-time informant. Both father and son would use their informant status to get away with committing their own crimes. Brennan was, in Michael's own words, totally untrustworthy.

Brennan managed to persuade the Met he needed a second handler, Detective Inspector Chris Smith, to inform. It resulted in John and Michael being accused of corruption by Brennan through the auspices of handler number two, DI Smith. The claim, later recanted, was that Brennan had to pay Michael, and later his boss, John, five figure sums to "cover" for him (in other words corruptly protect him from police investigations) from a theft of £400,000. It was a unique situation: a registered criminal with two separate handlers, where he managed to divert investigations into a theft he had committed by claiming £50,000 of it was corruptly handed over to the police.

A new anti-corruption unit at Scotland Yard, known as the Ghost Squad, had by this time been set up to counter the corrupt activities of some officers going back to the early nineties. The Ghost Squad failed to build a credible case against Michael and John and so resorted to desperate measures. They put out a bait, in the form of a specially marked confidential document in the hands of Michael's girlfriend and which would be of interest to the suspended officers. At the time she was a well regarded CPS caseworker. She took the bait – a transcript of a Ghost Squad interview with DI Smith, who the officers regarded as the author of their misfortune – at the end of a late afternoon legal conference at chambers. Unbeknown to Michael, his girlfriend or John, the Ghost Squad had learned, through their bugging devices, that Michael was coming over to hers for dinner and he had invited John over to cheer him up as by this time he was severely depressed. Michael's girlfriend took the transcript home and showed it to the pair.

After reading the document and not thinking much of it, the trio discussed burning it as rubbish. Unknown to them, the house was surrounded by anti-corruption cops, and their conversation was being listened to by senior officers in the Ghost Squad. On hearing the specially marked document might be destroyed, panic set in. Destruction wasn't a development they had factored in. It was decided that the offence of conspiracy to pervert the course of justice was being committed and the Ghost Squad signalled for a raid to take place. The operation's leader gave the 'go, go, go', the door was smashed down and the three were arrested.

The criminal charges which followed were all thrown out by the professional magistrate who didn't think much of the police case. The Met then spent a couple of years disciplining Michael and John for the incident. Seven years after their suspension they were "required to resign" over the marked document by the disciplinary board which heard their case, spelling an end to their long careers.

So what did any of this have to do with me? In 2003, former BBC crime journalist Graeme McLagan wrote his book *Bent Coppers*, published by Orion Publishing, which was intended to be the story of the Met's Ghost Squad. The book featured, among others, Michael Charman and John Redgrave. By the time of publication, Brennan had recanted his accusations against Michael and John. However, although McLagan did report Brennan's recanting of his allegations, it did not seem to count for very much in McLagan's eyes.

The following year, covering much of the same ground but in much more depth, Michael Gillard and Laurie Flynn published their book *Untouchables*. Whereas McLagan took the position that there were still reasonable grounds to suspect Michael and John of corruption (a view shared by the head of the

Ghost Squad, Roger Gaspar), the later book regarded the pair as wholly innocent and the victims of multiple cover ups.

Space does not allow me to describe the multi-layered history of the various police operations, the web of criminality involved and the immense efforts
made by the Met police's Ghost Squad against Michael and John. Readers
can read both books and the two libel judgments and make up their own
minds.

Michael sued McLagan and Orion for libel, claiming that the book bore
the meaning that he was a corrupt police officer.

The trial was hard fought after intense preparation. McLagan struggled in
the witness box at times with Hugh Tomlinson QC probing the freelancer's
investigations and exposing a tendency to rely on police rather than underworld sources.

McLagan and Orion lost the case before Mr Justice Gray, who decided
the book, so far as Michael was concerned, meant there were cogent (rather
more than reasonable) grounds to suspect him as guilty of corruption. It is
always embarrassing for an author to have written something *more* accusatory
than they think it is. But worse was to come for the publisher and author.
Gray J threw out the defence of what was then called responsible journalism,
where latitude is given to the publication if it is written responsibly.

But when Gray J delivered his judgment, I was unhappy with the word
'cogent'. If he was going to find for an intermediate level between guilt and
reasonable grounds, at least use an unambiguous word such as 'strong'.

However, the plain fact remained that the grounds to suspect Michael of
corruption amounted to not very much.

The elation at winning the trial was soon curtailed when Orion got leave
to appeal Gray's decision to the Court of Appeal. Another case called *Jameel
v Wall Street Journal Europe* had been decided on appeal liberalising the tests
for responsible journalism which the appellants could now catch the wind of
and use in their favour.

In the run up to the appeal hearing, the other side told us that if they
didn't win, they would concede the case because they would not fight the case

based on truth. In other words, the justification defence was to be jettisoned after years of maintaining the facts could be proved. The only way they could win was to show responsible journalism, even without evidence of the meaning of more-than-reasonable grounds to suspect them. We lost the appeal: the court ruled that McLagan did not depart from the standards required of a responsible journalist. Later, I heard that the original trial judge (now deceased) made it privately known he still stood by his decision.

When the appeal decision came out, it made several headlines, and my opponents were cock-a-hoop. Our short press release barely got any coverage: in essence we said there was still nothing, not a shred of evidence, that had been established against Michael (or John).

This remains the case to this day.

Brennan, the sole source of the withdrawn corruption allegation, eventually went to prison for three and a half years after the jury unanimously found him guilty of stealing £400,000. Even when goaded under cross examination, he refuted the suggestion the officers were corruptly involved with him.

Now in retirement, Michael Charman and his girlfriend, now wife, and their menagerie of pets, can look back with pride at his police service until the day he became Brennan's handler; and from then on in, he can look back in anger.

Chapter 10

Murder on The Bishops Avenue

The 'c' word in criminal law is circumstantial. This murder investigation was all about circumstantial evidence and whether it added up to a case against the dead man's widow or if she was (and remains) a much-wronged woman.

Sometimes you have to admit defeat after a long investigation which ends up going nowhere. The murder of Aristos Constantinou in the first hours of 1985 is one of those and still haunts his family, especially his brother Achilleas, four decades on. The years of frustration grind on, much like the murder of Daniel Morgan and the campaign fought by his brother, Alistair. I got involved in trying to help the Constantinou family in 2006. I didn't get very far.

Aristos' murder shook the Greek Cypriot community in London to its core. By then both brothers lived on the most expensive residential road in London's Hampstead, The Bishops Avenue, and had a thriving fashion business. They were famous in the fashion world, and their brand was a household name in London. Aristos Fashions (later re-named Ariella Fashions) was aimed mainly at young women and by the late seventies, the fashion empire was growing with a chain of shops developing.

My own mum and dad emigrated here as newlyweds in the coldest winter on record – 1947 – and the Constantinou clan arrived in a later wave. Weirdly, the families had a connection despite the clear difference between us in terms of social class and wealth. My dad had a tiny barber shop on the same street in Marylebone as the (then) up-and-coming Constantinou brothers.

It was only after I got involved in the case that my dad told me Aristos used to be one of his customers.

"Lovely man. Make sure you help them and solve the crime, Louis."

It was the only time he ever told me what to do about a case. Ever.

So, what happened on the night of the murder? Aristos and Elena, his much younger wife, arrived home from a New Year's Eve party in the early hours of 1985 after, witnesses maintained, she teased him on the dance floor. His annoyance resulted in him smashing a brandy glass when he put it down too hard on the bar as she continued dancing.

According to Elena, when they arrived back to their Hampstead mansion (complete with maid quarters and stabled horses in the vast rear garden) she went upstairs. She claimed she heard a bang and smelt what she described as "like fireworks" before being grabbed by a masked assailant, bundled into a bathroom and locked in.

Clambering out of the window and down a drainpipe, she raised the alarm by flagging down a passing motorcyclist and his passenger who turned out to be a gay couple, both from the long running production of *Cats*, on their way home from a New Year's Eve party. One of them got into the house in the same way Elena told them she had escaped. He broke through the bathroom door, went downstairs and found Aristos with multiple bullet wounds to his head and body.

He was dead.

The back door appeared to have been broken into, with glass debris on the floor near the lock.

A safe lay open. As Elena told it, the couple were the victims of a burglary which turned violent and fatal.

For the next few days, Elena was sedated and too unwell to give the police the help they needed. The *Cats* witnesses told the police she had said her assailants were "black men".

Meanwhile Achilleas Constantinou and his family rushed back from a holiday in France upon hearing about his brother's death. From the beginning he sensed something wasn't right about Elena's account. The family fractured quickly with Elena and her three young sons taking refuge with her parents in a less salubrious part of north London whilst Achilleas tried to make sense of it all, at the same time supporting his grief stricken mother, Efthymia, who went on to write a self-published book about the killing of her son and her suspicions that Elena was not telling the truth.

The police investigation was far from flawless, even by the standards of the eighties, despite the front-page headlines in several newspapers. *The Times* led with 'Burglary theory after wealthy businessman is shot dead'. There were criticisms about the failure to secure the house as a crime scene, the absence of any firearms residue testing on Elena and the officer in charge of the investigation deciding early on to treat her as a victim rather than keep an open mind.

As the police investigation developed, they were able to grasp a flavour of the couple's sometimes tempestuous relationship. Witnesses suggested an open marriage. There was talk of a breakup in the air. It was far from a happy, harmonious marriage and one theory is that Aristos revealed his plans to divorce Elena on the night he died.

But what about the means? According to some witnesses, Elena owned a small gauge handgun given to her by Aristos (who himself possessed shotguns) which she has always denied possessing. The main witness to this was a member of her staff who was horrified to have a gun casually offered to her by Elena in case she had any "trouble" on her way home from the tube station late in the evening after seeing her favourite show, *Trafford Tanzi* starring Toyah Willcox.

On another occasion the same witness saw the weapon and gave the police a detailed description. Silver and tiny with a pearl handle, it resembled a "lady's gun" from the movies. Size, in this case, is everything. A forensic examination of the bullets which killed Aristos were, unusually, small gauge. This matched the witnesses' description of a small handgun to a T. The murder weapon has never been found.

In fact Elena gave a new account to the police that her assailants were men dressed in black rather than black men. This was the prelude to an even bigger change of account from the widow. Shortly before the inquest she told the police it was time to reveal something very significant, now she felt protected by her new husband, a burly lifeguard she had recently met in Florida.

She now told the police she actually knew one of the masked men who had whisked her off to the bathroom after knocking her out. It was, she claimed, the father of two colleagues from one of the Aristos dress shops. According to at least one witness she had been having affairs with both these younger men although she denied it. The reason for her silence until nine months later was because, she maintained in her new account to the police, the lives of her children were threatened.

The police believed her. Tony Tooley and his father, Michael, were quickly arrested for Aristos' murder following Elena's change of evidence. However, the case against them fell apart when they were able to provide alibis for the night in question. It was, after all, New Year's Eve, the one night of the year most of the population can provide an alibi.

The police investigation was back at square one and one of the most unsatisfactory aspects was why the suspicion failed to now fall on Elena.

I was to find all this out when I went to see Achilleas at his home in Hampstead. He was still living there long after Elena had sold up next door, staring each day at the house where his brother was murdered.

I have never met anyone quite like Achilleas. Articulate and intelligent (he got himself a law degree from King's College, University of London before he became a fashion millionaire) he was utterly possessed of the case, keeping a vast amount of information about it both in his head as well as his physical archive.

Like many in his predicament, he also finds it very difficult to accept criticism of his brother.

The lack of a handgun, any worthwhile forensics or a witness to the shooting were problematic, I told him. But the evidential issues around Elena were also suspicious.

Achilleas took me to the vast garden to show me the drainpipe which Elena said she had climbed down after being locked in the bathroom. The

Cats witness accessed her home by the same means – up the drainpipe and into the bathroom through a small window before breaking through the bathroom door and going downstairs to find Aristos with six bullets in him. Two were in his temple and were found to have been shot at close range, as if he had to be finished off. The bullets were so small it is quite conceivable that the first four failed to kill the millionaire outright. The coincidence with the evidence of Elena possessing the small "lady's" handgun was, in my eyes, huge.

Achilleas had a long list of complaints about Elena's account. If it was a robbery gone wrong, why didn't the cash and jewellery get stolen? Was it because the intruders were so panicked after finishing off Aristos with shots to the head?

Why was there a vase still standing in front of the bathroom window Elena escaped from which surely would have blocked her escape route?

Why were the glass fragments from the kitchen door in the wrong place as if broken from the inside if the burglars had forced entry from outside?

Another theory supporting Elena was that Aristos was targeted by assassins out for revenge. A threatening call was made to Elena shortly after the killing with the caller saying that the rest of the family would meet the same end. If this was the case, why get caught in the middle of the burglary?

A further investigation in the late nineties resulted in more evidence which took things a little bit further. Achilleas told me there was a police recommendation that Elena should be extradited from Cyprus where she now lived with her third husband, arrested for her husband's murder and tried, but the Crown Prosecution Service decided against this course of action.

I became involved in the case in 2006 and worked on it for three years. My role was to seek a re-examination of the CPS' refusal to re-open the case and get evidence from the police to provide us with evidence hitherto withheld from Achilleas from the two earlier investigations. It was also to give advice on whether the media publicity route was worth expanding or not.

First, we decided to go down the private prosecution route. I instructed Keir Starmer to draft a powerful submission. Not long afterwards he became the Director of Public Prosecutions and was not only unable to assist further but precluded from any role whatsoever in the CPS decision.

The evidence that had been withheld arrived in dribs and drabs. This was because the new murder team had to get the consent of the witnesses to have their witness statements passed to us as wannabe private prosecutors. A bonus was the implementation of the 2003 Criminal Justice Act which allowed hearsay evidence to be used.

We considered that a powerful case was made when we wrote to the CPS in 2008. The cold case team which re-opened the investigation seemed sympathetic. Achilleas was convinced that whilst the police were onside and wanted to drag Elena back from Cyprus to be arrested, charged and tried, the CPS were having none of it. He even went so far as to claim the CPS had usurped the role of the jury. As the papers were scrutinised, including previously unseen material, I increasingly felt there was a circumstantial case to be put before a jury.

This was the big question. Achilleas and others believed the CPS' reluctance to prosecute was to avoid embarrassment over the initial police investigation. I have some sympathy with this view. My own theory was that the CPS did not want to have the history of the police investigation thrown back at them in front of a jury: first their acceptance she was a victim resulting in their abject failure to check her for firearms residue or treat her account of the burglary with scepticism; second, the embarrassment of the Tooley arrests on her say so and then having to drop the case against them so quickly. If the police had acted swiftly and kept an open mind about her suspect status so as to secure evidence about her possession of a small handgun, particularly when the bullets were so rare and small, there would have been no hesitation on the part of witnesses. Unfortunately, after so many years, the belated witness statements are prefaced with qualifications such as, "…but with the passage of time I cannot remember the details".

I brought in a new barrister from Keir's chambers, Alison Gerry, to replace him and she worked hard to come up to speed and present a case for prosecution. A date was arranged, and the venue was my office in Soho.

The CPS attended with the cold case officers and their QC, Peter Wright, who had a successful track record in some of the biggest prosecutions in recent years. Achilleas had his say, going on too long for some in the meeting, especially about his criticisms of Elena's account of her escape. Our barrister made some compelling points to back up our written submissions. I weighed in with some more. The police officers sat there grim faced. I could sense what was coming just from their frowns.

The QC delivered the bad news, saying that, despite everything we had put before him, he would not be recommending a prosecution. He wasn't willing to give it a chance. Our counsel, Alison, interjected with her criticisms of such a conservative approach. Wright didn't like anyone arguing back at him and he became verbally aggressive towards Alison. She fought back and said we were all meant to be on the same side, pleading with him to adopt a more optimistic outlook on the prospects of success. But there was nothing doing. Wright wasn't going to change his mind. After they left, we all felt crushed. It was either a private prosecution or nothing.

I again expressed my concerns about taking the private prosecution route. To get permission to start such a prosecution, it requires a professional magistrate to be convinced enough to issue a summons to commence the proceedings. The private prosecutor takes the case through every stage of the court process, just like a state prosecutor, and they have to follow the strict prosecution rules to ensure a fair trial. Here, the prosecutor would be Achilleas himself, represented by a team of solicitors and counsel. Two massive hurdles stood in our way.

Firstly, how to get Elena back from Cyprus. It is one thing for a state to ask another to extradite an individual, but my research had not come up with a single instance where a foreign state had acted at the request of a private individual. My fear was that a magistrate would refuse to issue a summons for this reason or, if persuadable, it would simply not be acted upon because of Elena's continuing absence abroad.

The second problem was that the CPS had the power to (literally) take over a private prosecution and then discontinue it if they felt there were grounds to stop it going forward. Given the negative CPS views all the way along, this risk could not be discounted.

I was also well aware of the experience of Stephen Lawrence's family when, in their prosecution of the men they considered responsible for murdering Stephen, the judge ruled they had no case to answer after hearing some evidence from at least one witness. It was very clear to me that a trial judge in a murder case would be punctilious in upholding the rights of a defendant who was being prosecuted not by the state (which didn't think the case was strong enough) but by a family convinced of the defendant's guilt.

And then, as always, there was the practical matter. The witnesses who had agreed to allow us access to their police witness statements were not the whole picture. What else might crawl out of the woodwork? Probably nothing of significance but you can never be sure.

So, with huge reluctance, Achilleas decided not to proceed with the private prosecution, at least for that moment.

In recent years Achilleas has had his hopes raised when a senior homicide counsel from the CPS considered the case was strong enough to commence a prosecution of Elena, a decision supported by a new cold case team, but then in a dramatic twist of events, the lawyer's decision was reversed. The family was told it was now within the remit of the head of the Special Crime and Counter Terrorism Division. The reasoning raised eyebrows, appearing to adopt a faulty threshold test for prosecution. It has left a very bad taste in the mouth among the officers and the family.

Unsurprisingly Achilleas, now retired and aged 75, has suspicions that somewhere someone is pulling strings to ensure Elena is never prosecuted. Like a dog with a bone, he will never give it up. If it was your beloved sibling, what would you do? It is a question I have asked myself many times in thinking about this most frustrating of cases. And, as time goes on and the fortieth anniversary of the murder came and went on 1 January 2025, memories fade and witnesses die. Achilleas and his family deserve to know what really happened.

Elena, still living in Cyprus, continues to maintain her innocence and criticises what she says are the family's grudges against her. But unanswered questions remain and a full account from her would help determine if there are still grounds to investigate whether the prime suspect label stuck on her is utterly unfair or not.

Chapter 11

The death of a war correspondent

There is no getting away from it – inquests are weird. In the England and Wales legal system, it is the only everyday judicial inquiry in which the judge is the investigator and not just the referee. In the Middle Ages judges were active fact finders; nowadays their officers, often former police officers, go looking for evidence under their direction. I have represented parties, usually bereaved families, in many inquests starting with mesothelioma victims of asbestos inhalation and then 'progressing' to suicides of over-stressed executives and clients in mental health facilities. But none was as strange as the killing in 2003 of Terry Lloyd, the well-known ITN war correspondent together with two of his colleagues during the Iraq War.

Terry was a regular on ITN news reporting from the Middle East and beyond. 20 years in, he was ITN's longest serving reporter and the first to be killed on assignment aged just 50. Like other war correspondents, he risked life and limb to bring us news of wars from the frontline. He had previously broken the news that Saddam Hussein had gassed the Kurds of Halabja using chemical weapons. I immediately felt a bond with him because of the time I spent with Med TV (see Chapter 2) which regarded Halabja as the worst atrocity Hussein had ever inflicted on their people.

In 1999 Terry was the first foreign journalist to enter Kosovo at the height of the Bosnian conflict. It was this war which changed the way news organisations supported their journalists in the field. Rightly, there was now an enhanced duty of care by employers who sent journalists and their support teams into battlefields. Risk assessments, hostile environment training, helmets and body armour all came into play to protect the war reporter. Terry was not wearing his helmet or bullet proof vest at the time of his death for the simple reason that no one in his two-car convoy thought they had reached the front line of the allied forces. Nor did they think they were in any immediate danger, as cameraman Daniel Demoustier was to explain in a later documentary.

Together with Frédéric Nérac and Hussein Osman, Terry paid the ultimate price. All three lost their lives as they followed the advance of British and US troops into Iraq whilst on the road to the southern Iraqi city of Basra. Only one of the team, Daniel Demoustier, made it back injured but alive. To this day, Fréd Nérac remains missing. The initial news reports the following day said the men's two vehicles – clearly marked with TV – came under enemy fire.

And let's not forget the context: Prime Minister Tony Blair had followed US President Bush into the invasion of Iraq using the justification that the President of Iraq, Saddam Hussein, had an arsenal of weapons of mass destruction and had to be stopped. British forces were deployed alongside the American military. Terry's quest for the truth of what allied forces would find was not only legitimate but also vital.

First reports of Daniel's account, just after his rescue, was that a vehicle drew up alongside the vehicle he was in and the occupants, Iraqi officers, appeared to want to surrender. At that moment shots rang out from the allied side, and he saw Terry, in the vehicle in front, fall out and onto the ground. A rapidly put together British Army investigation suggested Terry and Daniel were hit in crossfire. They were still classified as missing the next day. What was to emerge was a sorry tale of cover up and obfuscation which some in the Allied Command would much prefer to file under 'the fog of war'.

It would take an inquest into Terry's death more than three years later to get to the bottom of what *really* happened.

Initially ITN and the ITV network looked after Terry's family in terms of support and legal advice but, as often happens in cases like this, there comes a point when separate interests might call for separate representation and so it was here. Initially Anthony Hudson, a barrister who would go on to work with me on the Hunt case (see Chapter 21), was appointed for the Lloyd family. But he wanted to be proactive and got ITN's agreement to bring in a solicitor. He called me to get on board with him and represent the family as an interested party (as the deceased's family is termed) at the inquest, allowing legal representation alongside other interested parties.

What followed was a swift investigation for Terry's family as the date for the inquest was already scheduled. Anthony and I went to see Terry's widow, Lynn, at her home in rural Buckinghamshire. The village was quiet. I imagined such a tranquil spot would be a hugely welcome retreat for Terry after long spells in war zones. Lynn was still in the dark but at least relieved to know a date for the inquest had been fixed. We soon found out from her Terry's disdain for the embedded war correspondent (who attach themselves to the military unit and who are likely to give a more sympathetic perspective), preferring the independent life of the so-called unilateral journalist (who remain outside the official military press attachment). The night before his death he had spoken to her about his hopes to be the first western journalist to reach Baghdad whilst sending his love to their daughter Chelsey, then aged 21, and 11-year-old son Oliver.

Sadly, Lynn's illness meant she could not travel to the court in Oxford to watch the inquest alongside Chelsey. But she had already, in 2005, managed to slam the Ministry of Defence for their tardiness in resuming the inquest which had been opened and adjourned after Terry's body was brought back to RAF Brize Norton in Oxfordshire. She had been promised a quick and thorough investigation by the then Defence Secretary, Geoff Hoon, which in her eyes had not been forthcoming.

Fréd Nérac's wife, Fabienne, who was experiencing the same agonising silence that Lynn endured, had already made a bold move. She had personally confronted US Secretary of State Colin Powell at a NATO Press conference a month after the incident. He assured her he had ordered a military investigation into the circumstances of her husband's disappearance after she begged him to break his silence and tell her what happened that day. It was to take more than three years before it was dragged out of the US authorities.

Truth is at the heart of the inquest system. In coroner Andrew Walker's court it worked extremely well in the end. Initially, after hearing the confusing and sometimes contradictory accounts about gun shots which rang out at the convoy, we were left with more questions than answers, particularly concerning the role played by US soldiers on the front line.

As well as Terry's family, ITN was also an interested party to the proceedings. ITN's Editor, David Mannion, was a close friend of Terry and a huge support to the family. This made it even more difficult for Lynn to ask us to make sure we asked ITN awkward questions if they were justified. We said that such close ties should not deter her in the quest for truth. It was true ITN was funding us, but we were tasked to act independently of them. The potential for biting the hand which feeds you is not easy. But Anthony and I were determined that so long as Lynn and Chelsey instructed us, awkward questions were to be asked.

We interviewed ITN's hostile environment trainers and looked into every aspect of the support and training to journalists in the field to try and find out what, if anything, was deficient about the support given by ITN. Our assessment was that the news organisation had proper systems in place but there was, as always, room for improvement.

The inquest came on in early October 2006. Chelsey took on the role as family spokesperson and sat with me throughout the gruelling eight-day long inquest. This inquest was of a different order in terms of the content and public interest, especially as it was getting so much media interest.

It turned out to be the most high-profile inquest of its time.

We took final instructions from Lynn and arranged to meet Chelsey, then only 24, at a nearby hotel. The media, including her dad's own employer, ITN, would be at the entrance of the court to take our photos, film us and ask questions. I suggested we maintained a dignified silence at this stage whilst the evidence played out. Chelsey agreed.

The witness list was impressive and long. No wonder it was going to take several days to get through. Most inquests are over in an hour or two; this one was set to last for five days and, in fact, overran by three. My worry was that the witnesses lined up to explain the processes and systems might get in the way of what actually happened.

Coroners, as truth finders, have a monopoly on who to call. An interested party can only make suggestions. ITN was bringing out all the big guns: their Chief Executive Stewart Purvis, other news broadcasters including Trevor McDonald, David Mannion and many more. Several spoke about Terry's professionalism to his work. He was not a risk-taker, but he fiercely believed in the independence of journalism, we heard.

Stewart Purvis was one of the first witnesses and he told the coroner that the British and US military did not want unilaterals around for the simple reason that they preferred embedded journalists who were more likely to write up and broadcast their reports from a more sympathetic perspective. He also told the court that US military do not recognise or take responsibility for independent journalists not embedded with their troops "to such an extent they wouldn't recognise their existence". This, we later learned, was a key issue.

The court heard about what the ITN crew were doing: travelling into Iraq behind the front lines to find out what ordinary Iraqi civilians felt about the war. Remember, it was March 2003, a month after a coordinated day of protests held across the world in which ten million people in more than 600 cities marched against the war. In my city, London, protesters numbered more than a million.

Finally, the time came for direct testimony. The first and only on the spot witness to give evidence was Daniel Demoustier, the sole survivor of the convoy. Before taking the stand, he asked to speak privately to Chelsey. It was their first ever meeting and an emotional moment. Three and a half years on, he was still deeply affected by the incident although his physical injuries had healed.

In the hearing Daniel explained they were in civilian traffic heading towards the Shatt Al Basra Bridge when they suddenly and inexplicably saw Iraqi soldiers coming towards them from the opposite direction. Daniel was driving the vehicle with Terry in the front passenger seat and behind them, in a second 4x4, were Hussein Osman and Fréd Nérac. Both their cars were clearly marked TV. They had passed a line of US tanks, not realising this was actually the allied front line. They had no reason to think so as the highway was not closed off to traffic. Nothing was stopping them as they approached the bridge. They performed a rapid U-turn when they saw an oncoming vehicle, containing Iraqi soldiers, stop beside them. Weirdly, the Iraqis were giving him and Terry a thumbs up signal.

"At the same time gunfire started," Daniel told the inquest. "It came from a distance. Immediately I ducked under the steering wheel. Then all hell broke loose completely. The machine gun's fire was directly targeting my car. I was absolutely sure I was going to die."

He explained that despite having been shot he looked for his colleagues. First, he looked towards their other car behind and saw the passenger door was open. To his immediate right, Terry was nowhere to be seen. He was no longer in their car and then above him Daniel saw his car's roof was on fire. The machine gun fire had set their spare petrol cans alight.

Daniel hurled himself out just before his car, which was riddled with bullets, exploded. He lay in the sand and mud for 30 minutes, not daring to move despite carrying a bullet wound. He explained that the direction of fire was from allied lines: his inescapable conclusion was that they had been shot at and attacked by US soldiers after inadvertently crossing the front line. For some unexplained reason, the highway had not been closed off by the front line of US troops which explained how the ITN convoy had come across the Iraqi troops travelling in the opposite direction.

Daniel finished his evidence by explaining he was shot upon again by American troops in their tanks stationed no more than two hundred yards away when he got to his feet with his hands up. Eventually he was rescued by an Iraqi driver in a van which itself came under fire. He was then forced to bail out for a second time, and was eventually rescued by another press team containing a British journalist from the *Mail on Sunday*, Barbara Jones.

The British Army conducted its own investigation. We heard from Major Kay Roberts of the Royal Military Police who gave evidence that she had obtained footage of what she called the "fire-fight" from a cameraman attached to the US tank division who had filmed what had happened. It was handed to her several months afterwards and she was told this was everything the US military authorities had. But, she explained, a forensic video expert confirmed her suspicions that 15 minutes of footage had been removed.

The stench of cover up was upon us. We also heard that Colin Powell's promise had eventually been fulfilled: Fabienne received her promised reply. It was an outright written denial of their soldiers being at the scene of the fire-fight.

Someone here was lying.

To my mind it was deployment of the 'never admit, always deny' maxim or, to use a well-worn American phrase, pure bullshit.

The footage was shown to the court, beginning after the event, with both ITN cars already burnt out. Shouts of "that's media personnel down there" can be heard. From the footage you could clearly see that TV was emblazoned on every side of the vehicle, including the roof and the vehicles clearly wore Kuwaiti registration plates.

Then a mystery witness came into court.

Soldier B, whose name we never discovered, entered the witness box and gave evidence from behind a screen. He was special forces, from an SAS regiment. He had spent days in a ditch observing the events 500 metres away with high powered binoculars. He told the court he saw a US tank start shooting at the Iraqi troop's truck and the two ITN vehicles.

This was the big breakthrough, corroborating Daniel's account.

It was this witness who explained that the approach the British Army takes is philosophically (and fundamentally) different: shoot to kill is the last resort. The US approach, on the other hand, is that shoot to kill comes much earlier in their protocols.

Nicholas Walshe, who investigated the events for ITN, was also called. He had somehow managed to interview the driver of a green minibus who told him he had picked up Terry to take him to hospital. The driver told Walshe his vehicle had previously been commandeered by Iraqi troops and came under fire by American troops. He said Terry had lain in the sand between the two lanes of the road and had managed to walk to the vehicle but needed help to get in. He had been shot in the shoulder and appeared to have a broken arm. In fact, this was incorrect. It was later established that Terry had been hit in the stomach by an Iraqi bullet. It was a confusing second-hand account although Walshe spoke highly of this man's credibility.

At this point the coroner looked towards Chelsey and asked Anthony if we should break off to allow Chelsey to leave the court if she was feeling too distressed. It was a kind gesture. I turned and whispered to her. "No, carry on, I want to hear it all," she whispered back. I leant over and gave our counsel her instructions. Anthony explained to the court she wanted to remain and know "as much as possible".

Walshe then revealed that the Iraqi witness had told him Terry was shot in the back of the head by US troops as they tried to leave the scene to get to an Iraqi hospital.

I remember thinking this was no freak accidental shooting. This is a sniper with a target on Terry's head. And an injured target at that. My blood boiled but I had to keep it all in for Chelsey's sake. She was holding up amazingly well. Terry would have been immensely proud of her.

A ballistics expert backed up the green minibus driver. He told the court Terry was injured in the stomach by an Iraqi bullet fired from the Iraqi troop's truck advancing towards their vehicle which he could have survived with medical treatment. And then shot in the head by an American bullet which killed him outright.

The coroner then raised the highly contentious matter regarding evidence which had come to him from the US soldiers. Rather than permit any of them to attend the inquest where their evidence could be tested by being questioned by the coroner and cross examined by us and ITN, the US military instead submitted witness statements to the inquest. They would not even allow their soldiers to be identified.

We strongly objected to any suggestion that their untested, self-serving evidence could be used. Anthony submitted there would be grave doubts as to the accuracy of such evidence and suggested the soldiers may not be willing to come to these shores because they would put themselves at risk of prosecution for a war crime under the Geneva Conventions.

The coroner agreed with us. He would not read into evidence or take into account these highly contested witness statements. It would be another seven years before these first-hand accounts would be obtained, by Chelsey of all people, acting as both daughter and journalist. More of that later.

We had to then cross examine the ITN management witnesses to ask those awkward questions the family wanted answers to. They were relatively mild but one well known ITN news broadcaster, James Mates, appeared to give me a very cold shoulder the next day.

Finally, we had closing speeches which Anthony and Danny Friedman, the barrister for ITN, delivered hard and well. Both were uncompromising in their addresses to the coroner that he should record a verdict of unlawful killing which would amount to a finding of homicide by US forces.

The wait for his findings was relatively brief but still nerve-racking.

The coroner agreed with us. He praised the ITN team for their professionalism and dedication to journalism and were cleared of any blame. He found as a matter of fact that the initial fire-fight between US and Iraqi forces was justified given the hostile intent on the Iraqi side but that the civilian minibus Terry was being carried in presented "no threat to American forces" since it was facing away from them. "I have no doubt it was the fact that the vehicle stopped to pick up survivors that prompted the Americans to fire on that vehicle," he said. In other words, TV journalists picked up by the enemy were now fair game. The coroner ended by saying he was sending the papers to the Attorney General and the Director of Public Prosecutions to consider a prosecution against the US soldiers who shot Terry in the back of the head.

We could not have asked for a clearer verdict.

As he explained his ruling, I gave Chelsey's arm a gentle squeeze for reassurance.

We had spent the hours waiting for the coroner's findings composing a press statement for Lynn, which I was to read out on her behalf, and another for Chelsey which she would read herself. I could now tear up the other one I had prepared in the event the verdict did not go our way.

We were right to have asked awkward questions – to make sure the family got all the answers – but we did not attach any share of blame on the broadcaster. And I know the family felt properly embraced by this renowned news organisation which had suffered its first ever fatality of a journalist reporting from war zones in almost half a century.

Now it was time to face the media.

Chelsey and I got ready to walk through the huge white wooden doors of the Coroner's Court in Oxford. I had done this before many times, but she was a 24-year-old who had spent over a week hearing in grim detail how her father met his end. I did not need to worry. She had clearly inherited some of Terry's spirit and boldness, facing the bank of cameras and microphones without blinking or freezing.

I went first with Lynn's statement, which I read out to the waiting media:

"The evidence heard in this court establishes that the circumstances of his death from an American bullet whilst being ferried to hospital is a very serious war crime. How else can firing on a vehicle in these circumstances be interpreted? ... This was no, I wish to stress, friendly fire, blue-on-blue, incident or a crossfire incident. It was a despicable, deliberate and vengeful act particularly as it came after the end of the initial exchanges in which Mr Lloyd was hit by an Iraqi bullet. ... US forces appear to have allowed their soldiers to behave like trigger-happy cowboys in an area in which there were civilians travelling on a highway, both Iraqi and European."

Chelsey talked of her father's killing seeming "to amount to murder, which [is] deeply shocking".

The news reports carried their words far and wide. There were calls to make the deliberate targeting of journalists a war crime at the next United Nations summit and the Liberal Democrat leader urged a prosecution to get underway. The US Department of Defense said very little other than their soldiers "followed the rules of engagement". They said nothing about their change of story that they were not involved.

A prosecution was never brought. "Insufficient evidence" the CPS concluded. I told myself it was much more about embarrassment of both governments as coalition partners in the invasion of Iraq.

No one would be held to account for the deaths of these three men. Predictable and not surprising.

Chelsey went on to become a researcher and producer for ITV, following in dad's footsteps as a journalist. On the tenth anniversary of his death, she retraced Terry's last journey with Mark Austin, who also reported for ITN from Iraq in 2003, and Daniel Demoustier. In her own words, she told the *Daily Mail*:

> *I'd expected to hate everything about Iraq, but I was wrong. The people were some of the most hospitable I have ever met. I'd heard [dad] describe the desert, but never really understood. Now I knew.*

More remarkably was her trip, for the same programme, to meet the US Marine who gave the orders to shoot. She had written to Second Lieutenant Vince Hogan, leader of Delta Company's Red Platoon that day and in charge of 15 US Marines in four tanks. Hogan replied that he was willing to meet Chelsey after reading her emotionally charged letter asking to find out the truth.

Hogan, no longer in the army, spent four hours with Chelsey describing in as much detail as he could what happened that day. His orders were not to let anyone come over the river. Seeing a pick-up truck approaching at high speed over the bridge with a rocket-propelled grenade on the back was enough for him to give the order to fire. The ITN convoy had turned around so why, Chelsey asked him, were they fired on? His answer spoke volumes about the US military's refusal to recognise independent non-embedded journalists. He admitted that he was told all journalists in the area were embedded within the military, so his belief was that the clearly TV-marked Mitsubishi vehicles were full of Iraqi gunmen.

It was a remarkable admission.

To me this said it all: unless you are embedded and in our control, there to feed the official line, you are invisible to us, nothing more than a potential inconvenience. To be treated as hostile.

Hogan had no recollection of firing on the two Mitsubishi 4x4s containing the ITN team, nor had his former men he had contacted. As I watched the programme I thought: how very convenient. Nor did the programme explain why, with their high-powered equipment, the US soldiers hadn't seen Terry being shot by the Iraqi soldiers.

Today, Chelsey remains in broadcasting and making the film was hugely helpful in coming to terms with her father's death.

Terry was a dedicated seeker of the truth in the best spirit of fearless, independent journalism which is under appalling attack in so many parts of the world. Since 2000 as many as 16 UK journalists have been killed, including US born Marie Colvin working for the *Sunday Times*.

I wish I had met Terry when he was alive. Instead, sadly, I only got to know him in these circumstances. I obtained an artist's impression of the courtroom, with me sitting next to Chelsey in the row behind counsel. I keep it up on a wall in my home as a constant reminder about the importance of journalism and the costs of it, day in day out, all around the world. With well over 200 journalists killed in Gaza since October 2023 it is even more important than ever.

Chapter 12

Fergie, Andrew and stopping *Undercover*

One of my cases illustrated the best and worst of the Royal family. As a lifelong Republican, I have never had much time for them, but Sarah 'Fergie' Ferguson won my respect for the role she took in a TV programme. My client, well-known television presenter and journalist, Chris Rogers, found this out when he managed to get a working Royal to front a TV documentary. It was quite a coup (in television terms). In 2007 Sarah Ferguson, Duchess of York, agreed to go undercover in Romanian and Turkish children's orphanages to shine a light on the appalling conditions the children endured.

What could go wrong?

Sarah had asked Chris to a meeting after seeing his initial news reports on terrible conditions in Romanian state orphanages just months before the country was due to join the European Union. His ITV News coverage had forced the EU to demand changes, but he knew the long promised major improvements for children in state care were superficial, barely scratching the surface of the problem.

By then Sarah was officially an 'ex-Royal' following her divorce from Andrew 11 years earlier, but she was still dependent on her controversial ex-husband. She shocked Chris by offering her services which she had already put to good effect in Albania and Liberia in campaigning for children's rights. Sarah suggested going undercover with Chris back to Romania and Turkey and ITV commissioned an hour-long film if the unlikely pair could pull it off. Taking a Duchess into foreign countries undercover was more hazardous than going it alone, which Chris was used to, but weirdly, the filming of the

Duchess and her Princess daughters (then 18 and 20) went well.

Donning a headscarf, sunglasses and a dark wig she went with Princess Eugenie and filmed 700 unwanted, disabled youngsters in Turkey's Saray Institution. She did the same in Romania, this time accompanied by Princess Beatrice. Why, you might ask? She told Chris, "Could be the Celtic red-headed Irish in me, I don't know, but all I know is if I was lying in that bed and I knew there was a big, old battleaxe like me out there shouting for me, I'd be pretty pleased."

Post broadcast, both countries went full throttle into attack, complaining of smear tactics, privacy breaches and, in Turkey's case, threatening extradition proceedings. To her credit, the Duchess didn't back down and apologise.

Chris and TV producer, Marshall Corwin, followed up the documentary with a book called *Undercover* setting out how the extraordinary documentary was made. A courtesy copy was sent to the Palace, including a foreword written by Sarah who had co-operated with the writing process throughout.

The shit then hit the fan.

The Queen's favoured solicitors, Farrer & Co, wrote to Chris threatening to injunct the book. Regardless of the book's primary purpose, to highlight the plight of the children, the Palace threatened to kill the book and prevent it from ever seeing the light of day. Chris and Marshall had signed 'the usual' confidentiality agreement put in front of them when first meeting Sarah which, they were told, everyone agrees to as a matter of course without examining it or taking legal advice. Now it seemed, Andrew, through the Firm's usual attack dogs at Farrers, was dredging it up to look for reasons to object, including privacy breaches. Why he was bothered never became apparent to me. Perhaps it was protecting his good name despite this being his ex-wife's 'frolic'?

Chris and Marshall came to see me, understandably very stressed. We looked at the letter and they explained their odyssey from day one.

"But this claim letter," which I waved in the air, "is in Ferguson's name claiming breach of confidentiality." "Yes," Chris told me. "She keeps calling me to say Andrew is running the show, not her."

I advised Chris and Marshall to stand firm and regarded it as bluster. "Even if they sue, they won't succeed," I said, but we agreed the suggested changes to the book to mollify the Palace. It was another case of the Royal family taking a hammer to crack a nut. And, worse still, shutting the stable door after the horse (in the form of a widely seen audience all around the world) has well and truly bolted.

As the case went on, Sarah was still making secret calls to Chris behind Andrew's back saying she fully supported Chris. It was bonkers. Never in a million years did I imagine such a scenario. Nowadays, people might describe this as 'controlling behaviour' but when it comes to the Royal family I think it comes with the territory, even when you are only fourth in line to the throne (as Andrew was at that time). By then I had heard many rumours of his legendary unpleasantness, but this was another level. No wonder they call the family "the Firm".

Chris reported back to Sarah my advice to stand firm and only concede the smallest possible material. Her response was that Chris' lawyer sounded "amazing" which made this Republican laugh out loud.

Chris and Marshall were put under terrible pressure from many quarters including an extradition request from Turkey which resulted in Chris' wife getting a visit from Scotland Yard's international unit to notify Chris, then on another assignment, that formal proceedings were now being commenced. Between Turkey and the Palace, the duo were in deep.

The same week, Farrers issued legal proceedings in the Chancery Division (where intellectual property cases are handled) claiming much of the book was Sarah's copyright. I had a hearing in front of a High Court Master (just below High Court judge level) called Bragge, a suitable name to hear a media case.

We countered with a claim the Palace was abusing the terms of the template confidentiality agreement, which we argued was not intended for this type of arrangement. The agreement was a general NDA, and the understanding was to protect the Royal family from anything except the journalistic enterprise they were embarking on. Otherwise, it made no sense for Sarah to go to Turkey and Romania. We applied to have the case struck out. Not long afterwards, a without prejudice meeting took place in Buckingham Palace between Chris, Marshall, Andrew and Sarah which resulted in the Royals backing down and discontinuing the claim.

Bullies often climb down when faced with resistance. In this case, a change of heart occurred for reasons we will never know. Perhaps it was 'litigation bluff' and we called the other side's hand? I will never know. Sarah, in some senses still undercover, was no doubt cheering on Chris and Marshall from the sidelines in a case really brought by Andrew.

Best of all, the book was published soon afterwards.

The (now) former Duke and Duchess both got in very hot water over their Epstein connections in 2025 which make this episode look like very small potatoes.

Chapter 13

Robert Murat: "monstering" the innocent

I n 2008 and 2011 I acted in the two biggest multi-libel claims in modern times. Multi-libel claims relate to occasions where the media have gone in for the kill (let's expose the wrongdoer) thinking they can have a free -for-all thanks to inside information.

This inside info usually stems from secret communications – the cops and hacks like to call them "off the record" briefings – about a heinous crime. Invariably, when a journalist gets a tip from the police it is always on a non-attributable basis and on the understanding the police cannot be called upon to help corroborate or verify the story if the journalist gets it wrong. The beleaguered newspaper which has foolishly relied on the briefings without 'standing up' the story elsewhere stands fully exposed to a libel action. In all the excitement of the chase they forget the cardinal rule which is to get sufficient corroboration. More than once, I have told my opponent that when their clients publish in haste, they often repent at leisure.

With Robert Murat, many media outlets got it badly wrong resulting in record libel damages and profuse apologies. This and the Jefferies chapter (see Chapter 19) demonstrate why there has been such a significant loss of trust in newspapers in recent years.

Robert Murat was a resident of Praia da Luz on the Algarve coast of Portugal. When the terrible events of 3 May 2007 occurred, and three-year-old Madeleine McCann went missing, Robert was staying with his mother at her home a few hundred metres away.

As a Briton raised in Portugal, Robert is a fluent Portuguese speaker. When the alarm was raised, he was one of the first to join in the search for

Madeleine. The Portuguese police needed to take statements from British witnesses so Robert volunteered his services, quickly becoming an official translator. He selflessly stopped preparations for the launch of his new estate agency business to help in the search for Madeleine full time.

The British media descended on Praia da Luz and one of the pack thought Robert to be a suspicious character based on a hunch she had that he might be like the murderer of the two Soham schoolgirls. Like the murderous care-taker, the journalist decided he seemed to be "hanging around a lot". The reason why Robert was hanging around, just inside the police tape, didn't register with the journalist; he was on hand for translation and interpreting duties, so he *had* to hang around.

The pressure applied by the journalist turned the Portuguese police's attention towards Robert and he was designated a 'person of interest'. In Portugal, once you become a 'person of interest', you are given 'arguido' sta-tus with designated rights such as the right to be accompanied by a lawyer when questioned. An arguido is *not* a person under suspicion. The hungry press pack got wind of Robert's new found media-created status, ignoring the fine distinctions in Portuguese law by calling him a suspect, and the pile-on began.

His is the sad tale of the Good Samaritan who got badly mugged for his efforts, as I once told him. Madeleine's disappearance is probably the most heavily reported missing person's case ever. Any possible development makes headline news. The prejudice Robert suffered was intense and my job was to reverse it with maximum impact. This is that story.

In early 2008, the phone rang. It was another claimant solicitor asking if I could act for Robert. He couldn't because of a conflict of interest. Sometimes rivals can be friends, especially when they want the best for someone they can't act for. It was with an audible sigh that the details of the referral were passed to me. When a lawyer hands you a case sounding regretful you know they are passing up a biggie. By the time of this call, Robert's name was plas-tered over every report about the missing Madeleine for all the wrong rea-sons. To make things even worse, he had Max Clifford speaking up for him.

"Oh no," I groaned. At the peak of his fame Clifford was a household name and was renowned for talking loudly on behalf of clients in every media outlet he could get on. I knew this would be an obstacle and promised myself to sort it out if I got the case.

When Robert called, I could sense a man who was at his wits end. He spoke quietly, trying hard not to break down as he began to tell me the problems of becoming front-page news around the world as a kidnap and murder suspect.

"Robert," I cut in. "Look, this is going to take some time. Can you get on a plane and come to see me in London?"

"When?"

"Tomorrow or as soon as you can."

As soon as I put the phone down, I knew this was a race against time. In a case like this you have to put out the wildfires of suspicion as quickly as possible. By now, Robert's arguido status had been lifted and the media pack had moved on. Arrangements were made for him to come and spend a day with me to share his story and sort out how to fund the case.

* * *

When Robert walked through the door I saw a beaten man. It was as if he had just walked off a battlefield. His shoulders were hunched over and he avoided direct eye contact. I knew enough to tell myself to take it gently. He brought a box of newspapers with him. I had only managed to get the stories – without pictures and captions – from the internet service we subscribed to. The print copies were the real deal. Much more prejudicial than simply reading them from the internet. I admitted to being shocked at how bad they were. Trying not to be too diverted by the sensational headlines, we put them and the admin papers necessary to start a case off to one side, and I asked him to explain what had been happening.

It came. At first haltingly, like a tap coming back to life, and then it flowed. The whole nightmare.

Robert explained how he'd spent the fateful night at home totally unaware of Madeleine's disappearance and how he only found out when his mother woke him with the news which reached her quickly via Sky News.

His family home is surrounded on three sides by the holiday resort, so he had gone out searching the denser parts of his mother's large and, in places, overgrown garden. He soon bumped into a man connected to the McCanns doing the same thing. They got talking and the man took up Robert's kind offer to translate between the McCann party and the Portuguese police. He took Robert to meet the McCanns who gratefully accepted his offer of help.

Robert helped get the police to widen their search to other apartments in the resort. He took part in these searches and over the next few days became a full time volunteer assisting with the desperate hunt for the child. He informally helped the police with translations and explained how his reticence to give the gathering media more than his first name in between translation spells was eventually to be written up as a "refusal" which somehow gave them grounds for suspicion.

He was soon sworn in as an official translator and agreed to the confidentiality restrictions which came with the position which, he told me, was absolutely fine – he didn't want to speak to the media and now he had official backing. When approached, Robert steered clear of discussing what he was doing, sticking instead to explaining the differences between the British and Portuguese investigation process.

He remembered Lori Campbell joining in a conversation once whilst he was talking to another journalist and being snapped by a photographer at the same time, which disturbed him. Robert then noticed the same photographer talking to Campbell and so he approached them, insisting that they should not publish his photograph. Little did he know what was about to happen. Ironically, his preference for keeping a low profile was adding fuel to Campbell's fire.

Robert was soon tipped off that he had attracted police suspicion, but he had no idea how or why. He then noticed he was being followed and worked out it must be by plain clothes police. Soon afterwards he was shocked to discover the police had raided his mother's home which was swiftly followed by Robert being questioned for several hours at the local police station.

Retelling the story, I could see the agony and upset this caused him even now, after he was cleared of suspicion by the police.

It was, I told him, utterly despicable. He nodded and looked at the sea of articles in front of us. Eventually he continued.

"I just want one thing: to clear my name."

I replied I could do that and explained that the best way would be to pitch the demands for apologies as high and urgently as possible and, as a mark of the harm done to him, also require substantial payments of damages.

He gave me the green light to do my thing but he insisted that I made sure it was quick and his good name was restored. He didn't want a long court case.

We were singing from the same hymn sheet.

The next morning, we got down to it. Collecting and reading everything written about him was like mugging up for an exam where you hadn't been paying proper attention in class. The articles in the British press ran into their hundreds. Many newspapers wrote about him every day while the spotlight of suspicion fell on him. But how on earth did this happen, I asked myself? It didn't take long. The culprit was the single journalist from the *Sunday Mirror*, Lori Campbell, who took it upon herself to play Sherlock Holmes and 'dob' him in. *The Guardian* reported how she had "reported Robert Murat to local police officers in Portugal, as well as to the British embassy and Leicestershire police".

As any seasoned hack will tell you, never ever become the story. And Campbell fell right into the trap. Robert explained the very bored and story hungry press pack, cooped up in the local hotel and itching for any new development in the story, kept badgering him for information whilst he was interpreting for British witnesses during the first few desperate days. Robert was an innocent abroad when it comes to handling the press, as I told him at our first meeting. He can appear initially quite formal and shy on first meeting, and I immediately sensed why the likes of Campbell thought he might be an easy win in terms of solving the terrible crime. She even wrote an article, 'Why I shopped Maddy suspect' claiming there was something about his evasiveness and an unease about him that made her feel "extremely uncomfortable".

We found more evidence of Campbell making herself the story. She told Sky News: "It was very reminiscent of the Soham murders, that was my first thought."

She had lit the fuse and then stood back, claiming her police report was nothing to do with being a journalist and instead a gut instinct that she should share her suspicions. Either way, her actions set in train a disaster for Robert and his family. While Robert was telling me his story, I kept glancing back at the Campbell authored article seeking fame and glory for shopping him to two police forces and silently vowing to make sure her role was not forgotten.

By the time we finished for the day, although he was undoubtedly tired, there was now a glint in Robert's eye. He could see a way ahead. We had a plan. We set ourselves a tight schedule. Keeping everything under wraps, we would simultaneously hit all the newspapers and one offending TV channel on the same afternoon.

It was nose to the grindstone time, and we soon recruited two barristers, a QC and a junior, to work alongside us.

We decided that each news outlet should get a single claim letter setting out the multiple defamatory articles. Some of them were ludicrous. One newspaper found a witness from Robert's old school who claimed Robert was so weird he used to flick his glass eye in the air like a marble as a party trick. He didn't. He didn't even *have* a glass eye. There was lurid hypothesising about where Robert might have hidden Maddie (as the tabloids called her) in his mother's house with one 'expert' saying she might be being kept in a hidden section of the house. The stories also defamed his partner (now wife) Michaela Walczuch and the IT consultant, Sergey Malinka, who he used to help set up the website for his new online residential property business.

Finally, several days later, we were ready, and we launched the claim with letters before action to 12 newspapers and to one TV news channel.

With the letters all sent giving a short deadline for a response, it was now time to visit Robert in Portugal and get some first-hand evidence.

I admit to quite like going to the place where the events took place. It is always instructive and revealing, whether it is the scene of a crime, a factory where an accident took place or the client's home town.

Praia da Luz was no exception.

A more comfortable and safer resort you could not find anywhere. The notion that the abductor was looking out for opportunities and spying on the family was immediately rendered absurd by the setting. The surroundings of the Ocean Club resort would make anyone observing stand out a mile given how quiet and calm the place is, easily allowing you a sense of stability and security. None of this really comes through in the lurid news reports.

Robert showed me the bar where the journalists would hole up in, desperately trying to get some copy which their editors would accept. Once Lori Campbell let loose her suspicions, I could see why the rest followed like a wolf pack hunting its prey.

The next stop was to visit the aunt who had taken it on herself to contact Max Clifford, the well-known but not yet disgraced publicist, to act for the family. Robert apologetically explained that his aunt had reached out to Clifford in desperation because the family was being besieged by the press pack after his status as an arguido had been discovered. She was happy for me to tell Clifford he no longer acted for the family and to clarify he had never been instructed by Robert himself.

It was a most satisfying call and better still, short. The idea of listening to Clifford blathering on was too much and I didn't have the time. I cut in as Clifford started venting and told him firmly not to hold himself out as the family spokesman any longer especially as he had not been appointed as such by Robert. His indignant response – "I have never been treated so disrespectfully by a lawyer" – counted as a career highlight for me. I knew he was a wrong 'un from previous cases involving him (a client secretly filmed his account of various misdemeanours) but even I was surprised when he was arrested and jailed for eight years for indecent assaults on girls and young women.

Robert took me to meet others affected by the stories. I met Michaela and

Sergey when I was there. So desperate was the press pack that by the time they had got their teeth into Robert they had made the most lurid claims about Michaela and Sergey too. Michaela, a very religious individual, was deeply hurt by the made-up claims. Sergey was made out to be a mysterious and suspicious individual. I told them they each had their own standalone libel cases if they wanted me to pursue their claims as well. The press paid for this with abject apologies and six figure sums for each of them.

Back in London I received a letter from a law firm, RPC, which was representing the vast majority of newspapers. They had banded together to respond as one. A smile spread across my face. This could only mean one thing. They were going to settle. Not long afterwards I took a call from the partner, Keith Mathieson, asking me to visit him at his office to talk about the claims on a 'without prejudice' basis. In plain language this means talk turkey – openly – without any fear that something said would be repeated in open court.

I knew Keith from old. We had crossed swords many times. Before we began our confidential discussions he remarked, in his dour Scottish tones, this was not the press' finest hour. "You can say that again," I scoffed, telling him this had to be the understatement of the decade.

Several hours later, with the details having to remain confidential, I left the Thames side office with a good idea of how they saw the cases.

There was barely any comeback on our complaints. They couldn't stand up the stories very much or at all. And then came the figure to settle.

I was soon on the phone to Robert. I also consulted our QC who agreed the overall settlement figure was higher than we could get if we took on the newspapers at trial and got damages awarded by a judge.

I explained this to Robert, and he not only agreed the figure – £600,000 – but also allowed me to tell the world how much he was going to get to show how wronged he had been.

All that was needed now was to negotiate the content of each media organisation's apologies, how prominently they would feature in the newspaper and what each party would say in open court. The 'statement in open court' is a 100% stage managed production usually lasting no more than a couple of minutes where the claimant's lawyer explains to the judge what was said, how wrong it was, the fact the newspaper now accepted it was wrong and that if they now apologise, we won't take it any further. The newspaper's lawyer then stands on their feet and apologises to the claimant; the claimant's lawyer then gets back up and says they are happy with that plus the damages and costs, and the judge says yes, fine, "the record will be withdrawn".

This, however, was to be very different.

Robert is a big family man. His nearest and dearest were gathered for the occasion, in front of Mr Justice Eady who was then very well known as the senior libel judge. Although patrician and traditional in style and tone, I always liked his decisions which were perfectly crafted, to the point and nearly always correct.

On occasions like this, he played his role well as the silent referee, making sure everything went smoothly.

The court was packed with journalists, including some from the newspapers in the dock.

Both my opponent and I, each wearing our gowns and starched collars on top of our business suits, were up and down like a jack in the box. 12 times. Every single newspaper had to get up, through Keith, and individually apologise to Robert who sat beside me in open court savouring every moment. And what is often not appreciated is that even though the newspaper is the transgressor they still have to carry the story, although they give it much less coverage than the other media outlets.

We had a small press support team on hand to manage the media requests. They knew we would step out of the High Court to say a few words to the mob of press outside on the pavement of The Strand. I had been out on the steps of the High Court making statements many times before, but this was the biggest gathering so far.

Madeleine was a major story – even the news that an entirely innocent British man was getting the vindication he justly deserved made the headlines. The scrum was immense. I walked out with Robert and Michaela by my side to flashes popping, furry microphones thrust in our faces and court security holding the cameramen back. Both Robert and I had a few short words to deliver. Nervously, he made his debut as a public speaker in front of live TV, radio and press who clung on to his every word.

"The newspapers in this case brought about the total and utter destruction of mine and my family's life and caused immense distress…I am pleased that the publications concerned have today admitted the falsity of all their allegations and I can now start to rebuild my life…I can emerge from this action vindicated and with the recognition and acknowledgement that what was said was wholly untrue."

He paid tribute to me and my team and after a few words from me we were allowed through the pack to the waiting black cab. I settled in the back beside Robert and Michaela, thinking phew, glad we got that over when an eager photographer ran to the driver's side of the cab, ignoring the traffic on The Strand, opened the door and unwound the window. Without a word, he then slammed the door shut, brought his camera up and started snapping away at us sat on the back seats. We must all have been open mouthed, amazed at the guy's chutzpah.

The photographer packed up, still standing in the middle of the road, and walked back onto the pavement. As the cab pulled away, I turned to my clients and said, "He's probably going to sell those photos to the same newspapers you just took to the cleaners."

"You're joking!" Robert exclaimed.

"No, it is how the media works. The memory banks get wiped clean on a regular basis. Yesterday's monster becomes tomorrow's hero."

Robert was now in huge demand from the media outlets for interviews, especially those who hadn't libelled him. He agreed to talk to just one: Richard Bilton at the BBC TV news which he did back at my office in Soho before heading out with his family to enjoy a lunch at the restaurant attached to Bar Italia, just down the road on Frith Street. As they were setting up the lights and cameras, I was quietly watching the reporting of the case on the TV and online newspapers. I noticed the BBC was misreporting that Robert had been arrested in Portugal. I leaned over to Richard and whispered in his ear that if he didn't get this changed now, I would be making a new claim against the BBC. He scrambled to call the Newsroom where it quickly got changed and then resumed his one-to-one interview with Robert in our boardroom.

A couple of us from the office joined the happy throng. We all let our hair down that afternoon after a tense morning and a rushed few months, getting the case ready by mid-July before the end of the legal term. We wanted and got maximum publicity.

A few months later a much more relaxed and confident Robert was invited to speak at the Cambridge Union for the motion about the tabloid media: 'This house believes tabloids do more harm than good'. Robert and I went there together and we were up against Peter Bazalgette, a TV mogul, and Michael White, a *Guardian* columnist grandee. Neither of them fancied their task and told me so in private. Robert had never spoken in public before save for a few words outside the High Court, so he asked me to share the slot which I was happy to do. He needn't have worried: when he finished addressing them the audience gave Robert a standing ovation and the motion deploring the worst aspects of the tabloids was overwhelmingly carried. The President of the Union said it was the most one-sided vote anyone could remember.

A few years later Robert and I were both filmed for a Netflix documentary called *The Disappearance of Madeleine McCann*. It remains on the streamer's channel for everyone to see and hear Robert explain what happened.

As he said on the steps of the High Court and as he told his Netflix interviewer, we must never forget the most important thing is the disappearance of Madeleine and the continued efforts to find her.

This is all Robert was doing on the morning after she went missing, and he still says this remains his foremost consideration.

Chapter 14

The controversial Channel 4

I was enmeshed with the cultural phenomenon which television became, at least before the advent of YouTube and streaming began to undermine its hegemony, for about 20 years. If someone had told me I would be paid hundreds of pounds an hour to watch TV when I grew up, I would have kissed them on both cheeks.

By 2007 I had enjoyed being Channel 4's main external legal advisor in all criminal matters for five years. During this period, I had the best time and the phrase "Better call Louis" was coined.

Every week brought different challenges. One advice I had to give was whether a planned programme on the notorious 1993 House of Lords ruling in *R v Brown and others* might infringe the criminal law. The Lords were split 3-2 with the majority determining that consent was not a valid defence to assault in the case of sadomasochism. In other words, even if a participant in S&M consented to the act, it could still be a crime. I agreed with the two dissenting judges. If they wanted their penises nailed to a board and weren't forced into it, then why not? How much different was it to tattooing? Or enlarging ear lobes?

By then I had advised in lots of obscenity cases, but never did I think I would be getting paid to advise on the nailing of a penis to a board and whether consent was a defence. Channel 4 – back then a more inventive and outlier channel which did not obsess so much about ratings – wanted to make a documentary about the case (better known as the 'Spanner' case) and the defendants in it. Anyway, the Channel 4 executives were rightly not interested in my views but in whether the broadcast might be breaking the law.

Other controversial briefs also came my way. *Undercover Mosque* was an exposé of covert video footage taken in several mosques revealing instances of preaching and teaching which were highly offensive. Examples included rejecting the UK law of "the kaffir" (slang for non-Muslim), praising the murder of British troops and advocating attacks on Indian and Jewish businesses. It was classic 'hate speech' and drew headlines across the world. MPs demanded an official investigation.

After the programme was broadcast, West Midlands Police launched an investigation into whether any criminal offences had been committed by those teaching or preaching at the mosques. The CPS advised that there was insufficient evidence to bring charges. But then there was an extraordinary development: Channel 4 and the documentary maker, Hardcash Productions, themselves came under the spotlight.

West Midlands Police complained to Ofcom that the programme had been so extensively edited that those featured had been misrepresented, and that it was sufficient to undermine community cohesion. They also asked the CPS whether a prosecution should be brought against Channel 4 for broadcasting a programme which included material likely to stir up racial hatred.

Thankfully the CPS ruled against prosecution of the Channel on evidential grounds and Ofcom rightly rejected the unfair editing claims. Hardcash, alongside the programme makers and head of *Dispatches*, then launched a libel action against the CPS and West Midlands Police claiming that the statements made by them "were completely unfounded and seriously damaging to our reputation".

It was the first time senior individuals from the Channel and Hardcash had sued for libel. We were in the thick of the regulatory case, supporting Jan Tomalin, the head of legal, and her team. We succeeded in upholding the making of the programme and Ofcom gave a clean bill of health to the makers, Hardcash Productions. I was delighted. It was important public service television.

* * *

But the biggest controversy the Channel was ever involved with was the eruption of racial and class hatred between contestants in the *Big Brother* household. Launched back in 2000, it was 4's biggest hit, running for several weeks each season. I studiously avoided watching it, until the time I had to.

Jade Goody became famous after appearing as a contestant on *Big Brother* and then got invited onto *Celebrity Big Brother* a couple of years later. Even before this particular household blew up with Jade's attacks on Shilpa Shetty for what Jade perceived to be put downs of her based on class-based snobbery by the woman she called "the Indian princess", I was receiving calls from the production company, Endemol. They and the Channel were getting increasing interest from Hertfordshire Police about whether remarks from various contestants could constitute racial hatred under the Public Order Act 1986.

The Elstree studios were based in their county, and I used to enjoy getting into a taxi and being taken to watch eviction night in the studio. As the votes were being counted, I was instructed to liaise with any officers who attended and advise the ejected contestant when they came out about their rights and help them if the police wanted to interview them there and then.

Some nights I would just come home without having spoken to any contestant. However, following broadcasts which showed Jade verbally attacking Shilpa – all of which is well documented – it was clear she would be evicted in the next round. In fact, Gordon Brown, then Chancellor, declared that a vote not to oust her would be a vote "for tolerance".

On her final evening before the vote, Jade wept and told fellow contestants she was not a racist. When she heard she was to be evicted, she hugged Shilpa. I watched this on the monitors and turned to a producer and muttered, "This is good television." He agreed.

As Jade emerged, the usual fanfare of cheers, waves and breathless interviews were bypassed.

The Channel received over 50,000 complaints and a major diplomatic row broke out between India and the UK over Shilpa's treatment. Another contestant told Shilpa she could "fuck off home" and Jade weighed in, referring to her as "Shilpa Poppadom". Advertisers started pulling their sponsorship of the show.

It was cruel to put her together with, among others, Shilpa, when they knew Jade's anti posh people schtick would emerge. It was red rag to a bull.

Hertfordshire Police were successfully pacified on the night and, much to my bemusement, I was asked by an officer if I could get Jade's autograph. The power of TV was very evident. I told him it was "not appropriate" in no uncertain terms.

I was also in attendance on the later eviction nights and when the eventual winner emerged, lots of people asked me about my impression of both Jade and Shilpa. I shrugged my shoulders and admitted that if I had to have an evening out with either, I would prefer Jade, with whom I could debate her unwise words. Shilpa's superior airs and graces would much more quickly offend me.

Tragically, Jade died from cervical cancer two years later. Her funeral, at the church close to my (then) home, was attended by thousands. Sky News flew a helicopter above the ceremony to film it and the whirr of the engine and blades drowned out the quiet conversations of the mourners and birdsong.

Tacky and tasteless.

* * *

I was also asked to help Simon Brodkin, self-styled as Britain's greatest prankster. We had already met a couple of times to war game various scenarios for when security hauled him away following a successful hoax. He would come and see me for advice so he was as well prepared as he could be. By his own admission, Simon is the most meticulous of planners, with every possible outcome thought out, which is why his pranks are so successful. He was the epitome of a professional prankster, and I greatly admired his chutzpah.

Famous pranks included taking to the Glastonbury stage with Kanye West mid-headliner set, plastering Philip Green's superyacht with a 'BHS Destroyer' banner (soon after he closed down the retail giant leaving thousands without a job or staff pension, including my own niece) and handing

Theresa May a giant P45 mid-Conservative Party conference. He also managed to get close enough to Sepp Blatter during a major speech to shower him with US dollars as a comment on the crooked FIFA allegations at the time. The dollars swirling round Blatter's head made headlines around the world and was one of the pictures of the year.

This time Simon's target was Donald Trump whose security was at full max by mid-2016. The Donald was to fly into Scotland to give the main speech on the reopening of his golf course at Trump Turnberry. It was a quick break from campaigning for his first Presidential run and the day after the seismic Brexit vote to leave the European Union.

Simon, a chirpy and verbose Jewish Londoner and former junior doctor, explained to me his plan. His research had revealed that it was Trump's *modus operandi*, as the owner of multiple golf courses, to tee off at the first hole before giving a speech and then taking off in a helicopter. Simon intended to release several sets of golf balls just as Trump took a swing at his own ball in order to cause maximum confusion, with the moment captured by the cameras and reporters. But not just any golf balls. These were eye-catching balls with black swastikas on red.

Simon explained to me why. One of Trump's recent campaign declarations was that, if elected, he would ban all Muslims from entering the US. This, to Simon's way of thinking, made him both a racist and a fascist. The purpose of the prank was to make a serious point. Given how Trump's second Presidency of Trump has developed, Simon could also be lauded as something of a Prophet.

As I listened, I raised my eyebrows. I wondered how far this plan would get before Simon was discovered by the multiple layers of security surrounding Trump. If anyone could pull this off, it was him. He is an ingenious operator who was now taking on one of the biggest challenges of his career.

As Simon revealed afterwards on the E4 website where the prank can still be seen, he had to find a way to get round the huge security cordon. This he planned to do by assuming two identities: the first was to pose as a guest and to check in to the hotel the day before Trump was to land in his chopper. This was so that he could smuggle the balls, which took some effort to commission, into his room in a holdall. The second was to assume a different identity and acquire the uniform of a Trump Turnberry employee in order to move around more easily within the cordon. The staff were much more invisible to security, which was relatively lax once you were inside the cordon.

On the day of Trump's arrival, Simon returned to Turnberry in his grey sweater and tartan tie uniform as employee Frank with an identical holdall, this time containing nothing but innocuous items. He made his way to the hotel room with his guest key and switched bags (on the documentary he calls it "the switcheroo") and then set off for the assembled ranks of media to 'disappear' inside them until his big moment.

Amazingly, no one checked his holdall inside the cordon between the hotel and the location for the speech.

But then things started to go wrong: instead of the traditional tee off at hole number one, the media were to gather at hole number nine and Trump wasn't teeing off at all. Instead, no doubt for wide TV coverage purposes, he was going to make a major and, as it turned out, long-winded speech from a lectern just in front of a yellow lighthouse before the massed ranks of media, including a film crew from Channel 4 who were there to film the prankster.

Simon quickly had to decide what to do in these changed circumstances. He realised he had to carry on and at some point release the balls during Trump's turn at the lectern. He later found out that the location switch was to allow Security Service snipers an elevated position from the top of the lighthouse.

The footage shows Simon, in his uniform, pop up from a crouched position in the crowded ranks of the media, and release the first of several sets of swastika balls, telling the 45th President to be, "Sorry, Donald. These are the new balls you ordered as part of the Trump Turnberry range."

Trump was livid. Clearly furious and red-faced, he snapped at his baffled looking and rather burly secret service agents: "Get him out!"

Confusion reigned.

Some of the journalists started to laugh when they saw the swastika insignia. As Simon was taken away, he managed to say to the next leader of the Free World, "Sorry Mr Trump, I meant to give them out earlier. They are available in the shop." By now scores of balls were scattered all over the space between the press and the lectern.

Whilst Trump continued with his speech the camera showed security guards crouched, quietly gathering up the balls.

Simon was cuffed and herded off. He was later told by the police just how lucky he was not to have been shot by secret service agents. Funnily enough, I had warned him of the same risk. Simon, a brave soul, was always at risk of being roughly handled but not usually by men with guns and certainly not ones trained to shoot first if there is a risk to their 'boss'.

Luckily for Simon, he was hauled off by Scottish police rather than Trump's security and, once they realised who he was and that this was a prank, the cuffs were loosened by a sympathetic officer who, handing him a soft drink, whispered, "You're one funny man." Later, when released, Simon signed one of the balls at the officer's request.

Surprisingly, Simon was never prosecuted and received plaudits from people all round the world. It made headline news, and I breathed a sigh of relief.

* * *

Possibly the funniest case I was involved in for Channel 4 concerned a comedy show called *Balls of Steel*, which also featured hoaxers. One time I was called out following their arrest after they sprayed 'Tony Blair is a bell end' on Whitehall. It was the fag end of Blair's time as PM. I turned up at Bow Street Magistrates the next morning and represented them before the notoriously tough Stipendiary (professional) Magistrate.

After the hoaxers entered their guilty pleas to criminal damage, I thought I was pushing my luck when I asked if the magistrate could give each of them a conditional discharge; I explained that the paint was washable and they would pay for it to all be cleaned off. After all, "It was for telly!", I more or less pleaded. His response was unexpected. "Mr Charalambous, I will go one better and give each of them an absolute discharge." I was stumped. It was the first and only time I got a better result than the one I had asked for from a sentencer.

My other *Balls of Steel* case involved Tom Cruise and a fake penis. My Sunday afternoon watching the footie and cooking a barbecue was rudely interrupted by the phone. Channel 4 needed me to go down to Savile Row Police Station because the whole crew had been arrested for a fracas on the red carpet at Leicester Square Odeon.

In the cells I soon got to hear the story. They had been posing as a film crew when they stuck a furry microphone under Tom Cruise's nose and asked him a question. As he went to answer they pulled a lever and the fur parted to reveal a large fake and very pink plastic penis, which squirted the Hollywood legend full in the face with water. Filming in the can, they beat a retreat whilst laughing at the successful execution of their jape. Cruise and his people didn't see the funny side of it and called the police. At least Sharon Osbourne kind of got the funny side, one of the crew told me. After they pulled the same stunt on her, she ran into a nearby restaurant and then came barnstorming out with a bucket of ice and chucked it over the crew.

Now the crew had to face the music. I was in all the interviews and every time I asked the same thing: "Where is Mr Cruise's complaint statement?" After all, how can you proceed without it? The best they could come up with was a witness statement from his sister moaning that the liquid might have been much more harmful than London tap water. I said, "Not good enough" and we adjourned for the night, agreeing to return the next morning.

When we got back into the station it soon became apparent that Cruise wasn't willing to proceed and give the police a statement; the crew were all 'no further actioned' and released.

As we stepped out, we were surrounded by a group of men dressed in the same dark uniform adorned by Cruise in his *Mission: Impossible* films who had been hiding behind parked cars in the street. They squirted my clients with giant water pistols and soaked them to the skin. I stood to one side and laughed my head off.

Afterwards the squirters told me they had been hired by *The Sun* – which explained the presence of photographers to snap it all. The next day the revenge of Tom featured loudly on the tabloid's front page.

My final instructions were to be sent to collect the confiscated fake penis from the cop shop. It had been custom made and the production company's most valuable prop. I carried it back to the massive merc like it was the Crown jewels.

Chapter 15

Five: the new kid on the block

C hannel 5 was much more of a frolic than Channel 4 when it started. Labelled the "football, films and fucking" channel by its own Chief Executive, the irrepressible Dawn Airey, and "porn with purpose" by *The Guardian*, it managed to embroil me very quickly. As well as hits such as *Psycho Pussies: When Cats Attack* it made a lot of noise with the ratings hit, *Sex and Shopping*.

I was approached to be their 'talking head' and explain to viewers the history of obscenity laws and how they were being applied today. No problem, I said. By then I had what might be called a 'respectable' obscenity practice, operating in the interstices between criminal and media law.

For example, I had recently advised Taschen Books on its groundbreaking *Erotica Universalis*, a glossy tome with hundreds of pictures of erotica through the ages. Benedikt Taschen himself came over from Germany to be interviewed at Charing Cross Police Station about the educational and artistic merits of the book. The investigation quickly folded.

This time my role in the C5 programme was to be filmed in a studio by the maker of the series, Douglas Chirnside, on the laws around obscenity. I was told the series was a serious look at the global sex industry. It was explained to me that I would pop up from time to time in an early episode as a serious commentator. I sat and watched *So This is Porno Hell* with my partner and a glass of wine, with little inkling of what the rest of the show was about when it aired in November 1998.

The episode's 'star' was a Lancastrian pornographer who went to Hollywood and decided to make much harder core porn than anyone else in the US industry. It was the story of his success. My role, apart from a brief appearance in the studio at the start dressed in suit, shirt and tie (lawyers back then were less casual than today) was to be the voiceover for the hardest core porn – with a bit of pixelation – ever seen on terrestrial TV. It was a good lesson in the power of editing. With the grunting noises muted, you could listen to me calmly explaining the history of Britain's obscenity laws.

The furore caused by this episode and a couple of others in the series made sensational headlines, something which would have been on the filmmakers' and TV executives' agenda. Any programme with sex in the title always does well. Post transmission I was asked by their head of legal whether I was okay with the voiceover role I played. I laughed and told him I saw the funny side of being a legal pundit alongside much exaggerated grunting and fake orgasmic screeching.

Less amused was the Broadcasting Standards Commission which, in October 1999, ruled the explicit scenes were "unacceptable for broadcast at any time" and "beyond acceptable boundaries". The filmmakers were severely reprimanded and told to mend their ways. Weirdly, several friends (all male) said they had come across me on TV when channel scrolling. Funny that. I was even approached by members of the public asking me if I was that bloke on Channel 5's *Sex and Shopping*.

Channel 5 also pushed the boundaries on the crime front further than any other broadcaster back then.

In *Semtex For Sale*, Donal MacIntyre, a well-known undercover reporter, demonstrated how easy it was to buy Semtex on the black market in war-torn Kosovo. The legal team had cleared the expenses but were unaware of the team's plan to *actually buy* the explosive. They thought the undercover film would show them posing as criminals with a lot of cash – £10,000 – and the hundred plus sticks of the explosive, but that they would pull out at the last minute. They were wrong. The purchase went ahead and suddenly, the film crew had in their possession 13.5kg of Semtex, enough to wipe out a whole neighbourhood.

This was pushing the boundaries to the extreme.

Donal then called home and spoke to the head of legal, telling him not to worry, the explosive had been buried somewhere safe that same night. He added that he had told the United Nations peacekeeping force the whereabouts and were now to film them going to recover it safely. The rushes then show the moment the very pukka (Finnish) peacekeeper Commander turns to Donal and says, with classic understatement, "There's only one problem with where you buried it. It's in the middle of a minefield."

The camera then shows a bomb disposal team's robot making its way over the terrain to where the explosive was buried to dig it up safely.

I told the others this moment was TV gold and had to stay in the subsequent documentary. Thankfully it did.

My role was to represent the filmmakers when they came to give evidence before the UN-run criminal court, as key witnesses for the prosecution of the Semtex sellers. I was all for flying out there, but the legal budget meant I had to apply for an exemption to allow the filmmakers to give evidence by satellite TV and also to give it from behind a screen.

The application was successful, so we all attended a TV studio in Covent Garden, the screen was put in place, and I officiated at my end, satisfying the court chair of my *bona fides*.

The filmmakers gave their evidence over the course of a day, and the defendants were all found guilty and imprisoned. Despite spending hours and hours making sure the witnesses would remain anonymous, one of them just couldn't resist and stuck his head around the screen, showing his face to the defendants before I dragged him back.

* * *

Just as exciting was the time I helped to unsuccessfully defend an injunction application but then got it overturned in the course of the same day. It was another Donal special, this time looking into a notorious Manchester-based criminal gang.

The gang was led by a curious character who called himself Domenyk

Lattlay-Fottfoy although his real name was Dominic Noonan. His name change, which he had tattooed on his knuckles, is an acronym which stands for 'Look After Those That Look After You-Fuck Off Those That Fuck Off You'. He has more than 40 convictions and by 2013 he had spent 22 years – half his life – in prisons.

Remarkably, he allowed Donal to follow him around his 'manor' and answered candidly when questioned both about his personally difficult childhood and sexuality, admitting he was gay.

One Sunday night back in 2005, having just landed from a family holiday in Cyprus, I turned on my phone whilst collecting bags from the belt and saw that there were a score of missed calls and a handful of voicemails. Much to the annoyance of tired daughters and partner, I stood and listened whilst the bags went round a second time.

The messages spelt out the problem. Over the weekend there had been a gang killing with possible connections to the Noonan gang. Greater Manchester Police, anxious for witnesses, had freaked out that Donal's Channel 5 documentary, *A Very British Gangster*, due to be shown the next day would harm or ruin their efforts. They decided to try and injunct the programme and gave notice to the Channel that there would be a hearing in Preston Crown Court the very next day at 10.30am.

I had less than 12 hours to get it together and go and resist the attempt to block the broadcast. My secretary called Hugh Tomlinson to meet me at Euston at 7am and after a quick visit to the office and hurried calls with the client, the two of us headed north.

Experience told me that judges sitting in the Crown Court rarely had much truck with the media if they perceived any hint that criminals might get away with something. This is exactly what my opponents played on in their address to the judge. We put up a heroic battle, emphasising this was an important freedom of expression issue, that the concerns were fanciful, and the documentary would not dissuade witnesses coming forward (much more likely was the fear of retribution which comes with being in their orbit and helping the police).

Our pleas fell on deaf ears. The judge gave a short ruling which I tried to scribble down as he said it, permitting the injunction and banning the programme.

It was the first time Channel 5 had been injuncted. Knowing this was the likely outcome, I had forewarned the client. I then followed up news of the ban with strong advice that we could get the ruling, which did not properly address the issues we had raised, overturned but only if we moved fast. One of the main reasons was that there was no real risk a late-night documentary would interfere with police investigations.

Without bothering to wait for the Channel to decide, we took the unusual course of telling Greater Manchester Police to get themselves to London; the two of us were getting the next train to go straight to the Court of Appeal to get the decision in their favour overturned. The look on their faces, from self-congratulatory victory to bafflement that we could be acting that quickly, was priceless. We managed to get a super-fast hearing at the Court of Appeal because any delay beyond the scheduled time for broadcast would render the appeal academic. Once the scheduled time had passed, an appeal could not grant the remedy even if we won.

As we left the Preston Crown Court courtroom I shouted over my shoulder, "We're on the 4 o'clock. Suggest you get the next one which will get you to the Court of Appeal half an hour later – lots of time. We will call you once we've got a time fixed up." I tried to avoid a smirk on my face. I knew well how a sweet win can turn to bitter defeat in front of a panel of appeal court judges.

It wasn't until I was on the two-hour train ride that I managed to persuade the Channel that this was the best chance to win an important point and keep the documentary on air.

The Channel gave me the green light although the truth was we had given them little option. Meantime, Hugh rang the Court of Appeal from the train.

"Please can I ask the Court of Appeal be moved to meet tonight and hear our urgent appeal against the ruling of the High Court judge sitting in Preston?" was his polite request. The grumpy list officer at the other end said he would see what he could do and call us back.

For the next half-hour, I wondered whether enough judges could be rounded up at such short notice. Meanwhile I had to put together a note of what the judge had said in his ruling because, as appellants, it fell on us to present the papers to the court.

By 6.30pm we were back in London and hurried to the QC's chambers, quickly putting together an appeal bundle and inserting a typed-up note of the judgment in it. We also did something unusual: we gave the judges a recording of the documentary to watch. Usually this is a no-no because of the risk that a judge might start editing it down or changing it in some way. But here, as it was all or nothing, we decided pragmatism was the order of the day and with the benefit of having seen it, our arguments would carry more weight.

Our opponents, on the next train, were badgering us for confirmation of the hearing. I kept stalling, still not having heard from the court, noting that the GMP legal team were now en route to court having also disembarked at Euston.

At last, the phone rang: three judges would sit at 7.30pm prompt to hear the appeal, including the necessary application for permission at the same time (known as a "rolled-up" hearing).

With minutes to spare we dashed across the road to the mock Gothic pile on The Strand and into the wing which houses the Court of Appeal.

The other side was already there, still looking cross. We handed the papers round and the judges walked in. They agreed the length of time each side could take so as to allow themselves a cut off time to decide. The documentary was scheduled for 10pm. Everyone agreed the latest time for a decision, and we prepared an old film to show instead, just in case we lost.

Each side took the full amount of their allotted time slot. I got a hint at which way the judges might lean when, at the outset, the presiding judge, Lord Justice Chadwick, sniffily picked up the single sheet of paper containing the Crown Court judge's decision and asked both sides if this was agreed. Yes, both sides nodded. "Hmm, the *ratio* of his decision appears to be just the one sentence," the judge added. In other words, the reasoning of his decision was extremely short.

It was a good sign.

Just after 9pm the judges delivered their decision. The single judge below had erred, and the appeal would be allowed. The programme could go ahead. I think what swung it was the unusual decision we had made impromptu, on the train; let the judges watch the show for themselves. We hadn't even seen it ourselves as there was no time, but we had read the script. We had won them over. They were now in a better position to judge whether the police fears were well founded.

The makers of the documentary and head of legal had rushed to the court to watch the appeal and rang through to the Channel to keep it on air.

We got to Daly's wine bar over the road on The Strand for the first of a few rounds just as the documentary was being aired. Channel 5's head of legal came up to me after a couple, complaining I had given him little option other than to agree to go ahead with the appeal after telling the other side we were heading for London and then he laughed, "But fair enough, you got your own back on me after *Sex and Shopping*."

"What do you mean?" I asked.

He explained that back in 1998 Douglas, the director, had said to him, "Are you sure you don't have to check with the lawyer about us using his voice during those hard-core scenes? We really should get his permission. Even I know that." The lawyer in question was one of my closest friends in the law, Paul Chinnery, who was junior to me at Stephens Innocent and later became General Counsel at News UK before his tragic early death from cancer. The head of legal reassured Douglas he knew me well and that it wouldn't be a problem, saying "Ah, the Big Greek will be fine with it."

I smiled. "What goes around, comes around." It is a maxim which should be taught in law schools as a truism which repeats itself often in our world.

Chapter 16

BBC calling...

O ccasionally, TV documentaries and police investigations acciden- tally collide. In the *Funny Money* episode of the *Crooked Britain* series on BBC2 it was a head-on crash with serious consequences for everyone.

Undercover journalists and undercover cops work in the margins. Once revealed, arguments about entrapment, incitement and fakery abound. This time was different. Back in 2003 the BBC, hot on the trail of the source of counterfeit sterling notes, accidentally penetrated the inner workings of the gang behind it all. The series was an excellent exposé of the kind of scams which hurt us all. Fraud, counterfeit notes and the like all cause huge harm and worry to millions of people.

Reporter Phillip Wright was sure he was on to something when investigat- ing complaints about forged notes which innocent individuals were handling and then finding out they were fake. The problem was rife in Manchester at the time, where Phil was based. This particular gang boasted that the quality of the fake £20 notes was the best in the city. Phil also uncovered a link to another gang operating in London.

Phil's eight-month long investigation got to the stage where he could find out more about who was behind the operation if he sent in people passing as fellow counterfeit traders. He took meticulous notes of all his dealings with the two individuals he recruited for the task. In true pukka BBC style, it was all run past his producer, Fiona Campbell.

The necessary paperwork for justifying secret filming (a must in all TV undercover filming) was prepared and met with management approval. The two men then engaged with the gang and were taken to a location in Ashton where they could see for themselves the printing operation in action.

And, unknown to the counterfeiters, the two men sent in by Wright secretly filmed it.

The documentary was ready for transmission and, acting responsibly, Phil and Fiona invited the police officers (who they had found out were also looking at the same individuals) to a private screening. Several months earlier Phil had ascertained the police were interested in some of the fringe members of the gang but didn't have so much on the core members. It turned out the police interest was more than just local: the National Crime Squad (NCS – now called the National Crime Agency or NCA) and US Secret Service were also involved.

When the officers saw the film, their jaws dropped. They realised that here were the missing pieces of the jigsaw puzzle. They demanded the BBC stop the film going out and asked for all the film (the rushes) to be passed to them as part of their ongoing investigations. Unsurprisingly, the BBC agreed and handed everything over apart from source-identifying material and pulled the episode.

The core members of the gang, led by a Greek Cypriot graphic designer called Anastasis Arnaouti, were arrested and charged. The evidence linking them to the counterfeit operation was the undercover film.

As with so many cases in which evidence might be vulnerable to challenge, the defence teams called for a *voir dire* (a preliminary trial) to get a ruling on admissibility of evidence. Getting the BBC documentary excluded was their only real chance of an acquittal.

The rules for journalists using secret filming makes it easier than for cops. The authenticity and reputation of the media organisation behind the film and the soundness of the prosecution of the case, described as one of the most sophisticated counterfeit printing operations in recent years, were tied together.

There was however one massive glitch.

One of the undercovers Phil had recruited to pass as a fellow criminal called James Raven was now, two years on, locked up in prison for the murder of a cannabis farm owner. The other, Chris Guest More, was on the run and wanted for the same murder.

"It couldn't be a much trickier case," I had been warned in the pre-meeting call.

These were the dilemmas presented to me by the BBC's General Counsel, Sarah Jones, when she came to see me in 2005.

"Are you able to devote the next month to this case?" she asked. I quickly nodded, scrambling around for people who could cover my other work. This case was too important to turn down and absolutely my cup of tea; navigating journalists and their sources through the criminal process was my sweet spot. I was handed a dossier and film footage as my introduction to Operation Gait.

Together with Liz Grace, a dynamic and feisty young lawyer trusted with the trickiest cases by Sarah as I was soon to find out, we climbed, bleary eyed, onto the 7am train heading out of Euston to Manchester. Minshull Street Crown Court isn't in the most glamorous part of Manchester, but it was handily placed for the finest restaurants in Chinatown. Next door was a nightclub which promised evenings of cavorting. Sadly, my days and nights were instead filled with documents and rushes.

It was going to be a long *voir dire* – two to three weeks were scheduled. It ended up taking six.

Our first task was to chat up the prosecution. I had to make sure we were working together, side by side, except on those occasions when the journalism, especially the sanctity of protecting sources, meant we resisted their defence attempts at obtaining more disclosure than the BBC was prepared to give. Source protection was our watchword. How the BBC got into the gang was not to be disclosed, for the safety of those individuals.

Graham Knowles, the prosecuting barrister, played it straight and, with the CPS, made it clear that whilst he understood our position, his priority was to make sure the case got in front of the jury. Our sources were not his concern.

The second task was to meet the two key players in the film: reporter Phil and producer Fiona. I had to explain the intricacies of *voir dire* evidence and how it was sometimes the only weapon in a defendant's armoury.

Here, the defence had put together a position which, if accepted by the judge, would have sunk the case. They claimed that the BBC had been tipped off about the gang by the investigating police officers of the NCS so that the journalists could secretly film the gang. Their claim was that this was how the NCS could circumvent the strict protocols on the Regulation of Investigatory Powers Act 2000 (which we all know as RIPA) which governs police intrusion by undercover means and is much stricter than the rules governing undercover journalism.

There was only one problem: it was sheer bunkum. The fact is that the two investigations – BBC and NCS – ran parallel to one another, each unaware of the other.

However, the defendants, in their submissions to the judge, were able to make sweeping remarks and raise metaphorical eyebrows at our suggestions that this was mere coincidence.

Judge Lever presided over the case. He was quite remarkable. He claimed ignorance of certain laws and rules when asking counsel to enlighten him and then, in responding, made it obvious he knew them all along. He told one counsel to treat him like a two-stroke lawn mower, a simple soul, when asking for more explanation of the law. More worryingly he also indicated he was willing to permit the defence more latitude than usual to explore their theories with the BBC witnesses.

This added to the immediate problem Liz and I were grappling with: the redaction of the notes and diaries kept by Phil and Fiona to ensure the usual trio of no-no's were kept secret. Firstly, if the information might identify or lead to the identification of a confidential source, then it can be kept back by covering up the section of wording. The same applies if the material is otherwise private. The third is if the information could be regarded as irrelevant. If it falls into any of these categories, the journalist and legal advisors are at liberty to redact.

The source protection exercise took us several days, working in conjunction with Phil and Fiona but it was clear to us that Judge Lever was not well versed in those kinds of issues. Fiona refused to answer questions that might lead to the identification of their sources. I turned to Liz and said we need our own counsel to explain to the judge that she and Phil had the absolute right to refuse to answer such questions thanks to the HRA and the European Convention on Human Rights. Through the prosecutor, we got permission to bring in our own barrister to make submissions.

I told Liz it had to be Keir. She agreed and I rang Keir Starmer who agreed to drop everything and get on the next train.

I had worked with Keir on and off since the mid-nineties but now more on than off, especially since the advent of the Human Rights Act. He quickly got on top of the issues once we verbally briefed him. There was no time for the usual written brief to counsel.

I watched Keir make his submissions as to why Judge Lever could not sanction our witnesses for refusing to answer source-related questions which could identify them. The defence grins turned to grimaces as Judge Lever was gradually won round by the force of Keir's submissions and the case authorities which supported the principles at stake.

To speak to the judge without the defence being present, the prosecution applied for a Public Interest Immunity certificate which Lever agreed to. Remarkably, we were allowed into some of these hearings on conditions of strict confidentiality.

One of the most surreal moments of the *voir dire* was the appearance of James Raven as a witness. The Crown had no interest in putting Raven on the witness stand so, hoping it might help to show the BBC were mere stooges for the police, the defence did instead but to no avail.

Raven, as well as working on *Crooked Britain*, had previously operated undercover to help uncover a cannabis farm but was now a convicted murderer. Instead of appearing in person, he came on live video with a feed from HMP Strangeways. He was in what can only be described as a massive strop. Firstly, he refused point blank to take the oath to tell the truth. As he was already inside for life, threatening him with punishment for contempt of court didn't cut it. His answers were all self-serving. He had been a conduit for the BBC to get to the gang and been paid as a 'researcher' for this unusual access to a major gang, as the Liverpool Echo reported on 14 December 2021 in an article entitled 'BBC defends involvement with men who tortured a dad to death'. Previously, a BBC spokesperson called Raven a "covert operative" who they believed had become a reformed individual.

Lever had to then consider all the evidence and make a ruling; apart from two sections of film, he allowed the rest in. The judge ruled Raven could not be relied on as a witness of truth but that the secret film he had made could be seen by the jury in the forthcoming trial. And Lever dismissed the defence theory that the BBC was effectively working for the police so the film should be excluded for circumventing the normal protections under RIPA.

After six exhausting weeks we could pack our bags and only had to return when Fiona and Phil gave their evidence before the jury and later for sentencing after all the defendants were found guilty. Eccentric to the end, Judge Lever's sentencing remarks addressing Arnaouti (the brains who devised the sophisticated dollar and sterling set up, including all the graphics) were illuminating and he gave them with both barrels: "I've watched you now for several weeks of this case and I don't like the cut of your jib!" He sent the graphic designer down for eight years.

The judge commended the BBC for their investigation and assistance in putting the gang behind bars although he asked that in the future there should be better vetting of undercover operatives. He ruled the BBC had acted in good faith. The BBC could never have known that using intermediaries like Raven and the other man, More (who stayed on the run for a staggering 16 years), would come back to bite them when they went on to commit the murder at the cannabis farm.

Best of all was, after a delay of two years, Phil and Fiona got to see their film transmitted on the BBC in late 2005, with NCS officers appearing and praising the film for stopping the operation which threatened to undermine the economy due to the scale of the criminal enterprise. Fiona, a fast riser in TV (and now Controller of BBC3) was anxious to make sure she and the BBC came out looking good. Thankfully, they did.

* * *

The same can't be said about the Pollard Inquiry fall out.

One late autumn day in 2012, a very big cheese from the BBC called me.

"Louis, we want you to represent someone in the forthcoming Pollard Inquiry into what happened when *Newsnight* turned down a Jimmy Savile investigation into child abuse."

"Okay," I replied, asking for more detail.

My caller informed me that a galaxy of top media solicitors had been selected to look after the interests of the main characters who were involved in the decision and its extremely high-profile aftermath, when elements in the BBC made allegations of management interference in axing the film. Piqued at ITV going on to make a documentary of the same story, they had gone public with their criticisms.

On the outside it looked calamitous for the BBC.

"Who do you want me for?" I asked, thinking it would be for one of the journalists, given I was well known by then for looking after the interests of reporters.

"Helen Boaden."

"Blimey, the Director of News."

In charge of 8,000 staff all over the world, hers was a very tough gig. And to get there as the first female incumbent I knew she had to be bloody good at her job. The big cheese's final words about Helen were warm and affectionate. I was told in no uncertain terms to look after her well – she's the best we have.

The Pollard Report, when published, was book length. Close to 200 pages, it was a forensic investigation into the recollection of 40 plus individuals all of whom had to put in document returns, the polite request for, "Show us your emails, WhatsApps, texts and any other document you might have" about the Jimmy Savile investigation. They then had to give a sworn statement of their accounts. Finally, the individuals were sent a selection of documents to mug up on and be ready to answer questions about them before the Inquiry chair, Nick Pollard, and his team with questions from a QC on behalf of the chair. It was an exhausting process made even more difficult by the speed it went at.

By then, the Director-General, George Entwhistle, had been forced to resign. He had been embarrassed first by his role in the aborted film and then over another *Newsnight* cock up which led to grovelling apologies.

No one does naval gazing like the BBC. It is the biggest news outfit in the world. Its sheer size and layers of management mean that rivalries and sniping are inevitable. At its apex sat Helen, reporting directly to the Director-General.

She immediately impressed me on our first meeting with her fierce intelligence and steely determination that the Inquiry reach fair conclusions and not the wrong ones. Unafraid to take responsibility, she had already offered her resignation to Entwhistle after he told her he would make a public statement which inevitably would mean Peter Rippon, *Newsnight*'s beleaguered editor, would have to resign. She was willing to take the fall instead, even though her involvement in the decision-making process in the story not being pursued was minimal at best.

I warned her this would be a messy process and that she would need to steel herself for the attacks to come. They were soon upon us.

Driven by opponents of the BBC, in this case not just the usual suspects in the right-wing newsprint media but also ITN, ITV and *The Guardian*, she quickly became their main target. Some observers saw it as revenge for the BBC's exposure of the phone hacking scandal, but I didn't think so.

The BBC News division has to be independent of the Corporation when reporting on BBC stories, goes the mantra. Unlike other media organisations, *omerta* (never shit in your own backyard) isn't exercised when your own people are a news item.

Quite the opposite.

I spent most of one weekend negotiating on Helen's behalf a form of wording with BBC management and their legal and PR teams about her stepping aside from overseeing any editorial decisions in the Savile story. She was part of the *dramatis personae*. The next thing I knew the BBC were putting out a different version of events, making it sound more like an enforced removal than a mutually agreed process. I was furious and found myself shouting at the top of the hour Radio 4 news bulletin whilst driving my family to a restaurant, spending the next hour trying to get someone to take responsibility for the *volte-face*.

As well as having to endure the stepping aside business, in other words not being able to do the job you love and devote seven days a week to, Helen and the others had to endure a BBC *Panorama* special, *Jimmy Savile – What the BBC Knew* whilst staying gagged from saying anything.

My main role was to help Helen write her statement and stay calm under fire for the several weeks it took before the end of the Pollard Report. It wasn't easy. She and the others in the line of fire were subjected to all sorts of attacks, including from inside the BBC. Worst of all was Jeremy Paxman, *Newsnight*'s best known host. His animus towards Peter Rippon and management was obvious. The *Mail*, *Sun* and *Telegraph* all had a field day. It was a full-on feeding frenzy.

Come the day for Helen's evidence, Helen and I entered the Inquiry's hearing room. We sat in front of a large bank of lever arch files containing many thousands of pages. Alan Maclean QC began with a series of warm up questions and then got stuck in with the difficult ones. He asked Helen to look at and comment on numerous documents, especially emails, between other people which she had never seen before. This was much wider than the slim bundle they had sent us in advance so Helen could prepare to answer questions.

Half of me wanted to stop the hearing and require them to give us advance disclosure of the previously unseen documents. I was again in a state of fury. But the other half of me said keep it going because Helen is doing bloody marvellously in this verbal joust with the silver-tongued Scottish silk. I volunteered to get the files down from the shelves and open in the right place so that I could glance at them first.

I said nothing in terms of intervening to object and after a full afternoon we were done.

Like all the best journalists I have worked with, Helen knew her stuff and was hard hitting and decisive with her replies. She did not mince her words which were all published a few weeks after Pollard's report. That, I told her, was you setting the record straight.

We did not have long to wait for Pollard's *magnum opus*. His primary conclusion was that, while the decision to drop the original *Newsnight* investigation was flawed and the way it was taken was wrong, it was done in good faith and without any inappropriate managerial pressure or consideration that influenced Peter Rippon.

I received the report under strict terms of confidentiality and arranged for Helen to come to the office and read it. In printing it I was able to look at all the references to her and when she walked in looking anxious, I reassured her with a big grin that we were in the clear. Criticisms of her by Pollard along the lines of 'she should have been more pro-active' were piffling I told her. We'd all like hindsight; to have done more when something goes wrong at work is a luxury none of us have.

The usual suspects did their best to attack the BBC when the report was published but there wasn't much flesh on the bone. The Corporation got much more of a kicking when I was thankfully on the other side with Matt Wiessler and the Martin Bashir scandal many years later (see Chapter 27).

Helen was restored to her position as News Director, and the following year became Director of Radio.

A year afterwards the *Mail* tried its best to have a go at Helen and me with an article headlined: 'Head of radio treats lawyer to a taxpayer-funded thank you for representing her in Savile scandal'.

Blimey, I told her when we caught up with each other. Must have been a slow news day in the Kensington HQ of the BBC-hating title. Talk about a storm in a teacup.

The article claimed I joined her in a private box as a 'thank you' and that I was credited with saving her career. Directors of Radio are expected to invite the Great and the Good and send invites to hundreds of people each year. Looking down the distinguished guest list for the crowded box we were in, I realised I had well and truly 'arrived'.

And the *Mail*'s nibble was further evidence of the same which was quickly forgotten.

Chapter 17

Duck houses, moats and all that

Everyone got to know about the abuse of expenses by Parliamentarians back in the early noughties. You could say when *The Daily Telegraph* started drip feeding the story over several weeks in 2009, it did irreversible damage to the reputations of MPs. Or even that the scoop terminated the gentleman's agreements allowing MPs to make up on expenses what they lacked in salary. Greed had overcome some of them; some MPs even went to prison, so egregious were their sins.

But how did one of the "journalistic scoops of the decade" come about?

One day, in 2008, I took a call from Hugh Tomlinson QC, who was later on to become Davey Hunt's QC (see Chapter 21).

"Do you want to join me in making trouble?" he asked.

He explained what he had been doing *pro bono* for a journalist, Heather Brooke, by then three years into her battle with the House of Commons to obtain information on MPs expenses. Using the Freedom of Information Act, the efforts of Heather, together with another campaigning journalist, led to the information coming out but not as intended. Hugh had been to the Information Tribunal, the court which decides on data and information disputes, with Heather. The Information Tribunal gave Heather and the other journalist what they sought.

But the sting in the tail was an appeal to the High Court by the Speaker of the House of Commons, Michael Martin, who resisted Heather's attempts to prise out of him information about MPs' expenses claims against the public purse. Now the next stage required the services of a solicitor – me. One of my tasks was to persuade an insurer to protect Heather in case she lost her High

Court battle against the Speaker.

Heather described in an article for *The Guardian* being surrounded by a phalanx of lawyers and opponents in the High Court hearing against just me and Hugh. Security and privacy were the Speaker's mantra. The court ruled that the shortfall in transparency and accountability of the expense system meant the appeal failed. Heather told *Guardian* readers, "Fortunately, my case was so strong, and my lawyers so good, that I had confidence I would be all right."

Heather had been granted access to 10 MPs' unredacted receipts and was awaiting all the others. A date for the rest of them to come out was set for three months later. The date slipped by. Still nothing came. We looked at previous redactions from the Commons and steeled ourselves for further rounds of battles. More delays were threatened. Heather, a battler and data specialist originally from the United States, which has a much more open culture than we have, didn't blink.

But everything changed when a mole inside the 'redaction room' made a copy of the data and passed it to John Wick, a former SAS officer, who then passed it to *The Daily Telegraph*. In May 2009, they started to publish the full expenses files. Rumour had it that *The Times* was first offered the data but chose not to want the grief which comes with handling stolen material, especially if it was going to change hands for money.

Heather, ever the campaigner, was thrilled to see the material released. "But as a journalist, I was livid," she added. All her hard work had been scuppered by the release. I told her that, but for her determination, we might still be in the dark about Duck Houses and the other outlandish expenses being claimed.

The Daily Telegraph journalist who released the material was Christopher Hope, someone I knew from an earlier case. I called him after about the twentieth front page story to ask him how much more of this was to come. He laughed and told me this was the gift which keeps on giving. Asked if the gift was one he had paid for, he said he could not possibly comment...

Chapter 18

Dahlan, the strongman of Gaza

I t was to be my first meeting with the politician known as the strongman of Gaza. The Gaza Strip was called "Dahlanistan" by some, such was his control there. I had been summoned to meet him – VIP clients don't usually come to your office; you go to them.

Mohammed Dahlan was – and remains – one of the most controversial characters in the tangled web of Palestinian politics. Born in 1961 in the Gaza Strip's huge Khan Younis refugee camp with 61,000 other occupants, he was a leading activist in the eighties. Aged 19, he joined Fatah, the biggest component of the Palestine Liberation Organisation umbrella, then led by Yasser Arafat. He was detained by the Israelis 11 times, starting in his teenage years, spending a total of six years in Israeli prisons sometimes without charge and other times convicted by military courts. Determined not to waste his time inside, prison allowed him the opportunity to learn Hebrew fluently. This was to come in handy for his next step: negotiating with Israel for the Palestinians.

Aged 26, Dahlan was deported to Jordan by the Israeli Ministry of Defence and continued to be active in the PLO. He was keen to distinguish between opposing the occupation and his feelings towards Israelis who, he told me, he bore no ill will.

He rose so rapidly in the ranks of Fatah that he became one of Arafat's chief negotiators at the Oslo peace negotiations despite his relative youth. Overseen by Bill Clinton's US administration, the negotiations led to the signing of the historic peace agreement between Israel and the PLO in 1993. The Oslo accords, as part of the peace agreement, provided for the creation of interim self-government by the Palestinian National Authority (PNA) in the

West Bank and Gaza Strip, two chunks of land which Israel's government ceded limited autonomy to whoever the Palestinians chose in their first ever elections. I was soon to learn that elections in the PNA, especially Gaza, were very different to anything I had ever experienced.

It was a historic moment and allowed Dahlan to return from exile to Gaza where he was appointed the Head of Preventative Security to carry out the security of the second agreement. At that time Hamas was growing and becoming a more political than religious force. Hamas was also against the PLO's 'sell out' Oslo accords, regarding any compromise with Israel as treachery. They refused to participate in the first ever Palestinian elections in 1996.

In May 2003 Dahlan was appointed Minister of Security Affairs and later Minister of Civil Affairs, a position he held until January 2006, when Fatah lost to Hamas in the legislative elections.

Dahlan had hoped the election would allow him to shake off the mantle of the tough guy, the security chief who ruled Gaza, where Hamas was becoming increasingly active and popular. He decided to fight a very local campaign because he was popular among pro-Fatah voters in Khan Younis rather than win by being on the party list, a second way of getting elected. It seemed to me that he chose the harder route, which depended on his popularity, because he had ambitions to run the new Palestinian Authority in both Gaza and the West Bank. He ran a successful and hectic campaign, drawing increasingly large crowds to his rallies. Palestinians took well to their own elections which had only been allowed since 1996.

Dahlan stood on an anti-corruption ticket, acknowledging the mistakes and misdeeds of his own party. He came first in his district, narrowly beating his closest rival, polling 37,000 votes. But the shock, especially to the US who had overseen the process, was that Hamas beat Fatah, gaining well over half the seats.

A coalition government was formed because Hamas was not ready to take over the levers of power. Dahlan was appointed National Security Advisor in the Hamas majority government. The rapprochement soon broke down with fighting breaking out the following year.

Dahlan was accused by his detractors of attempting to mount a coup against Hamas in Gaza by bringing in Fatah controlled troops who clashed with Hamas operatives. Dahlan was in Germany seeking medical assistance when Hamas chose their moment to overrun Fatah troops. He was to soon find out that his home, which doubled as his office, was occupied and much of it turned to rubble. He had to re-locate his family to Egypt and divide his time between there and an office in Ramallah, the West Bank capital.

Dahlan was also accused of being a spy for the US or the Israelis because he frequently dealt with them in negotiations and of being an Israeli collaborator, a US puppet and coup leader. By the time I met him he had re-established himself in the West Bank as a Gazan MP in exile. Even then, Gaza was a no-go zone.

Probably his fiercest critic was a family doctor come political commentator called Dr Ibrahim Hamami, who made vote buying allegations on the politics show, *The Opposite Direction*. We claimed he was a Hamas supporter in our pleaded case. The show was broadcast by Al Jazeera TV, the Qatari run station which sympathised with Hamas at the expense of Fatah. The politics show was like those on our main channels on Sunday mornings, but much more popular throughout the Arab speaking world. When the interviewer asked Hamami whether his anti-Fatah criticisms were surely undermined by the fact Dahlan won his election fair and square by coming first, the medic replied no; Dahlan had *bought* his election through bribery and corruption and not won it. We complained the contribution by Dr Hamami accused Dahlan of corruptly securing his election in Khan Younis by spending $1.5m to buy the votes of his constituents (against his declared election expenses of just under the $60,000 official election limit).

Dahlan was outraged and decided to sue; he chose London, where he had earned a reputation as a highly placed negotiator and senior Fatah politician.

Why London you may ask? You can sue where you have a reputation (or one is made for you by the publication) and Dahlan indeed did have a reputation here although it was not uncontroversial. However, corruptly buying his seat was never in play as an allegation. And Al Jazeera broadcasts to the massive Arabic speaking diaspora in London and is very influential. One of the challenges would be to show by evidence how it had adversely affected him over here.

And why me? Initially Dahlan was recommended by a journalist contact to another libel specialist, Martin Soames, in a small specialist practice (like CCL) who soon realised he was not well enough resourced to take on a case of such magnitude. So his lawyer asked me to take over the case. As someone who revelled in political intrigue, and a former student of eastern Mediterranean politics, I accepted it gratefully.

Back to my first meeting with Dahlan. I got to the rendezvous, an Arab run coffee shop at the foot of his Mayfair hotel suite, early and took a corner table away from other customers, sitting with my back to the wall. When Dahlan walked in, I recognised him instantly from the various photographs I'd seen. Suave, handsome and engaging in a dark, Savile Row suit, he shook my hand vigorously and introduced me to the man on his right. He was Zaki Chehab, the London Bureau Chief for a major Arabic speaking TV station, Al Hayat, and the author of the first serious and highly critical history of Hamas, *Inside Hamas: The Untold Story of the Militant Islamic Movement.* Clad in a pilot's leather jacket and a red scarf, he cut a dashing figure. The third man, a bodyguard, took up a position close by.

Dahlan congratulated me on taking his usual seat – back to the wall and facing the entrance. A security measure, he explained.

We got chatting but he soon took over, explaining how many lies had been written about him by his detractors. Upping the ante, I asked him, "Well what about these allegations against you of torture in your prisons?"

"Louis, believe me, in Gaza I ran the *best* prisons in the whole of Palestine – no beatings, no torture. People would *ask* to transfer to my prisons because I ran such good prisons. Put that in my statement, I insist."

Trying not to shake my head, I continued to listen to his account, wondering why someone accused of torture was complaining about vote buying allegations. I admit I was a sceptic at first in this barely believable case which plunged me into the deep divisions between Fatah and Hamas. It was to take me to Ramallah, the capital of the West Bank Palestinian Authority, to try and defeat the allegations of election fraud made against Dahlan.

Until then my legal experience of corruption allegations by politicians was exposing the greed of some looking for extra money in undercover stings or helping journalists, like the redoubtable Heather Brooke who blew open the MP expenses scandal (see Chapter 17).

This was of a different order altogether.

So for the next couple of years, I was on the rollercoaster of Palestinian politics which was divided between Hamas-ruled Gaza (they had swept to power in 2007) and the Fatah-dominated West Bank.

My first meetings with Dahlan were intriguing. Clever, wily and charismatic he also had a good sense of humour. He was very charming and good looking. It wasn't easy squaring these impressions with his strong man reputation. His followers included a progressive feminist, Diana Buttu, a Palestinian-Canadian academic who then lived in Hebron, in the north of the West Bank. She was also a spokesperson for the PLO. She spoke highly of Dahlan and her presence certainly assuaged my liberal instinct to shy away from anyone accused of torture and extortion.

To get the case off the ground we needed to serve the papers on Al Jazeera and Dr Hamami. In the case of Al Jazeera we had to get the necessary approval of the High Court to dispatch the paperwork to Doha, where the Qatari broadcaster is based. And, likewise, the Hamas leadership.

The second problem was making sure there were sufficient funds lodged in court to allow the case to proceed. Security for costs was a standard requirement for overseas litigants. This was no easy task, but we managed to get over the hurdle.

More important was how we were going to counter the bad reputation that people like Dr Hamami were intent on sticking on Dahlan. Over the next few months, we built up a picture of him into a biographical statement from his earliest days till 2008. It is a story worth re-telling as it also explains the split in the Palestinian people between Fatah and Hamas.

From start to end everything about this case was difficult but, at the same time, fascinating. There was my client's reputation and the fact that everyone had a view on him. Good or bad but never indifferent.

The combination of not being able to speak any Arabic and every single witness save Dahlan unable to speak English was hard enough, but then, once we got through the early formalities, it soon became apparent that we were up against anonymous opponents in the form of witnesses who refused to identify themselves. And no one, neither us nor the major City firm representing Al Jazeera and Dr Hamami, could get into Gaza to get any evidence. It was, even back then, too dangerous as well as prohibited.

Luckily though, with the help of Dahlan's closest advisors, we soon decided we should interview West Bank based witnesses face to face and, with the advisors' help, conduct telephone interviews with witnesses in Gaza. As always, we needed evidence. Without it, just like our opponents, we'd be sunk.

By September 2009 the allegations had grown and the defendants claimed seven separate corruption allegations, fleshed out by both anonymous opponents ("Witness one, two" etc) and some named individuals all claiming Dahlan and his family had paid for votes in the form of bribes, telephone cards and distribution of free meat. It meant we had a vast amount of ground to cover. Dahlan told me not to worry, there were several witnesses to see.

So, in early September 2009, newly qualified Jeffrey Smele and I got on the plane for Tel Aviv and for the next week we were immersed in the cauldron of Middle East politics. We landed at Ben Gurion airport and filled out our landing cards. Destination: Four Seasons Hotel, Ramallah, West Bank. We knew it would be a red flag. Purpose of visit: business, we vaguely scrawled. At passport control we were told to step aside and wait on a nearby bench. About 45 minutes later we were called back to answer questions. Yes, we were here for business. Legal business. We were lawyers gathering evidence for Mohammed Dahlan in a case being heard in London. Sit back down. Not too long later it was decided we could enter the country.

We started to make our way towards baggage reclaim and had taken no more than a dozen steps when a plain clothes security official stopped us and asked us more questions. I guessed this was another branch of the security apparatus in Israel. Eventually he let us go and we met our driver who was one of Dahlan's team. He joked that our delay was pretty good and that usually it took longer than what we had been through.

We arrived at Dahlan's office after nightfall, passing through the security checkpoints going into the West Bank without delay.

Dahlan occupied the whole building which housed his round the clock security team provided by the Palestinian Authority. The protection was necessary because of his previous role as a Security Minister. We were shown up to an upper floor and greeted by Dahlan in his office. He sat behind one of the biggest desks I have ever laid eyes on.

Big man, big desk, I guess.

We were introduced to his closest advisors who would translate and accompany us everywhere during our packed schedule. Arabic tea, sweets and pastries were laid on.

"Okay," Dahlan said after the small talk concluded, "let's get down to business. We have several witnesses in Gaza who we will get on the phone to." Jeff, bleary eyed, whispered to me, "It's 11pm!" I muttered back to him, "When in Rome…"

We had arrived during the Ramadan period of fasting and so calling people after they had broken their fast meant it wasn't exactly bedtime. The interviews involved translators, sometimes on both sides of the phone given dialect issues. One of the interviews featured a very loud goat moaning in the background interrupting the Gazan based interviewee. By the time we finished we had managed to get several accounts from people who our opponents had implicated in voter buying, pointing out the absurdities of the new allegations. Every one of them utterly refuted the allegations. To offer a phone card to someone to buy his vote is an insult. To receive meat was a Muslim custom – for the rich to give to the poor – and not a bribe.

And then, as we were packing up, something extraordinary happened. A call came in from Gaza; it was a man demanding to speak to "Mr Dahlan's lawyer from London". He identified himself as someone who was meant to be a witness for Al Jazeera.

What was this? My mind raced. I know that sometimes traps can be laid by your opponents which can be followed up by accusations of witness interference. I asked our advisors to take it steady and ask him a few more questions before I was willing to talk directly to him. We satisfied ourselves he was genuine and then asked him why he was calling. What he told us was both heartening and, at the same time, depressing.

He explained that he was a poor man distantly related to the large Dahlan family and that he had been approached (i.e. leant on heavily) by Hamas. Preying on his poverty, he told us he was detained by Hamas and then 'interviewed' by one of their senior officials. They asked him to be a witness for Al Jazeera in Dahlan's libel claim and say he and others around him had been bribed with $100 bills. Not only did that not happen, he told them, but he also didn't bother voting. He was repeatedly pressed to sign a statement to this effect by a local lawyer who produced a contract which said if he gave evidence against Dahlan, he would be given a visa, accommodation and expenses including an air fare to London. It was clear to us that the man knew nothing at all about the Al Jazeera broadcast.

"They know I am poor but unless I sign, I won't be able to come to London." It was well known he wanted to get out of Gaza and the carrot was being dangled in front of him. We knew that if we could get him to sign a witness statement confirming what he told us, that would kill the other side's defence stone dead.

But the prospect of relying on a witness like this was both risky and uncertain. It reminded me that this dispute was not suited to the quiet confines and hushed tones in Court 13 of the High Court.

The next few days were hectic. We arrived at Dahlan's building the next day and went down to the underground car park. As we were getting into the car Jeff spotted bullet holes in the car door. He pointed this out to me, his eyes popping. I nodded, remarking we were in the middle of a battle. This was a libel case like no other.

The witnesses included officials, PNA ministers and the head of the

Election Commission. Each one explained just how implausible the allegations being made against Dahlan were. We saw campaign organisers who would testify about the popularity of Dahlan's election rallies.

One of the standout interviews was with a senior cleric who explained he was a former member of Hamas but he had left them because they were failing to fulfil their promises to help the people. He was now an independent but had been appointed by President Abbas to a ministerial role. He spoke highly of Dahlan and painted a picture of Hamas which was highly critical.

We also spent several hours with our client, getting a more detailed picture from him than we had been able to do on his brief London visits. He was clearly revered by those around him, and I felt his anti-corruption ticket and ability to admit to past mistakes was refreshingly rare in the region and, more importantly, genuine.

After four of the most intensive witness gathering days I have ever experienced, it was time to check out more of the West Bank. With no one left to interview and fasting by everyone except the odd non-Palestinian officials posted to Ramallah throughout the long days, I decided we should spend our last two days in Jerusalem. We checked into the American Colony Hotel, an Arab run hotel in the east of the most fascinating city of the Middle East. Between long spells tidying up the evidence we went out for a walking tour of our own and found ourselves in the middle of a row within half an hour.

As we stood at the crossroads of the Armenian quarter of the old city, looking at the remarkable stone walls, an Israeli man approached us. He was offering us his services as a tour guide. Before we could politely decline his offer, another Israeli came towards him and reproached him for working on the Sabbath. It was Friday. A full-scale argument then broke out between the two of them, both screaming at each other. Neither of them even noticed us quietly walking away, leaving them to it.

We wandered into the ancient market despite the stifling heat. We then got caught up in what we would call a hard police stop of a Palestinian youth riding his bike gently through the market. The Israeli soldiers who apprehended him had him on the ground, face on the stone floor, shouting at him and pointing their guns as if he had threatened to commit a serious crime.

It was, we felt, time to go and the next day we headed for the airport and an early morning flight. Our driver, an Israeli Arab, keeping to the speed limit on an empty motorway, was flagged down by police. The questioning was brief and routine. Afterwards, as we got to the airport, I asked him whether the stop was pure chance.

"No, my friend," he replied. He pointed to his number plates. "We are citizens here but we have to have different coloured number plates so we can easily be picked out despite me being a fully licensed taxi driver."

There was no need to say anything more.

Inside the airport, where security starts at the first set of external doors, we thought we had got through unscathed until the final bag search. Jeff was taken off with his laptop. Both of us were worried that our week's work might get snatched away in a security search. We had managed to forward everything on to the office, but the contents of the laptop contained important and sensitive information and, given Dahlan's senior status in Fatah, should not fall into the wrong hands. Anyway, it was also legally privileged but as I watched Jeff being marched away I didn't think this argument would hold sway.

The next 20 minutes were nail biting. I remained in the baggage area, having tried to intervene and been politely told to butt out.

Jeff came back, with his laptop, and we were nodded through. Luckily for us the laptop wasn't examined or interfered with. They had asked him a few questions and he had parried them well. He explained to me that whilst waiting he had struck up conversation with a Palestinian academic who had also been taken out of the line. The academic told Jeff somewhat phlegmatically that he was strip searched before every flight he took out of Israel but that Jeff, as a Brit, was unlikely to have to endure this humiliation. Luckily, he didn't but the academic's *sang froid* attitude put everything into perspective for us.

Back in London we discussed the evidence we had obtained with our counsel team. Our very sage QC, Andrew Caldecott, said that in his experience cases like this would be settled somewhere in the desert, not the High Court.

The next few months were hectic, getting ready for a trial. And then it went weird.

A pre-trial hearing was coming up in January 2010. A call came in as I drove along the motorway. It was Dahlan's number two who had accompanied us day and night of our trip, calling from Ramallah.

He asked me to pull over when I explained I was driving. I went to the next services and called him back. "What's up," I asked. He told me that I was now instructed to file a notice of discontinuance for the hearing on Monday. The case had been settled and each side would pay their own costs. He then called off before I had a chance to ask him anything more.

I rang the team to tell them the news and reminded our QC about his correct prediction about cases being settled in the desert.

It was the worst example of litigation interruptus I could remember.

The case ended not with a bang but a whimper. Mr Justice Eady approved the outcome without the blink of an eye, and the hearing was over in a couple of minutes.

Now, in 2025, with two years of heartache for both Israelis and Palestinians, started off by Hamas's appalling atrocities on 7 October 2023, I think back to this case and the MP for Khan Younis, and watch on my TV screen the refugee town which is mostly reduced to rubble.

Mohammed Dahlan, the implacable opponent of Hamas, lives in exile. Again.

I'm sure if he ever gets the chance he will want to get back to his home, his constituency, and re-build it. Or perhaps, as mooted in some quarters, he might become the ruler of a re-born Gaza or a new Palestinian state? Or is that mere wishful thinking on my part?

Chapter 19

The much-wronged Christopher Jefferies

S adly, nothing gets a news editor salivating more than a beautiful female victim and a creepy looking, posh sounding male suspect.

It's Beauty and the Beast.

So, when pretty, blonde-haired 25-year-old landscape architect, Joanna Yeates, went missing from her home on 17 December 2010 in Clifton, Bristol, the news media went into overdrive. Her body was found eight days later, on Christmas Day. She had been strangled. Every newspaper led on the search for her and the subsequent finding of her body which her killer had callously dumped by a quarry, no doubt hoping she would never be found. Her – and her murderer's – landlord, Christopher Jefferies, who supplemented his schoolteacher's pension by letting out two other flats in the same building he lived in, became my client not long afterwards. Like Robert Murat he was wrongly accused of being involved in a hideous crime. Just about every newspaper in the land called him, or at least suggested he might be, a murderer, based on just about nothing.

The case had dominated news coverage throughout the Christmas period that year. I was getting ready for the only sabbatical leave of my career. I left England with a round-the-world air ticket, starting in India and finishing in Brazil, and I admit I paid little attention to the headlines. I dearly needed to get away from my desk and the various courtrooms. I flew out just as the media were getting stuck into Christopher. I got back in February 2011. Not long afterwards the call came. Christopher had been urged by his criminal defence lawyers to get specialist advice about the matter of his "monstering", my term for the special category of individuals who are turned into monsters by certain sections of the media.

The call came in via a couple of sources who remembered my success with Robert Murat. I quickly arranged to meet Christopher and looked at some of the press coverage. As he later said in his evidence to the Leveson Inquiry, there was a frenzied campaign to blacken his character with headlines such as 'The Strange Mr Jefferies'. In his statement, which I helped him write, he said: "It was clear the tabloid press had decided I was guilty of Miss Yeates' murder and seemed determined to persuade the public of my guilt [with] allegations which were a mixture of smear, innuendo and complete fiction."

It was *all very Robert Murat*, as I told him at the time.

I was very happy to take on his case. As with Robert, I could do this by 'gambling' I would win on a no win, no fee agreement which meant a relatively level playing field. If I won, I would get my costs plus a success fee for taking on the risk of getting nothing if we lost. Neither Robert nor Christopher had the resources to issue writs against multiple media outlets worth billions of pounds.

* * *

Christopher is a really interesting and lovely man. He was, by all accounts, an exceptional English teacher at Clifton College, happy to correct your grammar – including one of my draft letters – and pass on his knowledge as he did to thousands of pupils over his long teaching career. I knew this because several ex-pupils got in touch to tell me. He reads voraciously and is a responsible citizen. His leisure activities include watching films, listening to music and the radio and he has no interest in television or newspapers. When the TV dramatisation of his story was released, I was asked whether it was an accurate portrayal; I nodded yes, that really is Christopher who was brilliantly played by Jason Watkins.

Christopher is a private and dignified man who stood out from the crowd. He sported a Bobby Charlton comb-over to hide his baldness and yet this mild 'infringement' was to become an aspect of how "weird" (in other words, probably guilty) he must be. He was perfect fodder for the tabloids, undoubt-edly fed crumbs by the local police as well as a crass attempt to implicate him by Joanna's murderer, Vincent Tabak. Although still familiar to many, his story needs a little unravelling to understand how he came to be arrested for murder.

Christopher's disdain for the print and television media made him an obvious target. His refusal to stop and speak to the media as he walked to his flat, just yards from Joanna's, made it worse. And his so-called "weirdness" sealed the deal. Nothing had been learnt from Robert Murat's monstering. The frenzy increased following Christopher's arrest. The contempt of court rules were abandoned by editors, and warnings by their internal lawyers ignored.

Take the *Daily Mail*'s coverage as an example. 'The teacher they called Mr Strange' was followed by 'Murder police quiz 'nutty professor' with a rinse'. The newspaper claimed he was obsessed with Christina Rossetti's poetry (in fact, he had a strong dislike of it); that he was "a loner" and "threw books and pens in fury". Not a *single* one of these allegations were true as the newspaper eventually had to accept.

The *Daily Star* went even further calling him an "angry weirdo" and anon-ymous sources claiming he was a creep who freaked out schoolgirls with an "over sexualised manner". It claimed he entered the flats of tenants without permission. Again, utter rubbish.

None of the eight newspapers we sued – *The Sun*, the *Daily Mirror*, the *Daily Record*, the *Sunday Mirror*, the *Daily Mail*, the *Daily Express*, the *Daily Star* and *The Scotsman* – tried to defend a single one of the 45 articles we complained about. It was a textbook example of a media pile-on, in which there was a firm belief by the titles that the initial smears about him could be amplified to make him sound guilty.

When the police finished interviewing Christopher three days after his arrest, he was released on unconditional bail which I knew to be a tacit admis-sion by the police that they didn't think he was involved, but releasing him without charge would be too much of a stretch.

When he came out of the police cells Christopher was still unaware of the furore his arrest had caused in the news, especially the tabloid media. In fact, one of the usually less excitable broadsheets – *The Daily Telegraph* – was borderline defamatory and there were lively discussions within our team about whether to include them in the subsequent legal action.

The only named source for the so-called inside information about Christopher was a former colleague who had unwisely called him "a loner". The rest were from unnamed witnesses who were happy to indulge in character assassination.

Evidence of Christopher being a totally normal and upstanding member of society was ignored: an exemplary 34-year record at a highly reputable school, active in Neighbourhood Watch, the Liberal Democratic Party and conservation campaigns. He was studying for a degree in French, enjoyed a large number of interests and had many friends. This reality was conveniently disregarded by a large section of the print media.

In the first few days after his release, Christopher dodged the chasing media. He told me it felt like being a recusant priest at the time of the Reformation, going from one friend's house to another. After a while the hostile articles started to slow down, but the damage was already done.

He was helped by a brave and assertive statement given by Joanna Yeates' partner, Greg Reardon, who laid into the character assassination and finger pointing by some sections of the media, a clear reference to Christopher's plight in a tribute to his beloved.

Christopher told one sympathetic journalist the impact of the allegations made against him which he started to become aware of after his release: "And then all these extraordinary falsehoods are woven around this now almost personality-less identity...here is this quite foreign, alternative personality which people are trying to foist upon you." He spoke of his identity being violated.

Christopher was unusual in one sense: he had managed to resist reading the terrible copy which had been written about him. When he came to see me in London, he had not read the vast majority of the offending articles. He was happy to "leave it to the lawyers". No other libel client has ever said such a sane thing to me after having their reputation trashed.

It took Christopher three months before he could return to his home after the intense media interest in him. It was not until after his other tenant, Vincent Tabak, pleaded guilty to Joanna's manslaughter (a plea not accepted by the Crown) that interest in Christopher evaporated overnight. Later, the jury found Tabak guilty of murder after a trial which put further strain on Joanna's partner and family. One detail which emerged was a call Tabak had made to the police trying to implicate Christopher in Joanna's murder. Just before his trial I bumped into Tabak's defence solicitor at a conference who told me I would be interested in the evidence coming up at trial.

* * *

The first thing I noticed about Christopher when he walked into my office was the comb-over. Thankfully it was under control. Then I told myself off for being so judgemental. So what if you don't want to follow convention and instead use what hair you have left to cover your centre baldness?

Christopher holds himself proudly aloft. His spoken English would get him a spot on the BBC (the World Service rather than Radio 1). I asked him to write about his feelings towards the media intrusion because they weren't initially forthcoming. We called it his distress statement. The word which really stood out was how *violated* he felt. As well as the police jumping to the wrong conclusion about him, aided and abetted by some sections of the media, he was understandably cautious. And reserved.

We pored over the articles together with one of my favourite barristers, Lucy Moorman, who joined our team at SMB after being in independent practice at the media Bar. She was rightly fired up to get Christopher the best possible result. Together we showed him the pile of articles, pointing out the allegations about him. Christopher's response was terse and short.

"Absurd…nonsense…utterly wrong." His abstention from reading newspapers (unless there was something he was seeking out) made it very different to what Robert Murat went through.

The next stage was to agree our priorities and the stages we had to go through.

Hugh Tomlinson QC and another junior barrister came in as we ploughed through the articles to knock out the ones which didn't make the grade, falling short of defamation.

The most difficult decision was what to do about *The Daily Telegraph*. There were two views in the team. Did we include them and gamble they would not put up a fight as their lawyers would recognise their story was borderline? Or did we drop them to clear a path to a quick and decisive win (like Robert Murat)? We were facing only a few weeks to the end of the summer legal term, the ambitious target we had set ourselves to complete the case.

The decision gave me a few sleepless nights. It felt wrong to let anyone off the hook and I was cross with *The Daily Telegraph*'s rather snide article which painted Christopher as a loner and a bit of a weirdo. It didn't go as far as the other newspapers but still, using quote marks as a distancing device, they repeated the false allegation that Christopher "let himself into tenants' flats" which was suggestive but not accusatory. In terms of whether overall it would make much difference to the total damages he might recover, the camp arguing against including *The Daily Telegraph* was right. A defendant can rely on 'mitigation of damages' for libel if more than one newspaper has said roughly the same thing. In short, despite one legal pundit saying publicly each newspaper should be shelling out the same level of damages thus awarding a multiple libel claimant a seven figure sum, the truth was it would only make a marginal difference if we recovered against eight rather than nine newspapers.

After weighing it all up, I reached the decision to give the pros and cons to Christopher and let him decide. He thought it over and then, with his steely blue-eyed stare, asked me what I thought. My reply started off, "On the one hand...and on the other" but I quickly realised my client wanted me to be decisive – as I would want in his shoes – so I came down on not including *The Daily Telegraph*. What won the day was pragmatism. If we included *The Daily*

Telegraph who would most likely put up some initial resistance, this could give the rest of the infringing newspapers an excuse to slow down and not settle quickly. It might even encourage one or two to resist. Christopher took my guarded advice, and we didn't send the broadsheet a letter of claim.

Lucy, who argued for including *The Daily Telegraph*, was frustrated with the decision and let me know in no uncertain terms.

We then had a race to get the letters of claim out to all the other newspapers before Easter. It was the evening before Good Friday and I was determined that every one of the eight letters be sent to the editor of each newspaper before the evening was out, so that the clock would be running. I wanted to get it all tied up within three months.

We managed it. Just. Those days we served by fax which made it tedious as we had to check the correct number of pages had been sent. By mid-evening we had finished and made it over the road to the tiny and ornate Dog and Duck in Soho, George Orwell's favourite boozer.

I toasted the team for a great job and a happy Easter.

Whilst the various editors and their lawyers cogitated over the claims, we decided it was time to go to the place where it all happened. Once a criminal lawyer, always a criminal lawyer. Go to the scene of the crime. Put yourself in the shoes of the various players. By now Christopher had been declared 'no further action'. Disgracefully he had to wait almost three months despite Vincent Tabak having been arrested and remanded as long ago as 20 January.

Christopher was now back in his home in Bristol and we agreed I would go to his flat, visit the crime scene and also talk to neighbours. Clifton is a beautiful stone clad suburb of Bristol. It is middle class, heritage loving nirvana. If I lived in Bristol, I would probably head there myself.

Christopher's flat is lined with books. Lots of them. As a book lover, I had to pull myself away and concentrate on the task in hand. I took a more detailed statement from him, snapped several photographs and went to the flat he had rented to Joanna and Greg.

I went to see a witness – a former colleague from Clifton – whose loose tongue had helped whip up the hysteria in the press by calling him a loner, with its obvious suggestions towards impropriety. He gave me a statement, explaining he merely agreed with a journalist's description of him as a loner because he was a bachelor. He was embarrassed. He also gave me useful information about how Christopher was besieged by journalists outside his home for several days.

On our last evening Christopher invited me and my trainee, John, to dinner. He cooked us a three-course meal which included a knockout French onion soup. Classical music played in the background. I wore my napkin tucked in my collar to prevent any stains on my shirt and tie, a tiny detail Christopher remembered and which was used to comic effect in the subsequent TV drama. Very civilised. If this is 'strange' bring it on, John and I agreed afterwards.

Back in London I predicted we would get a call from the same lawyer who was my opponent in Robert Murat. I was right. Keith Mathieson. In his quiet tones he explained he was acting for all but one of the newspapers as a 'job lot' – this time *The Sun* was going it alone.

"We must stop meeting like this, Keith," I quipped.

"Quite. Not the press' finest hour."

"Again?"

"Again."

We agreed to meet but this time it was to be on home turf. I told Keith he had to leave his city cubby hole by the Thames and come over to edgy Soho if he wanted to talk turkey. He readily agreed and we fixed a date. He couldn't really do otherwise. Although trial work is the most satisfying thing in litigation, having the upper hand in a case which is so compelling and will result in all your client's wishes runs a close second.

Word soon got round that Christopher was suing and being represented by us. Lots of people got in touch, many offering references to their brilliant former teacher, including senior lawyers and journalists.

The negotiation day was long and with the team and Christopher, we agreed the parameters and what we required to settle, here and now. Otherwise, we would see them in court. It was a protracted affair. We had to haggle over both sums of money and wording. It was relatively easy for us. Lots of dosh and full, unequivocal and grovelling apologies. It was undoubtedly trickier for Keith who, I guess, had to get sign off at every stage from competing newspaper editors. I assume they had pre-agreed the portion each one would be responsible for, with the biggest offenders taking the biggest hit. Maybe that was why *The Sun* was going solo? Keith, who always plays his cards close to his chest, wasn't letting on despite me baiting him that he was no fun and such a spoilsport. By the end of the day, with Christopher and our QC's approval, we reached a deal.

The other development, as well as Tabak being sent for trial at the Crown Court by local magistrates, was the Attorney General's decision to prosecute the *Daily Mirror* and *The Sun* for contempt of court for their articles on Christopher. This was sensational and a legal first: never before had this been done when charges were never brought against Christopher. And probably brought on by exasperation that the newspapers were getting away with too much.

It was probably another reason why *The Sun* decided to opt out of the group approach to settle. Back then their legal supremo was Tom Crone. It was well known among claimant lawyers – a parish I was soon to abandon – that if Tom calls, you know a settlement is about to be offered. And so it proved. We settled with Tom at around the same time as the others.

The last day of the summer term for the courts loomed and we got word that *Her Majesty's Attorney General v MGN Limited and News Group Newspapers Limited* (the *Mirror* and *The Sun* respectively) was to be heard by the Divisional Court on 29 July 2011, the very last day of the summer term.

I summoned the troops to the office. I explained that vindication day would be massively enhanced if, at the same time as the newspapers were making grovelling apologies, they were being hammered and lambasted by the Lord Chief Justice of England and Wales. It would also be a legal first. We had to race as quick and hard as we could to get permission to read the statement in open court by that date, preferably on the same day.

The team managed to do it. The libel hearing was set for 10am, again in front of the new senior media judge who went by the quaint title of judge in charge of the jury list. Again, I donned my robe, or Batman cloak as I preferred to call it, and fiddled with the starched collars, gold pins and weird tie arrangement. There was only one thing missing.

My client.

Christopher had very politely declined to come to London. I tried a few times to persuade him, explaining this was unmissable, his chance to explain how badly he had been treated and how glad he would be to receive such overwhelming vindication. He gave me his inscrutable smile and simply said, "I prefer not, Louis." He explained he would be happy for me to do it, and I could say a few words for him. He is essentially a private and modest man. What about letting me say how much he had recovered in damages? No. He instructed me not to reveal the figure he was getting for the 45 articles in the frame.

It was a whirlwind morning.

First up in Court 13 before Mr Justice Tugendhat, who had taken over as number one libel judge following Eady J's retirement, were the multiple statements in open court, just like in Murat. Classically trained, the judge insisted on calling me "Haralambous" as you would in Greek, not "Charalambous" as in chariot.

We repeated the apologies, up and down, up and down. One by one the wrongdoing followed by the apology. The journalists furiously scribbled away as the shocking accusations now being withdrawn were read out. At the end I looked back to the judge from my script – which we are obliged to follow word perfect – and got a little smile from him. Whether it was his wholehearted approval of the result or the fact neither Keith nor I had cocked up I couldn't tell.

The court was packed out with journalists, some of them whispering over to me, "Where's Chris?"

Outside court I had to let them down gently.

"He's not here but I have a statement I am going to read outside to the cameras." They followed me as I strode down the marble steps into the Great

Hall, a cavernous mock Gothic affair, removing my gown.

Outside, to cameras snapping and cameras rolling, I said my piece:

"Christopher Jefferies is the latest victim of the regular witch hunts and character assassinations carried out by the worst elements of the British tabloid media. Many of the stories published in these newspapers are designed to 'monster' the individual, in flagrant disregard for his reputation, privacy and rights to a fair trial."

The media – apart from the eight newspapers in the case – lapped it up. I went viral, so to speak. One friend from a TV newsroom messaged me to say I was all over every channel and could I please get off?

I went back inside and called Christopher. He was pleased it had gone well and asked me to make sure I passed on his best regards to the whole team. I explained it wasn't over yet – the *Mirror* and *Sun* were next up in the dock for their contempt of court after pleading "not guilty" and I was just about to go in and watch the case in another court in the same building.

The Lord Chief Justice at the time was Baron Igor Judge (I thought of him simply as Judge Judge, a bit like Major Major in *Catch-22*) and one of the most impressive and humane judges I have ever been before. The court was packed, and I managed to squeeze onto the back row. The atmosphere was charged, and I kept a close eye on the two legal teams. The Attorney General's side seemed to be enjoying the hearing. The newspapers' two QCs less so.

The Attorney General, Conservative MP Dominic Grieve, presented his own case rather than sending a QC in his place. Both newspapers tried to avoid being committed by arguing their coverage was not bad enough to warrant being found in contempt of court. In essence, we were rather naughty but not naughty enough, m'lud.

Grieve pursued his arguments on two limbs: firstly, if Christopher had been charged then there was a substantial risk he would not have got a fair trial because a jury would have been prejudiced against him; and the 'fade' factor – that the news reports would have been largely forgotten about a year later when any trial would have taken place – was not enough to get them off the hook. The newspapers also argued that a jury properly directed to ignore previous articles would have assisted in mitigating any remaining prejudice – the court called this the jury integrity point. Secondly, the AG submitted that Christopher would have been impeded in getting his own defence together since potential defence witnesses would have been prejudiced against him because of the articles assassinating his character.

The court listened carefully to the arguments of both sides and then came back with its decision. On the first point they decided in the newspapers' favour. They predicted that the fade factor and jury integrity aspect was enough to get them off the hook had Christopher been tried and convicted despite, as they put it, the "vilification" of his character. But on the second limb of the prosecution, potentially prejudicing his defence, they convicted both newspapers. There were no previous cases (or 'authorities') on this aspect so they were, in effect, making new law. In a Common Law jurisdiction like ours, this is exciting stuff.

The result was a £50,000 fine against the *Daily Mirror* – the more serious of the two – and an £18,000 fine against *The Sun*, who had the good grace to apologise in open court for their coverage, unlike the other tabloid.

Afterwards I made my way down to the front row of the court and introduced myself to Grieve. He is a super posh man who greeted me with a, "How do you do?" (which century are we in?) and we exchanged a few pleasantries on how good a day it was for vindicating Christopher – libel morning, contempt afternoon.

Outside I gave interviews to radio and TV. Several of the journalists afterwards spoke to me off the record to say how sickened they had been at the time with this coverage and how glad they were to see these prosecutions because bad journalism made their task and standing much worse.

Trebles all round, as they say in *Private Eye*.

Later on, I found out that Christopher received a note from the Lord Chief Justice – who sadly passed away in November 2023 – to the effect that he was pleased Christopher's libel case and the Divisional Court case took place on the same day. A very nice touch.

Four months later I helped Christopher compose his statement to the Leveson Inquiry, the wide-ranging inquiry into press standards. I went with him on the day he gave evidence, sitting with him beforehand in the witness waiting room and quietly at the back of the hearing. He was a star. Utterly calm and composed, he was able to lucidly articulate his experience at the hands of a section of the press. Like Robert Murat, he spoke about the crime and the victim in order to put everything into its proper context and remind everyone of the tragedy. Lord Justice Leveson picked out his ordeal as an exemplar of bad press standards because it was such a compelling case.

Not long afterwards I was contacted by the renowned writer, Peter Morgan, who would go on to write *The Crown*. Would I meet him for lunch so he could ask my help for his latest writing commission: an ITV drama over two lengthy episodes about what happened to Christopher?

I admit I was intrigued. It isn't every day a case becomes a major drama.

I agreed and we met in a rooftop restaurant in Chinatown. He explained his vision and how he wanted to make a film which would have Christopher's story at the heart of it; in order to ensure integrity Christopher and the lawyers who helped him at every stage would be consulted. He explained that Roger Michell, the brilliant director of *Notting Hill* and *The Buddha of Suburbia* among other TV and film classics, would be involved. I was to be a major character in the second film so I would meet Roger and the actor who would play me.

Roger told me he'd been taught by Christopher and was heavily invested personally in making the film. He also cast former pupils and friends of Christopher to play the press representatives. A nice Alfred Hitchcockian touch from a lovely man who sadly passed away much too early in 2021 at the age of 65.

After Christopher gave the go ahead to participate in the project, I told Peter I had two conditions: the first was that I had to be played by a British Cypriot actor. I was close to this small fraternity of actors and wanted to ensure one of them got the part. After all, it is incredibly rare for one of us to be cast in a serious role. The second was that I see his script so I could give him comments, again to make sure they were getting it right. Peter Polycarpou, a highly accomplished actor, was cast to play me. He was well known from *Birds of a Feather* (initially on the BBC and later on ITV) and numerous theatrical productions.

Peter Polycarpou and I met a couple of times so that he could 'get' my mannerisms and way of speaking as well as find out about the legal issues involved. Jason Watkins, another renowned actor, was cast to play Christopher. In 2014 I was invited to a private screening alongside a selected audience and the main actors. My only factual quibble with Peter's script was a meeting which never took place between me and Steve Coogan, another Leveson witness. The script had me meeting and greeting the star and being rather fawning, repeatedly saying "A-Ha". I asked Peter to change this, and the message came back that this would happen. So it was a bit of a pain to see the meeting with Coogan was changed to make it even longer than the first version. I shrugged my shoulders and accepted that docudramas have to give a bit of colour and invent scenes.

It was a great film, especially the portrayal of Christopher by Watkins. Afterwards I told the actor he deserved a Bafta as best actor. He did indeed get this accolade, and the two-parter also won Best TV Mini-Series.

Happily, Christopher is back to living his life and enjoying his retirement. He still gives talks about what happened to him and the need for press reform.

Chapter 20

Vindicating Luke

The jury looked flummoxed as the newspapers' QC told them that my client had "jolly well ring led" the protesters at the Tory HQ and his case should be dismissed. I gave my client a little nudge in the ribs. "Jolly hockey sticks, more like," I whispered.

My opponent's closing speech had an air of desperation about it. The newspapers in question seemed to have not a clue about the politics of the anti-government movement in the austerity years of the Tory-Lib Dem coalition that decided to jack up the cost of tuition fees soon after the 2010 election. I smiled and thought that at this rate we might even win over the very bored looking man in the white t-shirt on the jury.

I thought my client Luke Cooper's case would be the last libel case to be decided by a jury (his was the first heard for over three years when it came on in June 2012) but one more sneaked over the line before the axe of the Defamation Act 2013 came down on such cases. Although the Act says that a libel jury can still be convened in highly limited circumstances, it is now considered extremely unlikely. The jury room opposite Court 13 in the RCJ sits empty these days. Claimant lawyers I know love a jury and regularly lament their passing. The statistics for a claimant win have gone down since judges took control of the facts as well as the law.

In 2010, five months after the formation of the Coalition government best remembered by the Cameron and Clegg 'love in' held for the press at No. 10's Rose Garden, more than 50,000 people protested against the planned rise in tuition fees. The vast majority protested entirely peacefully and lawfully on that November afternoon. However, a tiny number broke away, got into the building on London's Millbank which housed the Conservative headquarters and, smashing some windows, got onto the roof where a fire extinguisher was thrown off. In the crowd fewer than 100 protesters burned their placards and threw missiles at police. The student organisers were furious, knowing this hijacking of the march would become the headline rather than the huge peaceful demonstration which had gone off so well. The NUS President described the violence as "despicable".

Luke Cooper was part of a feeder march which arrived at 30 Millbank long after the small group of protesters had entered the building. He mingled with other protesters outside the building and gave out leaflets. Also mingling were several journalists, all no doubt looking for an angle. One, from the *Standard*, spoke to Luke who answered his questions. With nothing to hide, Luke gave him his phone number and carried on with distributing his literature. He did not enter the building, engage in any violence, property damage or confrontation with the police.

Later that day the *Standard* journalist called him with more questions. Luke answered them and, as before, he was careful to distinguish between legitimate mass political protest against the fees hike and wider austerity issues and illegitimate acts of violence and property damage, making clear he was against the latter. As a self-declared Marxist, he deplored individual acts of criminality and was solely focused on building a movement to effect radical change in society. This subtlety was entirely lost on the journalist and his editor when, the next day, Luke became the personification of the mini riot because, it seems, he was the only one the journalist had managed to interview on the record.

Luke Cooper was the happy beneficiary of a unanimous verdict by his jury which decided the university tutor had been falsely described as the ringleader in the attack on the Conservative party headquarters. The newspapers in the frame were the *Daily Mail* (of course) and the *Evening Standard*, both reflecting the opinion of many of the public who deplored the attack. But here was the twist: it was the *Standard*'s story which the *Mail* 'lifted' (polite trade speak for stole) so much so that it put them in the frame alongside the original publisher. This practice often used by some newspapers of lifting stories from other titles can come back to bite them badly if it falls foul of the libel laws, especially because they haven't put in the hard yards of getting the story in the first place, leaving them at the mercy of the newspaper they nicked the story from.

The *Evening Standard*'s front-page headline screamed, 'Full' marks for the riots say lecturers' and 'Goldsmith's academics congratulate students on violent protests' and a smaller headline 'Ringleader: we attacked Tory HQ to send message'. The article began by describing how the *Standard* 'discovered' that Luke "was a ringleader in hijacking the student march". Luke was then directly quoted explaining why the students attacked the Tory HQ "in order to send a really strong message to this Government". He went on to describe legitimate targets of protest. A photograph of Luke, unearthed by the newspaper from a friend's Facebook page, showed him in a pub smirking and wearing a Batman transfer on his forehead. What the newspaper did not make clear was the photo was taken many months earlier on a social occasion. Instead, remaining silent on the context or its age, it carried a caption saying, 'Protest leader, Sussex University lecturer Luke Cooper, told the *Standard* of his role in plotting the attack on Millbank'.

The *Daily Mail* article was broadly similar, claiming it was unmasking the hardcore leaders of a student mob. It carried the same Batman transfer photo of Luke, calling him a protest organiser.

Luke is a serious academic who doesn't hide his Marxist credentials. When he came to see me in his mid-twenties, he was completing a PhD at the University of Sussex. He wasn't interested in damages. He just wanted the newspapers in question to apologise to him for trashing his reputation, the consequences of which might stall his career there and then.

I explained that newspapers being prepared to apologise was much more difficult than usual because of the ideological aspect: Marxism and right-wing tabloids do not mix very well. Also, a curiosity of libel cases is that if the defendant goes to trial and loses, they cannot be made to apologise which is the normal cornerstone sought by a claimant. However, they do have to report the defeat in the newspaper and agree not to repeat the allegation, otherwise they might face the wrath of the court in the shape of contempt of court proceedings.

Just like today, if a right-wing newspaper decides a complainant is politically hostile to their editorial stance and the biases of their readers then it takes a lot to shift their position.

And so it proved.

I don't suppose Luke expected to meet up with someone like me as his solicitor – with two politics degrees and an abiding interest in all things political. One of my early tasks was to sort out and understand the differences, sometimes subtle and other times glaring, between the various groups who marched to protest against the huge rise in tuition fees. Many of us still remember Nick Clegg's broken promise to the electorate in the 2010 election that he would not vote for a rise in tuition fees. Installed as the Deputy Prime Minister by David Cameron, he would have had no choice but to vote with the austerity package which included the rate increase if he still wanted to keep his job. When he voted for it and broke his word, he quickly became a hate figure among students.

But the real drivers of the price hike were Prime Minister Cameron and his Chancellor, George Osborne.

There is a natural tendency to play safe when it comes to political matters when you take on an 'all or nothing' conditional fee agreement. Prevailing wisdom is anyone on the 'far' left or right is unlikely to be favoured by the court. Even though I could see the coverage of Luke was highly exaggerated and most likely false, there was part of me which warned that his wish – for a revolutionary change in society – would alienate your average juror. But as well as completing his PhD and tutoring in his department at the University of Sussex, which made him both teacher and student, I could also see he was a thoughtful, pleasant and intelligent client who would play well with the jury.

It only took me to the end of my first meeting with him to decide I would take him on as a no win, no fee client. Like Mark Covell, he badly needed to set the record straight.

So it came down to an all or nothing fight between a 26-year-old tutor come PhD student and two national newspapers. And I relished the challenge.

Libel is judged by the entire publication: headlines, photos, captions and story, all of which have to be looked at together to arrive at the single meaning of the publication. However, the headline sometimes is much more aggressive than the story itself in order to grab the reader's attention. We argued the meaning of the *Evening Standard*'s article (or 'the sting') was that Luke was a ringleader of anarchists who masterminded the hijacking of a peaceful student march and the commission of violence and property damage.

We argued for a similar meaning with the *Mail*. The two newspapers disagreed saying that not every fact claimed about Luke was accurate (never a good start) and, in the *Standard*'s case, contended for three alternative meanings with subtle differences about the extent of Luke's pre-planning of the protest.

We thought this approach was unattractive. If they couldn't make their minds up about what the article meant then it was not, to put it bluntly, a good look. In the *Mail*'s case they settled for two alternative versions. And, where each article was defamatory of Luke, bearing in mind the allegations about being a ringleader who orchestrated violence were toned down compared with the *Standard*, each newspaper claimed they were true, thereby giving each newspaper a total defence.

We made an offer to settle early on – almost a year before trial – for only token damages of £5,000 apiece for each newspaper, plus an apology and removal of the articles from the two newspapers' websites.

But no – they were 'doubling down' and refused to countenance any settlement of this sort.

Telling the story clearly and openly was the most important thing for us. I worked on the case with Jeffrey Smele and Lucy Moorman. We all agreed that as this was likely to go all the way to trial, we needed a senior barrister who was a brilliant communicator, across all the detail and could tell Luke's story to a jury.

William McCormick, back then not yet a silk, was one of the most obvious names we discussed among the ranks of top libel practitioners. But there was a problem. This case was, at best, 50:50 in terms of whether we would win against these two newspaper giants who had huge resources. They were willing to chuck everything into a fight and try to dig up dirt against Luke and his fellow revolutionists. Would William take the case on if the only way he could get paid was by winning it?

We trooped off to his chambers at Ely Place, one of the last Georgian Streets in the vicinity of the High Court (which featured in the film of John le Carré's book, *The Constant Gardener* as a classic legal office location with its Georgian architecture all intact) and knocked on his door. We had sent him a small brief in advance and for the next hour listened to him hurl potential problems and pitfalls in Luke's case our way. We gave as good as we got. Good lawyers, especially in crime and libel, test a case by its weaknesses. Looked at another way, they put themselves in the shoes of the opponent. How would I attack this individual, probing for the soft underbelly of your own case?

By the close William decided that, subject to meeting Luke and satisfying himself my client could acquit himself well in the witness box, he would sign up to a no win, no fee agreement and, like us, be 'all in'. We were only a few weeks away from trial.

Luke described to me his first meeting with William as one of the most terrifying experiences of his life. He was subjected to a verbal bruising in order to give him some idea of the kind of attack he was likely to face from the newspapers' QC.

He came out of the 'beating up' well although when we emerged into Ely Place, he confirmed he now appreciated what he was up against and that he would prepare for the battle to come. Lucy and I helped him with the intricacies of the increasingly rare beast: a civil trial with a jury deciding meaning, liability and, if the verdict is for the claimant, damages.

What followed in the next few weeks was a barrage of attack from the newspapers. Their barrister team was obviously now at the helm and with experienced solicitors – RPC (again) – were chucking all sorts of material at us. Anything Luke had ever written, and any organisation he was ever affiliated with came our way. As is so often the case with litigation, it was mostly diversionary tactics. The central problem which they could not escape was that Luke had been clear about his political stance throughout: what he was for and what he was against. There were disputes between him and the journalist about what Luke had told him which the jury was going to have to decide as a matter of fact.

As well as having to handle the diversionary material being thrown our way, our opponents also changed their stance on how they put their case. They wanted to hang Luke on this material as well as what they claimed he told the *Standard*. Luke worried this was potentially a problem for us. I reassured him this was more likely to be a desperate scrabble to obfuscate the issues. I also predicted that masses of revolutionary literature would alienate a jury if forced to try and glean something from it regarding Luke's actions and words on the day and the run up to the protest. I told him that in the end it was simple things like who the jury believed or liked (or disliked) that determined decisions.

At last, we arrived at trial in midsummer on Monday 18 June 2012.

Trials are rare beasts for civil litigators. Most cases settle. I'm lucky in having been in more trials than most people. It is the real deal. Even more so when the fact finders are jurors. The plethora of documents relied on by our opponents to discredit Luke in the eyes of the court were abandoned after the judge indicated the bulk of it was unhelpful. The jury bundle – the papers which each juror would scrutinise and be taken through in trial – was now thankfully slim and free of political tracts.

Looks can be deceiving. One juror, the man in the white t-shirt, appeared totally uninterested throughout the case. I worried he might be against us. How wrong I turned out to be. He picked up his hitherto untouched pencil and pad the moment the judge started talking about damages. I broke into a smile. But I am getting ahead of myself.

The trial.

After opening speeches and a little trial management by the now retired High Court judge, Mr Justice Eady, we got underway. Luke was first on and gave his answers to William in a clear and straightforward manner. He told the jury what his beliefs were, his background and what he did that day before then describing his fateful meeting with the *Standard* journalist, Benedict Moore-Bridger.

Luke told the court he had been badly misquoted, in particular denying he ever said, "We attacked Tory HQ". The newspaper's case was on the contrary – he had said this, and his quotes should be treated as admissions. Luke explained that he was approached by Moore-Bridger as he was distributing his organisation's fanzine. The journalist said it was the other way round. Luke went on to explain the principles behind the protest and that he had no role in organising the protest, let alone be a ringleader or an anarchist. The latter probably offended Luke as much as anything else.

Anyone who knows the radical left will know the mutual disdain between the Marxists and the Anarchists. Even during the trial, I got the sense that no one in the other side's legal or editorial team got this. Likewise, they didn't get the difference between direct action and violent action. Everything and everyone were lumped together in their eyes; Luke and the tiny minority who used violent means were all the same. And someone had to be blamed. By agreeing to be interviewed by the *Standard* Luke was putting himself in the firing line especially because of his minor teaching role as an associate tutor whilst finishing his doctorate. I knew the importance of making sure the court understood the difference between political mass action and law-breaking violence and criminal damage.

The cross examination wore on. Now that Lucy Moorman was in-house with us, she positioned herself in the row in front of William – where solicitors traditionally sit – rather than behind him, where junior counsel normally sit. I took up my usual position at the back of the court so I could better look at everyone, particularly the jury.

In a short break during Luke's cross examination, I got a signal from my counterpart, Keith Mathieson, to meet outside court. "Louis, a quiet word please," and without waiting for my reply he wandered around the corner into a dark recess.

"What's up, Keith?"

"Your Lucy Moorman. My QC (Adrienne Page) is being put off by her constant turning round to look at her and flicking her fringe, whilst she cross examines your client."

I do not remember my exact reply, but I think it was along the lines of, "You are having a laugh, aren't you? Are you seriously asking one of my team not to look at your QC? She can look where the heck she wants."

Keith looked embarrassed. I'm sure he knew it was a silly request. Secretly I was delighted. Getting under the skin of your opponent at such an important juncture was good news. I had noticed what might be regarded as a disdainful turn of Lucy's head in front of me and she was in Ms Page's line of sight of the witness box. Afterwards I did speak with Lucy about Keith's approach. She confirmed that whilst she had no intention of putting off the defence QC, she was looking back to watch her asking what Lucy regarded as some damn foolish questions.

I burst out laughing.

Watching your client get cross examined is never easy and this episode broke the tension. However, as it wore on, Luke got better and better and was doing exactly what we had asked him: keeping it simple and addressing the jury with his answers. And not getting riled even when having to explain whether the use of violence was ever justified. Luke's answer that the uprising against the Libyan dictator, Gaddafi, was an example where force could be justified.

Eventually it came to an end, and the judge allowed him to take his place next to me. I motioned him to come outside court, and we swung open the large, creaking wooden doors which have probably been around since the late Victorian era.

I wanted to give him a hug for his time in the box. It is never easy having a skilled lawyer trying to assassinate your character. I remember saying this was the real deal and that most litigation is, to use the Latin, "*interruptus*" but that this was the courtroom equivalent of full-on coitus. I have no idea why I said this and that memory is a bit embarrassing. Luckily, Luke just laughed at my inane remark.

He confided in me that Page's cross examination was nowhere near as hostile or difficult as the session with William back in his chambers. I slapped him on the back and said there is nothing like your own team putting you through your paces.

The roles were reversed when the defence put up Moore-Bridger and William got stuck into him. He stood his ground as we expected him to.

It was one person's word against another.

After three days of evidence, it was time for speeches and the memorable "jolly well ring led" remark by Page.

The jury then listened intently to Mr Justice Eady's impeccable summing up and were told to come back in the morning to begin their deliberations. They would be required to answer a series of questions which indicated their decisions on meaning, the disputed facts and whether, if they found either or both newspapers liable, the amount of damages they were awarding. It was like a mini multiple assessment exam.

We did not have too long to wait. The jury came back and found in Luke's favour in relation to both newspapers and awarded him £60,000 damages. This showed they regarded it seriously. It was a massive slap in the face for these two newspapers. They should have settled for the modest £5,000 damages and even more modest legal costs we had offered at the early stage but they wouldn't, probably because the idea of saying sorry to a revolutionary was utterly alien to them and could not be stomached.

Whilst no apology can be extracted from a losing defendant, they were still obliged to report the court's finding to their readers which is at least something. Only the BBC and *The Guardian* reported the trial outcome. We hoped for a place in the libel history books as the last ever libel jury trial, but we happily settled on it being the penultimate one. And winning, which is the sweetest feeling for any litigator.

It was a massive relief for Luke who looked extremely happy. And equally a relief for the legal team. If it had gone the other way no doubt Luke would have felt crushed, and his academic career would have likely stalled.

Chapter 21

The Long Fella rides in

Aficionados of Jed Mercurio's TV series *Line of Duty* quickly learnt that OCG stands for Organised Crime Group. The fictitious goings on of earnest superintendent Ted Dunbar and his keen-eyed junior officers in an anti-corruption squad was a world away from the grim reality of real-life cops who investigate other cops. I was initiated into the world by the remarkable Michael Gillard, probably one of the most fearless journalists in Britain today.

By the time Michael's article about a crime boss appeared in the newspaper, I had already done several cases with him. The first was around the circumstances of his acrimonious departure heading up *The Guardian*'s investigation unit with fellow journalist, Laurie Flynn. After leaving the newspaper they sat down and wrote a 500-page blockbuster *Untouchables: Dirty cops, bent justice and racism in Scotland Yard*, first published in 2004 and re-published in 2012. Nowadays it is essential reading material for the new wave of anti-corruption officers, presumably filed under 'how not to do it'.

Scotland Yard's intranet immediately tried to ban officers from reading the book. This had the opposite effect. The hardback flew off the shelves mostly into the arms of cops wanting to read the amazing but true stories of some of the biggest cover ups involving anti-corruption cops and gangsters anywhere in the world. Every single complaint by people featured in the book was fought off successfully from my office in a rickety Georgian terrace in Soho where Michael became a regular visitor. Only passing mention was made of David 'Davey' Hunt in the book who made no complaint about being called one of East London's up and coming crime families.

All that was to change in May 2010 when Michael, now an investigative reporter for the *Sunday Times*, wrote an article captioned, 'Underworld Kings Cash in on Taxpayer Land Fund'. He alleged Hunt and the notorious north London based crime family, the Adams, were cashing in on a £20m government fund to buy up land earmarked for the 2012 London Olympics. The 21-paragraph article came with a police surveillance photograph of the rarely sighted David Hunt whose nickname was 'the Long Fella' because of his 6' 5" frame. His face was finally public.

And he was not happy.

A libel complaint letter soon arrived at the *Sunday Times* legal department. I wasn't a regular lawyer for the broadsheet title but had long been an admirer, particularly of their *Insight* team of investigative journalists. Back then I was still mostly acting for claimants. Michael, whose powers of persuasion to bend people to his will are legend, insisted I do the case for the newspaper because I had fought off all the other gangsters in *Untouchables*.

I looked over the correspondence between *The Times'* then head of legal and Hunt's lawyers. It was dense reading. But now Hunt had sued it was time for the external lawyers to front up for the newspaper. And I was to be plunged into the criminal underworld.

From time to time people would ask, "But aren't you scared?" My response was always the same: lawyers are replaceable, but witnesses aren't – they take the real risk here. But truth be told, I did take a few more precautions than usual.

My first move was to meet with the newspaper's favoured QC, Gavin Millar, to set out a plan of action. Gavin – brilliant, mercurial and not one to waste words or shower praise to 'get in' with solicitors – was already well known to me. Like me, he relished taking on tricky, difficult cases engaging criminal law and police procedure.

For the next three or so years we were catapulted into a rollercoaster of secret meetings, fights with and meeting large numbers of police officers connected to Hunt in some way or other, interviewing gangsters, hangers on and, most important of all, Hunt's victims. Most were too scared to talk or if they did, come to trial. An organised crime boss is not someone to cross.

Proving what happened to Paul Cavanagh, a lowly member of Hunt's OCG, back in 1997 was crucial. Michael's incendiary article alleged that David Hunt had personally sliced Cavanagh's face leaving a deep 15cm laceration from the tip of his chin to his left ear. Cavanagh hadn't followed orders to find Jimmy Holmes, Hunt's ex-partner in crime, the article claimed. Holmes was the author of one of the finest true crime books, *Judas Pig*, which was all about his life and times with Hunt before they fell out.

Cavanagh agreed to make a wounding complaint to police against Hunt which resulted in Hunt being remanded in custody. As he was to later tell the *Sunday Times* in 2014, in a remarkable article entitled 'I feared a beating – but 'the Long Fella' asked for a knife', Cavanagh soon regretted his decision and disappeared after making a withdrawal of complaint statement which resulted in Hunt being freed from remand. Cavanagh, however, was still afraid of retribution and went to live in Scotland. He stayed away from London for many years and was still hundreds of miles away when we located him.

Cavanagh agreed to a meeting with me and Michael who flew in from Mexico where he was living to keep out of the way of Hunt in the run up to trial. In his book *Legacy* which tells the story of the Hunt OCG in detail, Michael described our visit:

> *The reporter visited Cavanagh and found a broken man who needed an oxygen tank nearby at all times in case of sudden respiratory failure. His crippled hand from a car accident rested on his lap making channel hopping from news to racing results and back again more of a challenge than he would like at sixty. The light from the window illuminated the long, deep scar that ran from his left ear down to across his throat and then up to the tip of his chin; a disfigured reminder every morning of the attack.*

In the end, Cavanagh didn't give evidence at our libel trial. He was too fearful, even though it was 15 years on. And no one on our side would blame him.

We had better luck with Peter Wilson, a former *Sunday Mirror* crime correspondent, who also had a confrontation with Davey Hunt. His story showed
me why I love working for journalists and demonstrated how much risk they
are willing to take to try and get the story.

Back in 1992 Peter was following up a rumour that Hunt was responsible for a murder three years earlier for which he has never been arrested or
charged. He went to Hunt's crib – a gated, detached number in upmarket
Epping – and knocked on his door.

Bad move.

Hunt's wife answered, explaining her husband was still at work after Peter
explained he was a *Mirror* journalist and wanted to ask him some questions
about a murder. He left his card and went back later in the afternoon. This
time he soon learnt Davey Hunt was at home as Hunt rapidly strode towards
him. Without slowing down Hunt uttered some angry words about how dare
he come to his home and asking about murder and then CRACK!; Peter felt
a searing pain to his eye. Hunt had headbutted him so hard, it had caused a
fracture to his eye socket. Stunned, Peter staggered backwards into the photographer's car, who hadn't got his lens ready in time to capture the moment.

After receiving hospital treatment, the reporter unsurprisingly walked into
the nearest police station to report this serious assault.

However, someone was there to tell him this was a seriously bad move.

A sergeant, familiar with all the local villains, took Peter to one side and
asked him if he had any idea who he was going up against. Not just any old
gangster but someone who wouldn't flinch to take steps against anyone lay-
ing a criminal complaint against him. Was this a bent cop or just someone
acting kindly, telling him it would turn out worse for him in the long run?
My mind raced back to Paul Cavanagh. He too made a complaint which
resulted in Hunt being remanded in custody until Cavanagh felt the heat from
Hunt's associates and retracted his statement about who had slashed his face.
Peter weighed up the risks and spoke to some wise heads at the newspaper.
Reluctantly, he too withdrew his complaint.

But the anger burned inside and when I met him it took very little to persuade him to give us his account of what happened and to come to court and give evidence.

There were several other witnesses, the most notable being Billy Allen, an East Ender in the mould of the Arthur Daley character in ITV's *Minder*. One witness described him in court as that little fella who could milk a cow standing up, raising guffaws in court with the judge having to stifle a giggle.

Back in 2006 Allen got embroiled with a(nother) East End 'property developer', Charles Matthews, over ownership of some land and warehouses near the proposed Olympic site in Canning Town, which had featured in Michael's article. Allen refused to back down when warned the other guy had some heavyweight support. Both sides thought the site was potentially valuable because of the forthcoming Olympics. Allen lost the first round of his court fight with Matthews because he was bankrupt. Second time round, after winning the right through a court order to re-possess the land, the case came before a judge at Central London County Court located in a Regency terrace in upscale Regent's Park, which had featured in the film *Mary Poppins*.

Matthews came to court with his minders, who returned on day two again with the same heavies. They were led by David Hunt and his brother. It was a rare sighting of Hunt who now ran a number of waste management and entertainment businesses. A fight ensued and Allen's men were overwhelmed.

David Hunt and his thugs were careful to avoid being filmed dealing out the blows on the court CCTV. According to witness accounts it was bedlam for a couple of minutes. Allen escaped, running away past the millionaire Regency mansions. The case was postponed. Matthews, it turned out, was merely a front for the Hunt OCG.

This court corridor bust up featured in the article and we had to prove it was true. Billy Allen was our only witness. Michael persuaded Allen to come and see me and my number two, Gordon Clough, a tireless and stalwart ex-journalist who immersed himself into the case. After several meetings Allen agreed to be a witness for the newspaper and gave evidence at trial to rebut Hunt's version of the courtroom bust up.

Hunt's trial statement said:

"About 10 minutes after we arrived, a large group of men arrived separately. I recognised some of them, but they weren't with me. We had a friendly chat. They explained that Mr Allen owed them money and that he had been telling everyone the land was worth £100m and that he was going to win the case. I told them that was rubbish.

Mr Woollard and Mr Allen arrived around half an hour later. I had a brief conversation with Mr Woollard [Allen's security] and then some of Mr Allen's creditors began arguing with members of Mr Allen's group about the value of the land. Shortly afterwards, there was a commotion in the corridor leading to the Court but I couldn't really see what was happening. I wasn't involved in any way."

It was a crafty and clever get out – all he did was light the fuse by dismissing Allen's claim about the value of the land. Not down to him this fight – just a bit of civil war in the Allen camp, nothing to see here. A police report described the injuries of two of the participants as serious. Danny Woollard, his former minder, was to become a witness for Hunt, singing from the claimant's song book.

With Allen's own security turning on us, it looked hopeless until we got a massive break. We plugged away trying to get material held by the police. Michael had managed to get some but not much after years of investigating the Hunt gang. No one crossed Davey Hunt. Even though he had long since 'retired' from front line activities we knew from Billy Allen and the County Court dust up he was still willing to slip on the metaphorical knuckle dusters.

Earlier on in the case, we had lost almost a year in our evidence gathering because we decided to play it straight with the Met police and Serious Organised Crime Agency (SOCA). At Michael's suggestion, and being upfront (and no less than the *Sunday Times*, so ultra pukka), we wrote to them saying: "Just so you know we have got some sensitive documents of yours we've relied on in reporting this case and as we are now obliged to disclose them in our libel case we will shortly be doing so."

The proverbial then hit the fan with news of the documents which were now in our hands. Both the Met and SOCA demanded their material back. Immediately. We resisted, and Michael plus the newspaper suddenly became defendants in a breach of confidence case after both police organs got an injunction from a High Court judge. We were stopped from passing over any police paperwork to Hunt. The newspaper decided to fight it and asked – and got – a speedy trial to be heard in July 2011 after putting in a defence emphasising our fair trial and freedom of expression rights. Meanwhile we managed to stay (suspend) the Hunt libel trial.

A few months later a trial over the use of police material lasting several days unfolded. The Met put up flimsy arguments that certain classes of documents were too sensitive to disclose, which our barrister demolished. The police were at least willing to be a little flexible over other documents. SOCA, however, was obdurate and unrelenting, saying no to everything we asked for. In the end we got the judge to rule in our favour over some of the disputed documents for use in the libel trial but the key SOCA intelligence report could not be disclosed.

Back into the fray of the libel trial we threw everything into getting documents for use in the case against Hunt from the Met Police which hadn't been ruled impermissible.

But then we had a stroke of good fortune. One morning I took a call from the liaison officer at Scotland Yard designated to this case. Two boxes of material had been unearthed. Grabbing my jacket and Gordon at the same time, we jumped in a cab at his invitation to help look through the material to find what fell within the terms of the order.

We were greeted by the liaison officer in reception and taken along what felt like an endless corridor high up the old New Scotland Yard. The whole place was eerily quiet. It was the day of Margaret Thatcher's funeral so we guessed most of the inhabitants would be out policing the protesters or the mourners, or perhaps in mourning themselves. He showed us to a pokey room with a couple of large, dusty boxes. We looked at them and hoped to find treasure.

Within half an hour we knew we had struck gold. One stash featured the police records from the Billy Allen court fight. I opened a file of colour photos and found close ups of blood splattered on the corridor walls outside the courtroom, a witness statement from Allen's solicitor, Helen Porter, who witnessed some of the events and an initial account from one of Allen's minders which would have been taken whilst he was being bandaged up. In it he explained how he was not willing to finger his assailants.

Hunt's evidence about the dust up at court could now be countered. We no longer had to just rely on Allen.

The days and nights leading up to trial were intense. The sudden influx of new documents meant everyone had to play catch up. Both our counsel, Gavin and Anthony Hudson (who had helped me on numerous Gillard connected cases and brought me into the Terry Lloyd inquest), had to get on top of the new material as did our opponents, led by Hugh Tomlinson.

One morning, as I rushed to catch a bus, I heard a roaring in my right ear. A skip lorry thundered past only a few inches from me on a stretch of our High Road which is particularly narrow. I looked at it as it flew past. Hunt Skips. It was one of the legitimate branches of Hunt's business organisation. Coincidence, I told myself.

It was an all or nothing trial for both sides. Michael was and still is the most meticulous of evidence gatherers as the judge was to later observe. He devoted himself to helping us and was utterly on top of everything. Occasionally we wouldn't see things the same way but it was always resolvable, usually over a pint provided the pub wasn't modernised or 'gastrofied'.

David Hunt was now living comfortably in rural Essex, in a mansion (of course), with a string of respectable looking directorships. He hadn't been convicted of anything for decades and apart from the Cavanagh slashing which put him inside for six months on remand, he hadn't seen the inside of a prison cell. So proving he was a Crime Lord, responsible for serious criminal acts including murder, drug running and money laundering, was going to be difficult to say the least.

We had a vast amount of work to do which saw us call eight witnesses and summons another 19, who we could compel to attend against their wishes if they would not agree to come voluntarily.

The claimant, David Hunt, had to give evidence before anyone else. I couldn't wait. How would he answer the huge number of points about his past? I had no idea.

The designated liaison officer from Scotland Yard briefed us they were keeping an eye on things with regards to the security of our witnesses, particularly Michael. We had our own concerns on this score. News UK's Security Department was tasked with arranging a specialist security outfit to protect us from the start of the trial. I briefed them on the background. Members of the newly recruited security team sat in the public gallery while Tomlinson opened the case for Hunt on the first day. Keeping an eye on everyone, especially his associates, Hunt, who was immaculately attired, sat with his solicitor in the front row.

The next morning, as I made my way to court, I took a call from the security chief while I was on the bus.

"Stop Michael going to court," he said.

"What?" I replied, trying to keep my voice down on the packed top deck.

"The security team we hired just pulled out. They've been frightened off."

"How?"

"Last night two of the team were followed and when they were having a pint in a pub, they were approached by men who asked them if they were looking after the *Sunday Times* people in court in the David Hunt case. They were spooked by the approach and their boss just rang me to say they were pulling out."

"What, immediately?"

"Yep."

My mind was racing ahead. What if the security people had revealed the rendezvous point with Michael? I ended the call quickly and rang Michael, praying he would pick up.

He answered and I told him not to go to the agreed rendezvous in case it had been compromised. We agreed a new meeting place and I said I would walk him into the High Court. We met in a highly public place and strolled into court as if we didn't have a care in the world. A new security team was hastily recruited to look after us and we made sure they weren't compromised like their predecessors.

One morning Hunt was subjected to a humiliating warning by the Met police team watching the trial. A duty of care principle had been established following the tragic case of *Osman* which involved a murder victim who had not been adequately warned about threats to his safety after the police failed to pass on the intelligence they held. Henceforth, an *Osman*-style warning has to be given to potential victims of physical assault or murder. However, I had never before heard of a reverse *Osman*, but this was given to Hunt in the corridor of the basement court – specially selected for its security features by the liaison officer and other Met officers.

"Should any harm come to any witnesses in this, we will immediately arrest you. Do you understand, Mr Hunt?"

Hunt nodded gravely. The designated liaison officer had come through for us a second time.

Hunt was taking a massive risk in pursuing the case to the bitter end. Maybe, like Depp and Mitchell, he was gambling on the defence caving in given the massive costs and reputation risks for the losing party. I watched him closely throughout the trial – which ranged over 12 days – both in and outside the box. What struck me most about his appearance was his coal black eyes and his physique, justifying his nickname 'the long fella'. He came across as calm and measured. The violent temperament we accused him of was nowhere to be seen.

Every allegation we put to him in cross examination had a different explanation. No, he had nothing to do with Cavanagh's injuries – Paul, he explained, had taken shelter in the car showroom after being attacked by two Cypriot/Greek looking men. No, he didn't attack Peter Wilson fracturing his orbital eye socket with a vicious headbutt. No, he and his colleagues didn't attack Billy Allen's men in Central London County Court; he simply queried the valuation of the land at stake which caused Allen's men to start fighting between themselves.

Billy Allen and Peter Wilson both took the stand for us. They were crucial witnesses. With Paul Cavanagh absent, we had to make do with all the various witness statements and evidence of the abandoned wounding case against Hunt to make good the allegation.

We relied on both a justification (truth) defence and a responsible journalism defence. In other words, everything Michael wrote was substantially true (so justified) and it was all responsibly written. Once you put up the latter defence, the spotlight falls on the journalist to show how the story was put together. It was hard going for both sides. Hunt spent a few days in the witness box sugar coating his reputation. He tried to persuade the court that he was (just) a hardworking, family orientated businessman whom many cops bore grudges against. At one point he volunteered the fact that he had won a sparring match against an up-and-coming American fighter called Mike Tyson which led people to be jealous or vindictive against him in later years.

This 'they've-got-it-in-for-me' explanation took everyone by surprise.

Thanks to Michael's exhaustive digging, we were able to show several operations aimed at catching Hunt which failed for one reason or another. Hunt's QC tried his best to make a virtue of these failures along the theme of 'nothing to see' or because there was no evidence to support what was unfair attention on his client. His team characterised him as a "rough diamond". Our take was very different: we claimed Hunt was astute at knowing how to handle police probes, helped by a few friends making timely allegations of corruption against officers determined to catch him out.

One of Hunt's witnesses came close to showing how witnesses could be turned. Danny Woollard (now deceased), a cockney villain who had been Billy Allen's minder and with a string of convictions, was now giving evidence exonerating Hunt from any involvement in the court fight. Woollard had a witty turn of phrase. One of his more memorable, referring to his people being overwhelmed by the Hunt security team, was to complain, "If I knew they were going to be 20 handed I wouldn't have walked in with my prick in my hand."

Woollard and his men were beaten so badly that there was blood on the walls and floor of the courthouse which we could now prove thanks to the police archive finding. Woollard had been interviewed by the lead officer in the case against Hunt, chief inspector Dave McKelvey, shortly after the court fight:

DW: "We all met up with Bill in the morning, had a cup of tea. When we got round to the court there was Shane, Nicky and myself and then Billy and Mattie. When we got to the court there were about 20-odd of their side all dressed up like trainers, all like body building types. We could see what they were there for. So he said: 'I thought there weren't going to be any trouble' so I said 'No, it's just trying to frighten everybody'. When Shane looked back at them they pushed back, started arguing and shouting. It just went off. So we got Bill away. I think the idea was just to stop the case which they did do and frighten him and he thought he was going to lie down which he hasn't. He's a courageous little man. Well, ...we haven't seen him since…

"I was in the front with them just trying to do the best we can hold them and scuffle because as it happens they were in front and we was virtually blocking the doorway so they couldn't have got out after Bill in any case. There was a couple outside but Mattie got in the way."

DM: "Who did you recognise from the other side up there that day then?"

DW: "I see him, Davey, and [brother] Stevie Hunt. But I didn't know any of the others. I have seen them about but couldn't put a name on them."

By the time the parties had to swap witness evidence Woollard had completely gone over to David Hunt's side and was called by him as a witness to help exonerate his new boss from any wrongdoing at the court, making false allegations that McKelvey was corrupt and had forced him to give evidence.

Woollard's replies in cross examination by Gavin Millar were fantastical and utterly unconvincing; that the truth was David Hunt had done nothing wrong or illegal in the courthouse that day. At the end of his evidence, he gave David Hunt the biggest, most theatrical wink as if to say, 'There you go, I came good for you' before leaving the court. It was a great own goal by team Hunt which was not to go unremarked by the judge, who said in his judgment, "The knowing look that he gave the Claimant when he left the witness-box was telling."

Michael was brilliant in the witness box, batting away question after question with replies, often detailed and always incisive. As ever, once in the witness box I could not speak to him to warn him about increased police fears that his trenchant replies were causing concern for his safety. His cross examination allowed him to carefully explain his decade long research into Hunt as a crime lord (in police vernacular, a core nominal in the top 10 of crime outfits in the UK) and how he had put together his story responsibly, allowing him to reach conclusions which were entirely legitimate to make.

Alerted to an increased risk to his safety, I arranged with our new ex-military security team to have a black cab waiting in the courtyard of the Royal Courts of Justice. As Michael stepped down after a number of days in the box I beckoned him to me. He thought he would be resuming his normal place next to me and Gordon but instead I ushered him out of the door into the corridor. I wanted him out of court to lower the temperature given his effective and punchy response to prolonged cross examination.

I joined him straight after court and Michael agreed to come back with me as a precaution in case his home address was being monitored.

That night we went over the daily transcripts with a few beers.

Over the next few days we called our other witnesses. The two standout witnesses were Dave McKelvey and Peter Wilson. The latter gave his evidence calmly and lucidly, describing Hunt's attack on him vividly describing it akin to being "picked up and shook up like a rag doll". The cross examination of him by Hunt's team didn't last long. It was put to him he was "exaggerating" the headbutt. This was a difficult spin to put on it given we had a corroborating witness from his newspaper who saw the extent of his facial injuries. It was going to be an important decision for the judge to make.

After two and a half weeks the trial drew to a close with closing speeches to the judge. We were all exhausted. It had been the most difficult and complicated case I had ever been in. Had we managed to crack open the mansion-owning, respectable businessman veneer Hunt presented?

The judge, Mr Justice Simon, who had given few clues as to his thinking during the case, delivered his verdict two months later. My eyes lit up as I read his conclusion on the findings of our truth defence:

"In these circumstances, I have little difficulty in accepting that the Defendant has justified that part of the First Meaning which relates to the Claimant being the head of an organised crime network, implicated in extreme violence and fraud."

We had won, with a finding of truth for the most part (but unable to justify i.e. prove, that the murder and drug trafficking aspects were true) and a second finding of responsible journalism over the entire three-part meaning of the article. In other words, we would have won the case just by deploying the responsible journalism defence.

I was over the moon, reading the judge's very lengthy decision. It was the most fantastic vindication of Michael's journalism and resulted in him winning the Journalist of the Year and Investigation of the Year awards a few months later. Peter Wilson was described by the judge as "entirely credible" and he also concluded that Cavanagh had been viciously attacked by Hunt leaving him with life threatening injuries because we had proved it with witness evidence and police reports. The judge was satisfied that Cavanagh's belated "withdrawal" of his witness statement before going on the run was made out of fear of retribution. The judge also found for our version of events over what happened when Billy Allen's minders clashed with Hunt at Central London County Court.

It was a convincing win which, once publicly revealed, got a huge amount of press attention. The *Sunday Times* described the journalism as being on a par with their thalidomide exposé decades before. The following edition ran

Hunt related stories over several pages. Exhausted, we celebrated the decision long and hard into the night.

What then happened to the people at the centre of the case?

Nothing adverse happened to David Hunt. He continues with his life pretty much the same.

Paul Cavanagh emerged from the shadows to give the *Sunday Times* his account, both in print and video. The newspaper helped him to re-locate, as the article states in a note at the end. Sadly, he has since died from his chronic health problems.

Michael stayed in Mexico for a year after the case. He continues with his unique brand of journalism, focusing on crime and police corruption, writing both in established media and his own *Upsetter* website. No one can match his investigative journalism in his chosen field and, from time to time, he gets the odd complaint but his success in the Hunt case will make any of his targets extremely wary to take him on.

Chapter 22

Turning gamekeeper...fun with *The Sun*

I remember the call from Justin Walford in November 2011 vividly. He and I had clashed swords back in his *Daily Express* days and, for the last 10 years, *The Sun*. Even when I accused his photo editor of adding blue to Christopher Jefferies' hair to make him look like some kind of freak (see Chapter 19) we remained on good terms. His denial that they would do any such thing wasn't exactly convincing, but I had let it pass.

"Louis, are you sitting in your chair?" Justin asked in a concerned tone.

"Er, yes. Why?" What on earth was he about to tell me?

"I'm going to ask you something rather shocking so don't want you to fall off it or anything like that."

Hmmm, could this be some belated smoking gun on one of my cases that could lead to new litigation to reverse a decision perhaps, I wondered.

"We want you to become our new go-to external solicitor."

I silently gulped and tried to play it cool. By then I had no active cases against *The Sun* or *News of the World* and had steered clear of getting into the phone hacking litigation being brought mostly by celebrities against the *News of the World*. It really hadn't interested me.

"Why," I asked. "Isn't Farrer's on the scene any longer?" The Queen's law firm had been in the news recently in connection with their representation of *News of the World*. Ever the diplomat, Justin told me that both News UK and Farrer & Co had agreed to stop the relationship and move to a new law firm within two months. This time I'm sure Justin could hear my next gulp. I asked him to let me think about it for a day or two.

It would be a huge change. Acting for *News of the World*'s successor title, the

Sun on Sunday and the six-day-a-week *Sun* would be an enormous change, not just for me but the team I had built up over the years who were mostly used to working for claimants. My work for individual journalists and TV channels I tended to do alone.

That night I was due to go on the sleeper train to Cornwall for a short break. I had a few drams of whisky whilst the various scenarios I envisaged sunk in. I barely slept at all despite the gentle rocking of the ever so slow train.

By dawn, as I stared at the inky dawn through the grubby window, I had decided to go for it.

In the 'trade' of libel and privacy specialists, it is well known that it is much easier being a claimant than a defendant but being honest with myself, I knew I preferred the rough and tumble of justifying publication. I also perceived that post the Leveson Inquiry into newspaper standards and practices (in which Christopher Jefferies stood out as a shining example of an individual suffering from terrible journalism) that there would be a clean-up, and cutting corners – legally and ethically – would be a thing of the past.

And I was to be part of the clean-up. A clean skin as they say in the illegal drugs trade. Someone untouched by the bad old days, respected for having brought good claims for the likes of Robert Murat and Christopher Jefferies. I anticipated getting some stick from some colleagues on the claimant side of the fence and maybe some initial hostility from some quarters of *The Sun*.

Together with the head of our civil department, we made our way to Wapping for an early morning meeting to discuss arrangements. I explained that I would need to carry my team with me if we were taking over an existing caseload from Farrer's and then handling new matters.

I made sure everyone was in the office when I announced the deal, the pros and cons, how things were going to look and asked how they felt about it. There was a brief, stunned silence and then a spontaneous round of applause broke out. Nearly everyone was 'in' and I let Justin know the files could come over from Farrer's the day after Boxing Day so I could take over representation on 1 January 2012.

And, as well as some heavy libel and privacy cases like Depp, Mitchell and PJS described elsewhere in this book, we had a lot of fun with *The Sun*, Britain's largest selling newspaper.

* * *

Traditionally, solicitors have a safe at their office to keep their clients' deeds, wills and other original documents. Ours contain many sordid secrets and dick pics. So many that the nickname for it was "the dirty safe", containing a different sort of Crown Jewels.

Before the landmark *PJS* decision in 2016 (as recounted in Chapter 24) the safe was opened several times to reveal the photographs of numerous well-known footballers who, unwisely, had taken it upon themselves to send photographs of their penises to young women. The photos usually came to me after the newspaper had agreed with the aggrieved footballer to destroy all their copies save for the set retained by their solicitors. A bit like original works of art but much less endearing.

More interesting were the varied reactions of the footballers 'stung' by the kiss and tell women they had slept with. The newspaper always had to seek comment pre-publication. Some footballers were indignant and threatened immediate privacy writs. Others shrugged their shoulders and took a so-what attitude.

We rarely won when an application for an injunction was made but when we did it was guaranteed to make the headlines, both because the injunction attempt had failed to muzzle the media and because of the details behind the story. On one occasion a very high-profile manager, former England manager Steve McClaren, tried to injunct the newspaper publishing the story of his infidelity with a much younger woman.

It was a Saturday in August 2012 when we got wind of the threat to injunct. Saturday calls from the newspaper were always accepted with trepidation because often it meant 'cancel your day', and this was to be one of those. We scrambled, rushing to the office to put together a witness statement within a couple of hours. It focused on the fact McClaren had played heavily on being a role model so that the defence of public interest would win over the breach of the manager's privacy rights. There was also a hypocrisy angle, given McClaren's 'form' for extra-marital affairs.

Some libel and privacy cases can take months or even years, but the injunction beast is a different animal. It lives usually for just a few hours. The first few are taken up with understanding the story and getting to know both the key elements; where the person threatening the injunction is coming from and whether they have trump cards to play. The most common trump card is the impact of publication on young children. Stress would be laid on the fear the child would be ostracised or criticised for the sins of their fathers. One famous footballer gave evidence that his extra-marital fling with a teenager might trigger such a severe reaction in his wife, who suffered a nervous condition, she would likely take her own life.

After the initial adrenaline rush, the solicitor has to then juggle the other side's often frantic communications whilst, at the same time, keeping everyone connected with the preparation of the response to the claim. Counsel is usually immersed in preparing a written submission to persuade the judge as to their own side's arguments whilst instructions need to be taken from journalists and the internal legal team. And then it is for the applicant, here McClaren, to "move" the court (that is, ask a judge to hear the case over the phone).

Our Soho office was deserted. With a trainee to help me, we got ready as best we could in the short space of time before the judge announced when he would hear the parties.

The hearing went on for an hour in the early evening. It is strange arguing a case without being able to see your opponents or the judge. At the end of the hearing, given the presses have to soon start rolling, the judge must deliver a decision with detailed reasons.

Would McClaren's affair with a much younger woman, who claimed also to be an ex of another England manager, Sven-Göran Eriksson, be allowed to be reported? The other side's solicitors, Schillings, were screaming "set up" because the photo of the pair entering her flat was taken by a *Sun* journalist and in the hearing, we confirmed the informant for the story was the woman herself. Whilst this may appear unattractive (and possibly pre-planned) it also engaged the woman's right to have the story published. Just as the applicant had a right to privacy, she had rights to freedom of expression.

Back then, privacy cases were harder to predict. One of my partners represented Rio Ferdinand in his failed privacy claim against the *Sunday Mirror*. The newspaper won the case by claiming that as a role model there was greater public interest in telling the story of the Manchester United star's affair. We deployed the same argument against McClaren.

In his judgment, Mr Justice Lindblom went through the submissions of both QCs. The judge laid some emphasis on the fact that McClaren had himself put into the public domain the story of another extra-marital affair to *The Sun*, although according to the newspaper's counsel, when he was Middlesbrough's manager McClaren had actually sold the story for £12,500 through Max Clifford. McClaren's counsel disputed the payment claim which he called contentious.

We argued that McClaren was unlikely to win a permanent injunction at the end of any trial several months, if not years down the track.

The judge found, without any difficulty, that McClaren's Article 8 privacy rights were engaged. The real dispute was the balancing exercise between the woman's right to freedom of expression versus McClaren's rights to privacy. Despite McClaren's arguments that there was no public interest in the mass media publishing a story about the private life of a football manager and his relationship with a woman who was not his wife, the judge came down in favour of publication for two main reasons. The judge accepted the argument that McClaren was a prominent public figure and a role model for whom the public can expect a higher standard of conduct; and he didn't injunct last time, instead giving his story to the newspaper which would otherwise have revealed it.

Would this be the same outcome today on these facts? I am sure it would not, given the development of privacy law in the intervening 13 years, especially with reputational damage being allowed in as a reason to favour applicants.

As soon as the judge finished the hearing, I rushed to call the newspaper. They were able to carry their exclusive in the later editions of the *Sun on Sunday*. They were rightly delighted with the decision which was a rare win for the media. With my trainee, we stumbled into the bright lights of the West End and celebrated into the night.

Celebrities, their agents, PR teams and lawyers kept us busy at weekends so much so that I used to organise a Saturday injunction team rota because there were so many threats. One Saturday morning whilst trying to get the weekend shopping done, I was juggling two cases with both claimants threatening to alert the High Court judge on call for a hearing. I had to dart into quiet corners of the supermarket to speak in hushed tones about the latest developments.

Nowadays, there are fewer injunction threats not because there is less terrible conduct (to employ an umbrella term) but because the balance has shifted towards privacy rights at the expense of freedom to publish. Or, to put it another way, they are now, apart from the exceptional cases like Matt Hancock, getting away with it.

Chapter 23

Plebgate: blue conspiracy or red mist descending?

There's no getting round the fact that *The Sun* has traditionally been a pro-Tory newspaper. But when their political editor Tom Newton Dunn got a whiff of a story that would be inconvenient for the political party they always support (Tony Blair and grudgingly Keir Starmer apart), they were not going to pass it up.

Scoops trump allegiances.

It was no surprise then that they decided to 'roast' Andrew Mitchell, David Cameron's Chief Whip and previously Secretary of State for International Development, who was accused of being verbally abusive to a police officer as he left Downing Street on his bike on 19 September 2012. The allegation was simple: did Mitchell call PC Toby Rowland a "fucking pleb" or not? The story reached Tom Newton Dunn and *The Sun* ran it as a front-page splash, also filling several inside pages. The banner headline read: 'Cabinet Minister: Police are Plebs'. Tom called it an astonishing rant, and it was to remain their front-page lead for weeks as the denials and conspiracy claims from the Chief Whip gave the story even more oxygen.

Context is everything and as Bob Dylan wrote, "The Times They Are A'changin'." The political period was peak Cameron/Osborne unpopularity, a couple of years into the austerity period. Cuts to public services, including the police were being felt. As Nadine Dorries, at that time an unusual right-wing back bencher and later chief cheer leader for Boris Johnson wittily remarked, the PM and Chancellor were "two posh boys who don't know the price of milk". The story was an example of just how some "posh people" were not, as Cameron proclaimed in 2011, "…all in this together".

As they say on Fleet Street, this story has legs.

We take the print edition every day at the office and watched how the story developed over the next month into a bitter confrontation between the newspaper and Mitchell, who continued to deny the story and instead accused the Police and the Police Federation of an almighty stitch-up. Like Johnny Depp, the conspiracy imagined by Mitchell seemed to change shape and character as the story developed.

It is well known that, as a cabinet minister, you can only survive hostile front-page headlines for so long before someone taps you on the shoulder and says, "Sorry old thing, it's become something of an embarrassment. It's time to resign". And so he did. Operation Alice, the Met's exhaustive enquiry, then got going into the multiple allegations flying around about police malpractice and what role it played in the incident. It became one of the biggest political scandals of the past two decades.

And I was in the thick of it. Delicious. This was the kind of case I hoped to get, working for a national newspaper. I was a student of politics for many years, so with a political journalist as a client, this was manna from heaven.

Or, as they say more colloquially, right up my alley.

Tom Newton Dunn is a live-wire journalist, always ready with a smart remark and a nose for a story. As *The Sun*'s political editor, he was based at Westminster with a small staff and was part of the parliamentary lobby which is fed stories both officially and unofficially by the governing party and, increasingly, by the opposition. His own political inclination was right of centre but on the liberal side. He soon sniffed out that I was a Labour supporter, and from then on friendly sniping and jibing ensued. But he was a journalist first and foremost, hence his lack of hesitation in following up the lead about what happened at the gates of Downing Street.

The incident began when PC Gillian Weatherley, a member of the Diplomatic Protection Group tasked with round-the-clock protection of the PM's office/home, refused to open the large and very heavy metal gates for Mitchell and instead directed him towards the side pedestrian gate. Sensing a need to defuse the "stand-off" as Mitchell was standing firm, PC Toby

Rowland took it upon himself to intervene and instead gently usher the angry and insistent MP ("I'm the Chief Whip and I'm going through that gate!") over to the pedestrian gate. The whole incident lasted no more than a minute or so.

The fallout and subsequent investigation cost the public a seven figure sum (and all this during the midst of the 'austerity years'), a cabinet resignation, several parliamentary appearances and the usual grandstanding by committee members that goes with it, as well as two libel cases and a joint trial. Mitchell's defeat set him back well over a million pounds in costs and it took him 11 years to get back into government. All in all, it told you a lot about the state of Britain in the early part of the Cameron administration.

Wikipedia even has a very lengthy entry which says Plebgate was a "British political scandal". Too right. Some would say this was a mountain made out of a molehill by the press in general (and *The Sun* in particular), but I would say the blame for this lay at the hands of a foul-mouthed Chief Whip.

Instead of responding to media requests for comment by saying the smart thing, "Oh my God, I don't know what came over me, must have been a red mist and I am terribly sorry. I will apologise personally to the officer. They do a great job guarding us, etc, etc", Mitchell decided to double down, denying that his F-word was aimed at the officer and saying that he had not used the pleb word at all. Both directly and via No. 10 he failed to outright publicly deny the allegation he called the officer a "fucking pleb".

Mitchell later described suing *The Sun* as his "fatal mistake".

Early on in my investigation of Mitchell I heard many things about him being crochety if he didn't get his own way. I also noted the famous public school he attended – Rugby – was in the habit of calling 'townies' plebs. Of course, this was simply confirmation bias – the tendency to search for information that confirms one's beliefs. And no one could prove he had used the word learnt in schooldays. Against this was the obvious thought: would he be so stupid as to 'lose it' with a police officer at the most heavily guarded entrance in Britain, potentially within earshot of other police officers and onlookers? Did the copper mishear? Might the officer have had it in for Mitchell and be making it up? All these thoughts went through my mind as I mulled over the letter of claim from Mitchell which screamed libel, demanding damages and an apology from my client.

First thing I did was interview Tom and take a long statement from him. I had to ascertain how he had put the story together. How were we going to prove the police version of events, which the newspaper had tied itself to hook, line and sinker? The police log told PC Rowland's account of what Mitchell said to him:"Best you learn your fucking place. You don't run this fucking government...You're fucking plebs."

The log also described the officer warning Mitchell he could be arrested if he continued to swear at him. Mitchell's parting shot was a threat: "You haven't heard the last of this."

Later I found out that this threat was what persuaded Rowland to write up the log, egged on by colleagues. He was to tell me when we finally met that he wasn't inclined to write anything up as this was just another grumpy politician after a long day, letting off steam. His sergeant, who was on duty during the shift, told him the threat to take it further meant he had to get his contemporaneous account down in writing. The subsequent leaking of this log entry was to become a huge focus for Operation Alice.

The letter claiming libel from Mitchell followed three months after his resignation in October 2012. It was one of the angriest letters of claim I have ever seen and sounded like it was penned by Mitchell himself and then turned into the third person by his law firm. It was to be followed by the particulars of the claim itself which was a hot mess of conspiracy allegations and rage. Mitchell decided to claim that the allegation he had abused PC Rowland, calling him a fucking pleb, was somehow cooked up first by the officers – including Rowland – and then by the Police Federation.

When I put this allegation to Rowland, his response was scathing: "Sir," he said to me in a serious and respectful tone, "we can't decide between us whose turn it is to buy the milk for the teas and coffees in the hut on a morning, let alone conspire to bring down a member of the government." I fell about laughing, knowing full well that this had what criminal lawyers like to call 'the ring of truth' about it.

Operation Alice stopped Mitchell's attempts to restore his reputation in its tracks for several months. There was no way round this because he had so publicly accused the police of having it in for him so there had to be a full-scale investigation. It would find and make revelations of some officers close to the incident (including PC Weatherley) leaking information and, in one case, another officer posing as a member of the public to complain about Mitchell's conduct at the gate. That officer was not only dismissed but also jailed for 12 months. It cast a shadow over Rowland's position because Mitchell's side were then able to point at this in making their claims about invention of the core allegation. If one officer was lying or had it in for him, then Rowland must be too, went the thinking on Mitchell's side.

In charge of Operation Alice was a savvy Detective Superintendent. He and I were to get to know each other very well through calls and emails as he sought to get evidence from Tom about how he had obtained the story, as this aspect fell within Operation Alice's terms of reference. Of course, as soon as we received the police request formally, we responded by explaining we never reveal confidential sources. The Super knew this was coming and over many weeks we developed a mutual respect for each other's opinion and position, despite Tom's anger that he was being investigated as potentially being accused of Misconduct in Public Office (MIPO) by police officers on the most flimsy "aiding and abetting" basis.

They have to do this post-hacking cases, where MIPO was the dish of the day, I explained to Tom. It did not take long for the senior prosecutor to declare "no further action". We made it crystal clear that Tom had nothing to do with any aspects of the police misconduct which Operation Alice might uncover, and they did not pursue this aspect further after fully investigating but were, they maintained, duty bound to look into it given Mitchell's stance.

One of the quirkiest moments in this extraordinary case came one morning when the friendly Superintendent rang me out of the blue, laughing whilst talking, and telling me to grab a copy of *The Daily Telegraph*. The previous day I had watched with mouth agape as Mitchell and his buddy David Davis, the avuncular veteran MP and former Shadow Home Secretary, conducted a press conference. The press conference was covered live on Sky News, and *The Daily Telegraph* headline the next day derided David Davis for Inspector Poirot-like attempts to solve what happened at the gate during the press conference. Sketch writer Michael Deacon captured the occasion brilliantly:

> *So Poirot is not dead after all. What fools we were to believe that he was. After an absence of 38 years, the brilliant Belgian sleuth is back among us.*
>
> *In exhaustive detail, the detective talked his audience through the Downing Street CCTV footage, in slow motion, from several different angles, while reminding them of the fate that had befallen the victim.*
>
> *"Five seconds!" he cried. "According to Rowland, 40 words were spoken in that five seconds. Most people speak at two to three words a second. No one speaks at eight words per second. So PC Rowland's account does not fit the facts. Forty words do not fit! Forty words cannot fit in that time!"*
>
> *In this vein he continued, for 10 dazzling minutes...[giving] the impression he was unravelling the greatest murder mystery of the past half-century, rather than commentating on CCTV footage of a middle-aged man on a bicycle saying a rude word in the presence of a policeman.*

The press conference proved to be a spectacular own goal.

Operation Alice had determined that no action should be taken against PC Rowland, which was absolutely the right decision, as he had nothing to do with the misconduct of other officers. But during the presser, Mitchell declared he would pursue his claims that Rowland was lying by reigniting his libel claim against *The Sun* and making Rowland give his version of the altercation in court.

This, it turned out, was the final straw for Rowland who had already been advised by his lawyer, Jeremy Clarke-Williams – someone who had stayed a friend despite my poacher-turned-gamekeeper move a couple of years earlier – that if Mitchell went any further with his allegations of lying, Rowland would be entitled to bring a libel claim. The press conference also helped with my attempts to get Rowland give evidence for *The Sun*.

The claim against *The Sun* got under way and we received an extraordinary pleading drafted by David Sherborne, by now a regular opponent given his popularity with claimants. The document caused me to rub my eyes and read it a second time over. Contained within Mitchell's Reply to our defence of truth (to show that the alleged defamatory statement was substantially true) was a theory which was at the heart of his case: "It was obvious that these police officers had a serious axe to grind…in wanting to smear a government minister."

This was a wild accusation to make, and in doing so Mitchell set his team a very high hurdle to jump over. Once you allege conspiracy – 'Infamy, infamy, they've all got it in for me' goes the quip (Kenneth Williams playing Julius Caesar in *Carry on Cleo* for those of you young enough to remember the films) – it is incumbent on you to demonstrate how this worked in the factual scenario.

Gavin Millar, my number one go-to Queen's Counsel, was brought in early on to lead our team and he took the same view as me – Mitchell's team had just set themselves a much harder task than if they had just focused their fire on the hapless PC.

Meanwhile I was making increasingly desperate pleas to meet Rowland at Jeremy Clarke-Williams' office on Chancery Lane. When I finally got to meet the officer in the middle of the maelstrom, I realised straight away that what others had told me about him was spot on. Rowland was, as they say, straight as a die. He was a big fan of the Electric Light Orchestra outside of work. Otherwise, I was reliably informed, he was a quiet guy.

His main interest in his police work was road traffic regulations and their interpretations. He told me he was mostly a bike cop in his Diplomatic Protection Group role, patrolling sensitive locations.

On that fateful day he had been brought in to do gate duty for a few shifts. He explained to me in detail what he was later to tell the court; how he was simply trying to defuse the anger of a man on a bike. After the incident he had to go and look up Mitchell's face to confirm that he was who he was claiming to be. Why? "Because I didn't recognise him or know who he was." Not a good start for the conspiracy theory fans on the other side. Once I finished getting his account, I was satisfied he was telling the stone-cold truth, especially when he explained he had to have his arm twisted by his sergeant to write it up in the log after being told by Mitchell that he hadn't "heard the last of this".

The case even made a bit of legal history in the procedural stages.

Nowadays, in an attempt to control the ever-spiralling costs of litigation, each side has to obtain a budget approved by the court. Conscientiously, me and my team prepared ours and sent it to Mitchell's lawyers and the court within the normal time frame. We waited and waited for theirs. It was late. Eventually we got it on the eve of the court appointment. On my way in to court I took soundings from my costs lawyer, Andy Ellis. "Complain loudly," was his short and sanguine advice. "I intend to," I told him.

Mitchell was represented by a lawyer called Graham Atkins. When I arrived in the dark, wood-panelled corridors, known to regulars as the "Masters' corridor", (these deputy High Court judges are called Masters, regardless of gender) I came across Graham and wished him good morning. He looked ultra-relaxed for a solicitor who had only just got his budget sent over at the last minute. In fact, he was so laid back he was reading a newspaper. Up against me was counsel, David Sherborne, and our assigned Master was Victoria McCloud. It was my first time appearing before her and I had not picked up just how much of a stickler for rules she was.

After the introductions and my complaints about the lack of time I had had to take my client's instructions on their suggested budget, the Master turned to me and asked: "What do you think should happen for this breach?" I replied they should suffer some kind of sanction rather than get away with it. Sherborne tried to brush it off with a breezy, "Well, it's here now so let's just get on with it." McCloud was having none of it. She made an extraordinary zero budget order for breaking the rules. It was within her powers but rarely, if ever, used.

Behind us I could hear the most audible groaning from Graham. This order meant that even if Mitchell won, they couldn't recover costs from us (apart from getting a refund of court fees). Essentially, if we eventually lost the newspaper would be saving several hundred thousand pounds. I knew it would also engender animosity and division between Mitchell and his legal team as they were now hampered by this devastating costs order. It was hard trying to stop myself from breaking into a smile as we shuffled out into the corridor. Graham's face looked like thunder.

Unsurprisingly, Mitchell's team rushed off to the Court of Appeal complaining about Master McCloud's punitive order. Leap-frogging the High Court judge, we all turned up in a three-judge court to thrash it out. This time both sides had senior costs barristers. McCloud's decision was upheld, and the legal press went into overdrive about it. The phrase "getting Mitchelled" sent a chill through tardy litigation lawyers. The message being sent was simple enough: delay at your peril.

The case was all about the witnesses, but my problem in persuading Rowland to give evidence was solved by Mitchell himself. His ill-advised press conference had provoked Rowland into suing him for libel. Rowland was now a claimant and Mitchell a defendant. As the officer told me and, later, the court at the trial, once the allegations that he was lying had been so publicly made, he could no longer give evidence in cases without Mitchell's taint being thrown at him. He had to clear his name both as a professional police officer and an individual with an otherwise untarnished reputation.

Our team then had a brainstorm meeting and thrashed out a plan. Gavin and junior counsel, Adam Wolanski, made a novel application. In view of the exact same facts – what happened at the gate – now engaged in the two cases, why not have a trial of the facts with everyone involved? This would mean Rowland would be giving evidence on his own behalf as a libel claimant. And Mitchell would be the claimant in our case and the defendant in Rowland's case. Another legal first as far as I could remember.

Before we got to trial there were a couple of efforts made to settle the case between the newspaper and Mitchell. The first was all very hush hush. George Osborne wasn't just the Chancellor of the Exchequer but also the number one mover and shaker in the Conservative government. He was the Fixer. Through his auspices, attempts were made to informally settle the case with a senior police officer, Sir Hugh Orde, acting as the go-between, which came to a head over a hot summer weekend. But this failed. Since then, Mitchell has written about this failed attempt in his autobiography.

A more formal attempt was made through mediation. I'm prevented from recounting the exchanges which took place over a very long day but again it failed. One thing I can report was Andrew Mitchell coming into our 'retreat room', where I was sitting with another lawyer from the newspaper.

We were taken aback by his entrance, but he explained he simply wanted to apologise for the amount of time this was all taking and that he hoped a resolution could be found. We said nothing other than acknowledging his ultra polite break with etiquette by smiling and nodding in agreement.

Litigation has been likened to war without the bloodshed. You inevitably end up demonising the opponent, so this appearance, I admit, threw us temporarily. And I appreciated the gesture. Politeness, as my dad drilled into me, is a pre-requisite for human behaviour.

A huge amount of time was spent during the case on what the CCTV cameras showed of the incident and what was said. Audio experts were deployed by both sides – ours flew in from the United States. But it was the cameras run by MI5 that we believed were trained on No. 10 and Downing Street which proved most elusive. We never got confirmation either way that there was a missing film held by the Security Services, but we felt that there had to be at least one camera trained on the most sensitive street in the UK. Despite a visit to No. 10 and a good look around, we made no progress on locating such a film. The No. 10 staff seemed well disposed to us and even let us leave by the famous door with me urging my high-flying junior, Erica Henshilwood, to get a photo at the door for her folks back home in New Zealand.

We spent the next few weeks interviewing witnesses who were on the gate or were otherwise involved. One – the senior PC on the gate who advised Rowland to write it up in the log – was hard to contact and had retired, so difficult to trace. We managed to track him down through the police pension fund and summonsed him to attend. We offered to meet him just before he went into court to make it a much more civilised occasion than calling a reluctant witness 'blind'. Fortunately, he accepted our offer and we met him, obtaining his account at the very last moment the night before he had to answer his summons. His account was to prove important in the trial judge's decision.

The House of Commons' reputation for being a place of rivalry, jealousy and intrigue soon proved to be right when we tried to find people who had spoken to Mitchell about what had happened. We managed to get two Conservative MPs to give important evidence concerning their discussions with Mitchell about the incident.

One, a Deputy Chief Whip called Sir John Randall, gave evidence that Mitchell had admitted to him he did not remember clearly what happened at the gate. This was important because the frank admission was so soon after the story broke and in stark contrast to Mitchell's almost second by second account which emerged in the case. The other MP, the most famous blonde in the Commons, Michael Fabricant, had a very similar account. I did not get the impression there was much love lost between them. Importantly, Mitchell decided not to challenge them in cross examination because to do so would involve calling their recollections false and impugning their reputations.

A late witness for Mitchell, who we didn't challenge, was Bob Geldof. The former pop star turned Live Aid organiser remarkably remembered a call with Mitchell shortly after the incident in which the MP mentioned an occurrence involving a police officer just a few moments earlier. This didn't amount to much, but Mitchell tried to turn this into a point in his favour. "So what?" was our position on his evidence.

The trial of the facts took place over eight days in November 2014. It was a three-way fight, with a police constable in alliance with a newspaper and Mitchell fighting as both claimant and defendant. There were several witnesses on both sides.

To impress the judge – Mr Justice Mitting – Mitchell lined up a host of character witnesses to give evidence saying he was not generally potty-mouthed or inclined to call a police officer a "pleb".

Sherborne had, by now, been replaced by James Price, a silk with a smooth tongue and patrician manners. Rowland was represented by Desmond Browne QC, one of the top silks of his generation. There were no matters of law in dispute between the parties – just a plain old fight over the truth of those 11 seconds. The judge's role was to decide the facts, nothing more. There was going to be a lot of mudslinging at the police generally by Mitchell because of the misconduct involved in leaking the story to *The Sun*, the way the Police Federation reacted and the frankly over the top way the newspaper reported it day after day.

The courtroom, inevitably number 13, was packed every day. A strained looking Andrew Mitchell surrounded by friends and family was ever present. Rowland, with colleagues and Police Federation representatives present in numbers, was also there all the time. Both were looking like they would rather be anywhere else although Mitchell was much better at putting on a brave face. One reflective piece in *The Guardian* captured it well:

> *We had 26 witnesses, astonishing piles of documents and three legal teams. That was the sledgehammer. The nut was a short conversation that took place on 19 September 2012...CCTV footage suggested it began at 19:36:45, and lasted no more than 11 seconds. Mr Mitchell is accused of uttering three "toxic phrases", a total of 20 career- and life-defining syllables, one of which counted above all the rest...The establishment of the legally accepted facts that would resolve these parallel cases, and with them bring some sort of closure to a dreadful parable of class and entitlement that has haunted the country for more than two years, has run up a total legal bill of about £3m.*

Looking back, I can now see the whole case was, in one sense, ridiculous. Rowland was desperate for it to be over, setting out the trauma he and his family had experienced in his trial witness statement. *The Guardian* article went on to describe Rowland's cross examination by Mitchell's lawyer, James Price QC:

Whereas Rowland is stout and damp, with an obstinate set to his jaw, Price – Eton, Oxford – is vulpine, ruthless, and even posher than Mitchell. He dissects Rowland's testimony with the abstracted interest of a child operating on a fly with a pair of tweezers. Indeed, while his case is that his client never said "pleb", his tone seems to imply it would have been jolly well merited if he had.

"You must have known," Price says – laconic, nasal, one leg casually hitched up on the bench, endlessly jingling coins in his pocket – "that to give a senior public figure an arrest warning could lead to a complaint direct to the commissioner's office."

Price's pomposity is well captured with the article's imagined rhetorical questions:

Do you not see how important Mr Mitchell is? Do you not see the trouble you've caused him? I'm waiting, boy.

The strategy was a familiar enough litigation tactic: first, pick off the least credible parts of your opponent's evidence – the 'wounding' – and then go full pelt for the kill after this nibbling at the edges has weakened your opponents. Both the protagonists stuck to their guns.

The three officers on the gate at the time were crucial in helping the judge decide who was telling the truth, together with the footage of the incident. Gillian Weatherley, who had lost her career over the case because of her ill-advised role in leaking the log Rowland had written to another colleague (who then passed it on to *The Sun*), was a remarkably good and measured witness for us. She had been an officer for over 20 years, and this one small error had cost her dear. Despite this, as the judge was to remark, she gave her evidence – of how she stopped the Chief Whip on his bike before Rowland wandered over – without rancour. However, it was the last-minute witness, the now retired Mr Richardson, who helped us hugely.

Price cross examined him in the same way as he had interrogated Rowland, suggesting that the threat Rowland had issued to arrest Mitchell if he didn't stop swearing at him was so serious it could not be true. Richardson disagreed with Price, replying that in fact it was only a trivial incident, a "Mexican stand-off. It wasn't a murder scene. It wasn't putting tape up. You must appreciate it was a quirky incident with a gentleman on a bicycle who had the hump. It wasn't a crime scene." Even the judge could not help but laugh at this reply, pricking Price's balloon.

Price then continued by criticising Richardson for not taking fuller notes of his role in the incident during his break. Again, the droll retiree deflated the attempt to inflate the scene to make the same point: "I was eating my sand-wiches. I couldn't be arsed to write too much more – laziness."

Richardson said he asked Rowland later whether there were any witness-es, not, as Price suggested, to justify the arrest warning given to Mitchell but because the officers "needed to be bomb-proof" if the MP complained. This defensive response – get it all down in the log and notebooks – rather than the "conspiracy" to bring down Mitchell was ultimately preferred by the judge.

Mitchell, as we expected, stuck firmly to his guns and did not concede any-thing in his evidence. The judge would need to find between the two versions of the truth.

After the closing speeches by each side's QC, the judge said he would deliver his decision at 2pm, straight after lunch. Bloody hell, he's obviously made his mind up quickly we decided. But which way is he going? Who was he going to decide had lied in his court? I thought we had won given the more convincing and plausible account, but I could tell the Mitchell team were also confident of victory. They looked pleased, as did we. This is rare. Our conference room was quiet whilst we sat with our private thoughts and Pret sandwiches over lunch.

Court 13 was groaning with bodies. There was not a single space left in the upstairs gallery, the press benches and the rest of the seating in the court itself having been taken. A hush fell over the court as Mr Justice Mitting walked in, all of us straining to hear every word to glean the decision if he didn't tell us at the outset. These days it is uncommon to get an *ex tempore* (Latin for impromptu). A decision via email, as in *Depp v NGN*, means that we can zoom to the end in private surroundings and find out, but here, over the course of two hours, the judge explained his finding of the facts of what happened at the gate.

As such long judgments are delivered you start to tick off the judge's findings which have gone your way rather than against you and eventually you reach a tipping point when you know whether you have won or not.

For me, the standout sentence was when the judge, quite early on, described his view of Rowland as a witness calling him a rather old-fashioned policeman who was well suited to his job as a DPG officer. "He is not the sort of man who had the wit, the imagination or the inclination to invent on the spur of the moment an account of what a senior politician had said to him in a temper." He added the officer was not inclined to "perform the pantomime which their invention would require".

In other words, he was finding that Rowland hadn't made it up and he had not started a conspiracy to bring down Mitchell. Likewise, towards the end of his decision, the judge lavished praise on Richardson as a witness.

He was gentle on Mitchell, finding that his stance when told he could not go through the gate on this occasion was childish, resulting in him throwing his toys out of the pram and that his version of events was inconsistent with the CCTV. "I am satisfied that he did lose his temper," and the politician's part-admission under cross examination that, whilst he was ill-tempered, he hadn't *lost* his temper, was mere hair-splitting, the judge decided. Despite finding against him the judge could not have gone easier on the former Chief Whip.

Mr Justice Mitting finished his judgment and said he was going to rise for 10 minutes. You could hear a pin drop as the decision was being taken in by everyone.

The MP had lost but there was no clear declaration of the winner or loser at the end; however, it was obvious to the legal teams, at least. I had put myself in the very front row which meant I could slip out and go straight to Rowland because he was looking bewildered and some distance away from his lawyer, Jeremy, who was crammed in on his row, seated behind his silk.

I could see Rowland wanted someone to confirm the outcome to him, so I shook his hand and said congratulations. His puzzled frown turned into a huge smile, and any lingering doubts were dispelled. He then quickly and quietly said to me, "Did he," pointing to the vacant judge's bench, "say I was too thick to have made it up?"

I replied, as diplomatically as I could, "Well, kind of. I think he was saying it's not in your personality to invent this." He gave a shrug of his shoulders and said, "Fair enough," before being surrounded by well-wishers.

I slipped downstairs to watch Mitchell give his brief statement to the press on the outcome. After a round of thanks, he said little other than that he was bitterly disappointed, but it was time to move on. He wore an upside-down smile which most newspapers put on their front page in their reports the next day. Momentarily I felt sorry for him. Here was another well-resourced litigant who thought he could bend the truth his way and it had come back and slapped him hard in the face. But then I remembered how, if it had gone the other way, he would have torn into Rowland and the newspaper using his customary eloquence and verbosity.

Now it was our turn to speak, a bit like the Wimbledon tradition at the end of a championship final. Stig Abell stepped into the fading late November light to the massed ranks of photographers and reporters to say his bit for the newspaper. Now a well-known broadcaster and author, Stig was then the managing editor of *The Sun* and its chief clearer upper of messes. This time he was on the winning side.

He is a remarkable individual. Erudite, humorous and switched on, rising to the top so young without the usual leg-ups given to the elite, it was clear he would not be stopping in the troubleshooting exec position for long. It is rare indeed for the editor of a tabloid to be able to come out of the High Court in smiles, able to vindicate his paper's journalism. We carefully worked on his few sentences to be delivered to the waiting media. We walked out on to the familiar steps at the front of the High Court and the camera flashes started popping.

This was when it all went wrong.

A familiar figure outside the High Court and on other occasions where the press pack gathered was a middle-aged Christian pacifist protester who always arrived with a banner and his dog. The dog, a yappy pug, wore a 'No Nukes' emblazoned coat. The flash bulbs sent the dog berserk, and it started barking and straining at the leash, so much so that the cameramen, on first-name terms, told its owner to can it.

Nothing doing.

The entire statement given by Stig was drowned out by the barking of this little but very loud beast which, at the same time, managed to drag its owner across the pavement to try and take a chunk out of Stig's ankle. He had to perform a little pirouette to avoid its teeth. The rest of us couldn't help laughing as he came back into the High Court whilst he cursed the "fucking dog trying to take a lump out of me" and drowning out his words. He too then saw the funny side. The next day, *The Sun*'s front page headline was 'RIGHT SAID PLEB'.

Since then, Mitchell has written a chapter of his autobiography, *Beyond a Fringe*, describing the case from his perspective. The chapter is called Forty-Five Seconds to Disaster. It is clear he still does not accept the judge reached the right verdict. Which is a shame. But hubris has a big part to play in such decisions on whether to sue which, given the impact on his health and finances, which he so honestly writes about following his defeat, I am sure has taught him some lessons.

The takeaway from the case was simple enough and often repeated in the privacy of counsel's chambers and solicitor's offices: don't sue for libel if there is a good chance you might lose. It will make things much worse for yourself reputationally and, given our 'loser pays' system, financially. This could be applied to many infamous cases from the past and will no doubt be the same in the future. Suing for reputation can be a tricky business.

Chapter 24

PJS and the fall of kiss 'n' tell

"The Court is well aware of the lesson which King Canute gave his courtiers. Unlike Canute, the courts can take steps to enforce its injunction pending trial. As to the Mail Online's portrayal of the law as an ass, if that is the price of applying the law, it is one which must be paid. Nor is the law one-sided; on setting aside John Wilkes' outlawry for publishing The North Briton, Lord Mansfield said that the law must be applied even if the heavens fell: R v Wilkes (1768) 4 Burr 2527, 98 ER 327 (347). It is unlikely that the heavens will fall at our decision."

With these opening words from Lord Mance, the Supreme Court brought about the end of Kiss 'n' Tell stories, (although happily, as we will see later on, not altogether). The case of *PJS v News Group Newspapers*, which was widely reported in the media, changed the landscape for the right to tell such stories. In the eternal war between privacy rights against freedom of expression, this was a low moment for the media. It also featured the tension between an injunction in one jurisdiction against the worldwide nature of the internet breaking such injunctions. And it was a case everyone was talking about.

In four hectic months *PJS v NGN* went from win to lose to win and then to lose for News Group. That is how litigation sometimes unfolds.

In Kiss 'n' Tells, proof of the frolics (in tabloid speak "romping", a curiously old-fashioned term) was usually in the form of photographs and breathless accounts by one half of the coupling.

All this changed in 2016 when the judges of the Supreme Court (the new name for the House of Lords) sitting at the apex of our legal system decided almost unanimously to put an end to Kiss 'n' Tell (absent an overriding public interest) with my case of *PJS v NGN*. It was the first time one of my cases made it to the highest court of the land. Losing is never easy and losing in the highest court of the land was tough. And like other litigation addicts, I was a sore loser.

Let's go back to the beginning. Unsurprisingly, the publication of Kiss 'n' Tell stories was under attack once privacy became a thing in English law. When *PJS* got going, most cases fought were won by claimants. After the Supremes (as legal wags are prone to calling the judges there) ruled in 2016, the question wasn't even asked. It was nearly always a no-no.

The call came in from Justin Walford, director of legal at *The Sun*, about PJS, the acronym given to a well-known man in the entertainment business who is married to YMA, a very well-known entertainer. The newspaper wanted to publish a story about PJS' sexual frolics whilst playing away. Previously I had been involved in other cases about one of the spouses, so I barely raised an eyebrow.

So who was PJS? I can't ever tell you because my client agreed a permanent undertaking never to do so. PJS started sexual encounters with another individual, AB, who had a partner, CD. PJS then asked AB for a three-way sexual encounter with CD which took place soon afterwards. The sexual relationship between PJS and AB then ended.

AB and CD, in true Kiss 'n' Tell fashion, then approached the newspaper to sell their story. The editor, having bought their story, contacted PJS to get his reaction. His response was to instruct lawyers to stop the story because of breach of confidence and invasion of privacy. The newspaper refused to agree to the demand to prevent publication, relying on there being a public interest in the story which focused on PJS' public position being entirely at odds with the true, private position.

Unusually, we won the first round in front of Mr Justice Cranston in January 2016. The High Court judge agreed with our position that the image PJS portrayed of being in a committed relationship was false and there was a public interest in correcting the image by permitting the story of PJS' casual sex exploits. PJS made an emergency application to the Court of Appeal which resulted in the decision being reversed. The two appeal judges decided that the first judge hadn't taken their children's rights properly into account and concluded that one of PJS' pronouncements (that whilst he was committed to YMA this "may not entail monogamy") was not to be held against him. Holding the ring (maintaining the current position), the names had continued to be withheld until the outcome of the claimant's appeal and now, with PJS getting the injunction from the Court of Appeal, there was a ban on names until the full trial of the privacy claim which would be at least a year away.

Meanwhile the massed antennae were up with other media organisations and individuals who liked to guess who PJS and YMA might be.

AB then decided to get the story published in the United States, where privacy injunctions are unheard of, through *National Enquirer*. The First Amendment free speech rights would never allow privacy rights to flourish as they do here and elsewhere in Europe. PJS and YMA were named in the process. The newspaper published a series of articles complaining about the absurdity of the situation it found itself in.

NGN decided to go back to the Court of Appeal and ask them to lift the injunction because the names were already in circulation on the internet and print media outside of the injunction's jurisdiction, the geographical entity of England and Wales. The names were even starting to appear in Scotland as well as other anglophone countries such as Australia. This was Lord Mance's inspiration for the reference to King Canute and the incoming waves.

The US agreed to geoblock the story so that it only appeared in the US publication or hard copy editions over the water (but not in England or Wales). It didn't stop the story taking off elsewhere. A storm was whipped up by the print media here and a survey found 20% of those surveyed already knew who PJS and YMA were. Given these statistics we returned to court to get the injunction lifted.

The identities of PJS and YMA were popping up everywhere and there was a rumour that an MP was going to use (some would say abuse) Parliamentary privilege to name them. It must, the argument ran, be in the public interest.

Opponents would say no, it is just of interest to (some of) the public.

By April 2016, pressing Article 10 freedom of expression arguments, we put together a case to lift the injunction. By then, the Court of Appeal wasn't a happy hunting ground for me. I had lost more than I had won there. A letter was quickly put together telling Carter Ruck on the other side that we were going to apply to the court unless they conceded the names, given everything happening outside England where the injunction had no force.

The same two judges who had granted PJS' permission to appeal, Lords Justice Jackson and King, were now joined by Lord Justice Simon, the judge who had ruled so decisively in our favour in the Davey Hunt case. I hoped that perhaps this augured well for us.

The three judges were won over by our arguments despite a history of past decisions against the media at this level, with tabloids in particular getting a rough ride. Lord Justice Jackson and the other two judges concluded that PJS would most likely win a privacy breach trial because private sexual lives were afforded the highest level of privacy and this story, he commented, and public discussion of such goings on had very limited public interest. But, with the situation which now prevailed where we had demonstrated the relatively high level of awareness of the couple's identity, it was unlikely they would get a permanent injunction at the end of trial. This is the litmus test for granting or refusing an injunction.

"Confidentiality has probably been lost," and much of the harm the injunction had been intended to prevent had already occurred, the judges concluded. Damages would be the claimant's remedy. The waves were now winning against King Canute 30-15. The variation application was successful; we could now identify them, subject to a higher court reversing their decision.

Pragmatism seemed to have won the day. Lord Justice Jackson said, "…the court should not make orders which are ineffective…it is in my view inappropriate…for the court to ban people from saying that which is common knowledge." Basically, they agreed with our proposition that the genie was now out of the bottle and couldn't be put back in.

It was, of course, too good to be true. Again, applying the principle of holding the ring, the injunction remained in force whilst the Supreme Court reached a decision following an urgent application by PJS.

The Supreme Court fast tracked us, deciding they would deal with the permission application at the same time as the substantive appeal in a rolled-up hearing. We arrived there within a record breaking nine days of the Court of Appeal decision in April 2016. They then took exactly four weeks to deliver their verdict.

We lost 4-1. The only judge on our side was Lord Toulson, who thought the leakage of the names had gone too far and to maintain otherwise would be illusory. But he, like the other four judges, did not think much to our public interest arguments.

I knew we would lose as soon as Lady Hale, now a Baroness, intervened. She picked everyone up on the inadequate role that the rights of the children of PJS and YMA had so far played in the case. She spoke of their free-standing privacy rights in all of this. As soon as she brought up children's rights my slender hopes of winning now vanished.

The thrust of the majority decision was that whilst there had been significant leakage there was still something to protect and worth protecting from blanket, universal coverage.

Their decision was so tightly embargoed that only the two QC's, Gavin and Desmond Browne, were allowed to read the judgment in advance. The rest of us were only told when the court would publish its decision by handing it down in open court. It would take just a couple of minutes, so we decided not to go and instead gather at Gavin's chambers, Matrix chambers (launched at the turn of the century by several legal high-fliers including Cherie Blair QC and which is housed in the old Holborn Police Station). As soon as he was able to, Gavin gave me the bad news. We then spent a miserable hour reading the judgment before watching the handing down on court TV.

You can never pick and choose these things. The news of their decision filled the airwaves and front pages. *The Sun* screamed about the injustice of everyone outside England knowing what they could not tell their readers. They were right to do so.

It meant there was now even more pressure being applied on identifying the couple. Overseas newspapers picked up on it and published the identity of PJS and YMA. It took less than five seconds of online searching to locate the names. Nonetheless, the injunction route in the digital age remains an effective if not blanket remedy to this day.

On reflection, Kiss 'n' Tell stories are an invasion of privacy rights which should only be permitted where you can demonstrate compelling public interest grounds that are unconnected with the private sex lives of the individual concerned (see Chapter 28 on Matt Hancock). The judgment sounded the death knell when it said that public interest should be effectively disregarded and is incapable by itself of outweighing privacy rights of the individual. As Lord Mance put it: "There is no public interest in the publication of the material, however interesting it might be to some members of the public."

My old colleague, Mark Stephens, now unofficially the legal pundit laureate, made a good point when he said: "This ruling drives a wooden stake through the heart of kiss and tell stories but only in England and Wales. Information about global superstars is still going to come out around the world. But in England, where people enjoy their daily morning dose of gossip, they are no longer going to get it."

It must be hugely satisfying for a claimant lawyer when writing to complain to *The Sun* to cite *PJS* as the authority in maintaining privacy rights in this area. I groan every time I see reference to it.

There was, as always, much more detail to the story, some of it rather salacious, than they were able to threaten to publish. If only I could tell you what it was, but sadly, I can't…

Chapter 25

Amber and Johnny: the trial of the century

Since the trial in London brought by Johnny Depp against *The Sun* and the second trial he took against Amber Heard in the US, whole books and documentary series have come out, fascinated by the two contradictory outcomes and how that came to be. So this account does not dwell on the ins and outs of the two cases. The evidence and the rulings are all on the internet, in full, for people to read and make up their own minds. Instead, this is an inside account of how we – the team representing *The Sun* – built a defence from very modest beginnings to end up with an overwhelmingly outright win for the newspaper following a detailed and well-reasoned judgment by Mr Justice Nicol, one of Britain's finest libel judges. Afterwards, Johnny had just one comment to make in response: "It was just one man's opinion." He was clearly hoping a US libel jury would swing the other way to redress the wreckage of the defeat he brought upon himself.

But first, to the beginning.

* * *

The call came out of the blue. It was May 2018.

"Louis, we've got a bit of a problem with Johnny Depp." On the other end was Justin Walford, chief editorial lawyer at *The Sun*.

"What's up?" I asked.

I was soon flicking over the pages of my daily copy which was hand delivered to my office every morning. Dan Wootton, newly promoted to Executive Editor, had written an opinion piece and, just from the headline, I could immediately see the problem with it:

GONE POTTY How can JK Rowling be 'genuinely happy' casting wife beater Johnny Depp in the new *Fantastic Beasts* film?

The internal lawyers like Justin are the ones battling with everyone to get stories out safely without butchering them to pieces. But sometimes things slip through. The 'externals' have to remember never to rely on hindsight, the most annoying science ever invented. Many people in and outside Hollywood may have shared Dan's opinion, but few would dare to say it.

Depp was – and remains – a powerful player in Hollywood. And highly litigious.

"I need your help with this one," Justin pleaded. I replied, as always, that I was happy to help and thanked him for asking me.

When I put the phone down, I admit to wanting to punch the air. I gathered a couple of my team around my desk and told them, "Looks like we've got a big one: Johnny Depp and JK Rowling and I'm not sure we can get rid of their complaints that easily." Together with my brilliant junior, Jeffrey Smele, we got down to it: a line-by-line scrutiny of the article, the headlines, the captions – in libel, it's the whole kit and kaboodle of the piece to ascertain the meaning. In other words, what is the sting of the piece in respect of each complainant and is it defamatory of them?

JK Rowling didn't sue in the end but Johnny was a different matter. He was already on record for being prone to sue. We call these people serial litigants. Adam Wolanski, our go-to barrister for *Sun* cases quickly came on board. A response was formulated and we responded to Depp's law firm, Brown Rudnick, who had an outpost in Mayfair.

I was brought up – in terms of my legal training – to specialise in getting the evidence even if it means jumping through fire, travelling to the other end of the world or even brown-nosing potential witnesses, as they say in *Private Eye*. Luckily, I usually manage to avoid the buttering up process but this time I had to deploy every trick in the book. One thing was crystal clear: we could only win the case if Amber Heard was willing to give evidence for us and, most important of all, she was believed over Johnny Depp who was spending fortunes on declaring his innocence.

The stage was set. Ahead, the mountain we had to climb was steep. And the path circuitous.

* * *

Divorces are bad enough. Celebrity divorces are even worse. But a US divorce featuring Johnny Depp was a nightmare. Scratching my head, I read everything I could lay my hands on about the divorce. Although there were hundreds of articles in US, British and European media, none of them amounted to very much. Back in May 2016 there was a highly publicised trip to Amber's local court earning headlines such as 'Amber Heard Seen with Black Eye Leaving L.A. Courthouse' and a joint statement by the couple a few months later in August saying:

> *Our relationship was intensely passionate and at times volatile, but always bound by love. Neither party has made false accusations for financial gain. There was never any intent of physical or emotional harm. Amber wishes the best for Johnny in the future. Amber will be donating financial proceeds from the divorce to a charity. There will be no further public statements about this matter.*

That was it. It was clearly a statement cobbled together by PR advisors and lawyers on both sides, straining hard to say nothing damning. As sure as night follows day, the rest would be tied up and bound by confidentiality agreements.

And so it proved to be.

All our efforts to make contact with Amber's divorce lawyer came to nothing. Our calls were not being returned and our emails went unanswered. Whilst we tried to stall him in correspondence, Depp was moving fast and issued writs (now called claim forms) against the newspaper and Dan.

It is exactly what I used to do in my claimant days to apply pressure. If you're gonna do it, do it fast. In the years when I worked on the side of the claimant, like Depp the best way to show you mean business is to sue quick. It carries risk. If you want to pull out, you have to pay the other side's costs. It showed us he meant business. With the clock ticking we were forced to rely on the filings we were able to get from the LA Courthouse where Amber got her restraining injunction. Unlike here, in the US once a case is filed – lodged at court – the paperwork which goes with it is publicly available unless a judge has designated it private (and to remain 'sealed').

Depp issued proceedings quickly which meant we had to submit a defence not long after. As I explained to the court in a witness statement in the first hearing of the case, we had to plead our defence of truth without access to Amber due to legal restrictions because of her divorce settlement with Depp. Instead, as I further explained, we relied on Amber's detailed account of abuse at Depp's hands from her sworn declaration to the court in Los Angeles.

This is known in the trade as a holding defence.

We needed Amber.

But then we caught a lucky break. One of my partners was a regular visitor to Los Angeles, the epicentre of the music scene. Richard Baskind is a big cheese in the world of music law. He makes it his business to know all the major players in entertainment law. He knew of my desperation to get in touch with Amber (I moaned about it around the office enough) and one of his lawyer contacts knew Amber's main lawyer, someone altogether grander than her silent divorce lawyer.

First, I made a call to Richard's friend and convinced him of my *bona fides*. It was not the most promising start.

"You do know they all hate *The Sun*, don't you?"

Of course, this was an exaggeration, but I had to play along. The truth is that when it is going well many celebrities love the limelight the tabloids shine on them. When it is going less well, they can scream blue murder. But he agreed to put me in touch with Amber's lawyer and effect an introduction.

Eventually I was granted an audience with The Man, as I liked to call this lawyer. He came on the phone and sounded even louder, brasher and self-confident than the average American lawyer with a Hollywood client roster. I explained our request to speak to Amber and our client's desire to support her account of the downsides of life with Johnny Depp. I could hear the sucking of teeth at the other end of the phone. It went along the lines of, "Well we sure do appreciate your support for Amber but you have to understand she just cannot speak out or say anything to you because she is bound by confidentiality restrictions he imposed on her in their divorce settlement." Was he, I asked, willing to put it in writing as this put us in an impossible position in our case? My thinking was simple enough: if we were prevented from getting Amber to speak to us then Johnny should not be able to proceed with a libel claim in which he, through the divorce case restrictions, is stopping us from speaking to the one witness who could win us the case.

The Man wrote us a letter. It was enough, or so we hoped. We then issued an application in the High Court to 'stay' Depp's case in its tracks. A hearing was arranged before Mr Justice Nicklin which would take place in open court. The number of lawyers assembled showed this was truly a *Clash of the Titans* type of case.

When we arrived in court the first thing we saw was that the Americans were in town. Johnny Depp was a no-show. I nudged Jeff in the ribs and asked, "Who's that guy, the dead ringer for Walter Matthau?" "Search me" was his response. We quickly found out when his presence on the lawyers' bench was announced by Depp's smoothy chops QC, James Price.

"We also have in court Mr Depp's US lawyers, Benjamin Chew, together with his principal lawyer, Adam Waldman." I turned and looked at Waldman. So that's him. Depp had given an interview in *Rolling Stone* which sought to re-establish his cool credentials. The journalist described Waldman, who was "hanging out" with Depp during the interview, as appearing to be Johnny's closest confidant. The assessment was spot on.

Unknown to us at the time, Waldman was going to play a large role for the next two years.

The hearing itself was an uphill struggle for us. We couldn't make our arguments stick. The judge said he didn't have enough evidence to help him make a decision to stay the case. The other side's QC took a long time to say very little. It was an easy decision for the judge: the case would go on.

Then two sudden turns of events sharpened things up. The first was a settlement meeting at their suggestion. It was to take place at Depp's law firm in Mayfair the very next day. What goes on in without prejudice (WP) meetings – where parties are free to settle cases without it having any impact on the case should it progress – can never be divulged unless everyone agrees to do so. However, there are two things I can say about it: first, it was the shortest WP meeting in my career, taking less than five minutes and, secondly, it was the first one I had done which was conducted by a US lawyer on the other side.

Adam Waldman waltzed in wearing a black t-shirt and matching trousers like a Tech Bro straight out of Silicon Valley. Thanks to a waiver of privilege made by Waldman in a later communication, I told him their case against Amber would have her on a par of pre-planning and conspiracy with Rosamund Pike's brilliant performance of the protagonist in the film *Gone Girl*. After the end of the WP meeting we casually exchanged criticisms about the other's case for a minute or two before leaving with both of us promising to, "See you in court, counsel". Jeff and I were still laughing about it with both of us guessing (correctly, it turned out) there wouldn't be another WP meeting in the case.

While all this was going on, we had been keeping a watching brief on everything written about the two main protagonists in the case. This included the only time Amber made reference to her situation in an opinion piece in *The Washington Post* which hadn't named Depp but said that she wrote as someone who was the victim of domestic violence.

The second sudden turn was the headline news from across the pond. Depp had filed a libel suit against Amber (but not against *The Washington Post*). Depp's claim is what we call a form of SLAPP lawsuit (SLAPP stands for Strategic Lawsuit Against Public Participation). In other words silencing your critics by burdening them with the risk of a huge costs bill to persuade them to settle fast rather than fight. Here, by not taking on the newspaper, Depp was signalling the target was Amber, which is straight out of the SLAPP playbook. I judged it to be a deeply cynical move especially as he would have known his ex-wife's financial position.

No wonder James Price aloofly pronounced relative neutrality about our application for a stay. He surely would have known there was a libel suit about to be launched in the US. They must have been holding off and waiting for Nicklin's decision first. They would have known we'd make maximum use of his libel suit against Amber if they issued it before the hearing (or indeed if news of the libel suit had leaked out) to get the judge better disposed towards us.

By suing Amber in the US, her lawyer's objections to speaking to us about her difficult relationship with Johnny fell away. Now the gloves were well and truly off. It was time to make our next move: ask our clients to let us go and meet Amber to persuade her to give us her account and become our star witness. And persuade The Man to let us do so.

In July 2019, after weeks of haggling and negotiating, Jeff and I boarded a plane to meet Amber. With us was Amber's newly appointed English lawyer, Jen Robinson who is, in fact, an Australian. Her role was to give Amber independent advice on English law and act as a go-between with her US lawyers in the libel case launched against her.

We all met at Heathrow's Terminal 5, and I glanced up at the giant screen in departures. It was Johnny's face ten metres high, advertising Sauvage, the new eau de parfum by Dior. Oh, the irony. And there we were, off to California to prove he was indeed a wife beater who put Amber in fear of her life.

As the plane took off for LA I knew it was make or break time. Jen was an important bridge to Amber. That evening we were scheduled to meet Amber at the iconic Chateau Marmont Hotel, probably the most famous meeting place for the rich and famous in LA. It was also notorious for having the most infamous celebrity benders including a clutch of sudden deaths – John Belushi and photographer Helmut Newton among them. It was a favourite haunt of Harvey Weinstein. A young Marilyn Monroe had her trysts there with author Arthur Miller.

And now we were to meet the one person who could turn the case around. Outwardly I stayed calm as Jeff excitedly snapped up a branded 100 dollar t-shirt and told me the details of the hotel's illustrious residents. Inside, I was worried. If it went wrong, I didn't fancy the meeting with the Editor to say we didn't have a case. Nor did I fancy the financial fall out which would follow.

Tabloids break as well as make celebrities. It is a love-hate thing. Was Amber going to put us through the wringer? In her shoes, I might well do. I thought she would arrive with a phalanx of helpers: at least one assistant, a PR boffin plus security and a driver. So it was a surprise when she walked up to us, on her own, in the hotel's gardens holding out her hand to say, "Hello, I'm Amber, you must be Louis." Her accent was Texas modified by California.

She is a former model (for many years the face of L'Oreal) as well as an actor and activist but she was also a model of politeness and sincerity to every-one. We took our seats in the courtyard garden, ignoring the stares of others, with the restaurant management making sure we had space to avoid people listening in.

Described as having the most beautiful face in the world by matching the 'Greek Golden Ratio of Beauty, Phi,' with 91.85% accuracy, Amber carried herself with grace and modesty. I was pleased to find she was not a prima donna, like so many celebs I've met.

Quite the opposite. She was delightful company and happiest with friends and family.

It was a hugely important meeting for us. Once we got the introductions out of the way, it was time to choose the wine. I had no idea that Amber was such a wine connoisseur, and she took control, ordering a top end wine with matching price. I explained our brief in coming to see her. We didn't have to wait too long for her verdict as we drank the next bottle of the extremely expensive wine and crossed our fingers.

"Come and see me tomorrow at my place in the Hollywood Hills and let's talk," she said as she departed. The relief on our faces afterwards was like you see on someone who has passed an entrance exam. On Richard's recommendation we had taken rooms at the Sunset Marquis Hotel – another iconic venue and the hang out of rock stars. It was very cool but by the time we got back there at around midnight, and with the eight-hour time difference between London and LA, it felt like the longest day ever. But getting on with Amber made it sweet.

Hollywood Hills is mostly gauche. Huge mansions on curling hills. Tiger Woods crashed his car on one of its bends as recently as 2021.

Amber lived in a small house with her girlfriend and their two dogs. Getting in was a problem. She lived there anonymously and with threats against her a daily occurrence she was wise to make sure she was secure. Inside was tasteful and relaxed. Nothing ostentatious, I noted. As we gathered round a huge table, where both dogs pressed their wet noses against our shins and gave off a distinct odour, we spent the day talking about her time with Johnny.

Life with Johnny was worse than we imagined. Amber gave us a dark, brutal and utterly convincing account. Living with an addict is never pretty whether a pauper or a millionaire. This conversation was the first of many which resulted in her trial witness statement some months later and released publicly when she took the stand in July 2020.

It was an emotional day. At one point Amber disclosed to us something very private about Depp's conduct towards her which she hadn't ever told anyone else and became the subject of a private hearing in the trial. Amber's sister, Whitney Hernandez (Whit), was on hand to support her in telling us. In fact, Whit was one of our best assets in the case – not just a key witness to events but also an all-round brilliant person to have helping us despite juggling a full-time job and a young family. She is funny and observant and like Amber, rounded and grounded.

As well as Jen watching out for Amber, we also had a young and very switched-on lawyer from Amber's law firm who observed our careful traipsing around life with Johnny. At one point another close friend, the writer iO Tillett Wright, arrived all the way from Joshua Tree, thirsty from the long desert drive. He too was to become a key witness to one of Depp's rages when he called the cops on Johnny, the first time anyone had ever dared to do this.

By the end of the day, we knew that in Amber we could win the case based on a truth defence: always the most satisfying way to win a libel case especially when a powerful man is insisting it's all a lie. But we couldn't get ahead of ourselves. There were lots of other obstacles to overcome, the next of which was to get The Man's approval; our second entrance exam.

So, the following day we went downtown to meet The Man. His assertions on the restrictions Amber was under hadn't impressed Nicklin J enough to stop the case. Now we hoped with the new lawsuit brought by Johnny, he would agree everything had changed. The next 30 minutes was another do or die occasion.

You get to know the different types of lawyers in the media and enter-tainment world. This one wanted you to know he was the Big Cheese. First sign was the actual meet. We were kept waiting for a while in their expansive reception at the top of yet another LA skyscraper. Instead of popping out to greet us in the normal way, he had us brought in for an audience with him.

"Howdy," he intoned. "Fabulous to meet you guys." And from then on, we didn't get much of a chance to say a great deal, not even brown-nose.

He brought out a book that had been written and just published by a female colleague and presented it as a gift to Jen with great fanfare. Then he showed us landmarks of LA looking out over the amazing view from his office; "And over there is the golf course where Jews were excluded and to the right is the one the Jews had to use…" It was a weird thing to point out to us.

Then he told us to hang on; we had to meet 'The Governor' who was in the next room. Jeff's eyebrows raised and I envisaged him bringing in a prison boss.

In fact, it turned out to be a former Governor of California who was a Republican from the Reagan era. The penny dropped: like calling all ex-Pres-idents Mr President, the former Governors keep their title. Despite the so-called classless nature of US society, I always get the feeling that status and titles count for a lot, especially in California. So, The Governor was wheeled in and small talk and a nip of whisky – apparently customary on a Friday afternoon – soon followed.

Eventually we got down to brass tacks in the last few minutes of the meeting. With Depp suing Amber for libel and our case much further advanced than hers, two things followed. Surely The Man now agreed that the divorce settlement gag preventing Amber (and Johnny) from talking about their marriage was now in the past, blown apart by the well-publicised writ against Amber? Yes, he had to agree.

Second, it would hugely help their case and Amber if she became our star witness in London, and not just because of the principle of your enemy's enemy being your best friend. In the relatively sober world of Court 13 – the main libel court in the Royal Courts of Justice – we explained how Amber could give her evidence of the relationship before a specialist media judge whose sole concentration would be the evidence on each side. No jury. Just a judge. I told him this had been my parting message to Waldman a few weeks previously. He rubbed his chin, considering. I explained that from my initial assessment of spending the day with Amber, she would make a great witness.

The Man would, as all lawyers in his position rightly say, take instructions.

Shortly afterwards we got the go ahead. Amber had liked and trusted us and wanted to do it, especially as she was now going to have to do the same in the US court anyway at some point in the future. We promised her we would be back to take her witness statement.

I reflected on what motivated anyone to shine a light on their troubled past. Surely it was a 'no win' for Depp, who must have known what was likely to come out about his turbulent past?

My own theory was simple. Never underestimate the rage of a rich, addicted multi-millionaire man who has had his image punctured. An added twist was his jealousy. The damage he caused to one of Amber's paintings by a former lover relatively early in their relationship to me spoke volumes.

Back in London we started to pore over newly released documents from Amber now we had made the breakthrough. The new information allowed us to amend our pleadings and strengthen the factual claims which we had been relying on from the limited picture we got from the divorce settlement.

But then something utterly unprecedented happened.

Once you have finished with the pleadings stage in which both sides set out their cases and the parameters of the issues in dispute are crystallised, each side has to send to the other the relevant documents which help or harm the issues in dispute. In this case, anything which went to proving or disproving our truth defence – that Johnny was indeed a wife beater – was in play.

We sent our list – pretty short, mostly filed court documents from the divorce case – and got theirs in return. It was weird. A lot of it was irrelevant and there were indications from the headings that it came from another case where Depp had sued a former manager. Unsatisfactory, Jeff and I agreed but first things first. Let's analyse what we have got and also fire off a letter about the things they must have but which were missing.

What you have to understand about litigation, especially complex cases like this, is that the detailed leg work is done mostly at a junior level. It is like an apprenticeship, learning from the bottom up. In Enfys Jenkins, a switched-on young Welsh woman, we were blessed with someone who was engaged and enthusiastic. And, importantly, happy to take on the hard yards of disclosure. She was also our social media monitor, plugged into anything Depp related. She kept us up to date with the PR/social media war launched by Team Johnny.

We were in the eye of the hurricane which I told everyone to try and ignore. Let the raging storms rage. His Justice for Johnny campaign was at full max volume. We were to discover Russian bots were apparently being deployed to inflate his following. As if he needed it, I muttered. Grumpily.

We worked open plan in Soho, helpful when working in teams on big cases. One morning Enfys called me over.

"Louis, there's something a bit odd going on here." I peered at her screen. The electronic document Enfys was going through was in Excel format and if you clicked on certain rows, a drop-down list of other documents appeared which could then be opened and read.

"Are they relevant and at all interesting?" I asked.

"Not so far. But there looks to be loads of them."

Keep going, Jeff and I urged her. The rules about establishing whether a document might be inadvertent disclosure, which I knew well, permitted you to read on because, equally, it could be intentional disclosure. How so? Some litigants do what we call a document dump and say, "There you go, find the needle in that haystack."

Not long after, Enfys struck gold.

"Oh my god, look at this. I've just come across some messages between Johnny and the actor Paul Bettany about Amber."

"And?" I asked.

"Just read them."

I looked again at her computer screen. What they revealed was an extremely misogynistic exchange in which Johnny joked with one of his best friends Paul Bettany (who happened to be married to a #MeToo activist and Hollywood star):

"Let's burn Amber!!!" wrote Depp. In reply to Bettany he added, "Let's drown her before we burn her!!!" And then, "I will fuck her her (sic) burnt corpse afterwards to make sure she is dead."

My jaw was on the ground. In three decades of media cases, this was the craziest exchange I had ever seen, especially coming from a man who wanted his reputation about being a southern gentleman who would "never harm a woman" to be believed. In private he was indulging in the most hateful misogynistic abuse.

It was a turning point.

Depp had boasted about an almost saintly approach to women in defence of his own character. Now we had him.

The unravelling could begin.

There were oodles of documents revealed in the drop down; Enfys estimated there were about 70,000. Right, time to get some extra help. Another trainee lawyer was brought in and between them they sorted out the relevant from irrelevant documents and filed any lawyer-client communications into a separate category. Special rules apply where you receive such documents because the receiving partner has to work out whether there has been a deliberate waiver of privilege or not. I read them and decided these were inadvertent as none of them related to the relationship.

Now I had to tell the other side. I explained that in the documents received, we had found and permanently deleted the privileged material and would disregard the mostly irrelevant material, but we would be relying on the relevant material about the relationship, including the Bettany exchanges.

Within minutes the phone line was buzzing. I was out and several repeat calls and emails followed. The partner on the other side made it clear that the material was unintended disclosure and demanded immediate destruction and an agreement not to use it in the litigation. But the disclosure could not be simply passed off as unintended and the rules permitted us to look at the material. We composed and sent our reply accordingly.

Tough. You've given it to us now and some of it is clearly relevant and will stay in the case. It should have been disclosed anyway under the 'not helpful to your case' rule. Depp's team threatened an injunction to prevent its use. 'Go on then, see how you get on with that,' was our position. Their mistake was enormous and hugely embarrassing for them, but our retention of the material documents was utterly legitimate, and they knew it.

Caught with their pants well and truly down.

The Bettany messages plus more were now in the case. We took the trainees out for a drink to thank them for the comb through and toasted Enfys' bloodhound instincts.

It was time to report back to *The Sun.* Unsurprisingly, they were hugely cheered up by this latest turn. They were used to setbacks in litigation rather than golden gifts. Enfys was quite rightly lauded for her enterprise and nowadays does regular night lawyer stints at the paper as well as her day job with us.

Appointing a lead counsel for the trial was the next step. I pulled up the list of the best criminal silks in town because the case would turn on what was, in essence, a series of criminal allegations

Sasha Wass was the name on the top of my list.

She was already a legend. One journalist described her to me as a cross between Helen Mirren in *Prime Suspect* and Carol Vorderman in *Countdown*. Her no nonsense, unimpressed by celebrity approach was just what we needed. "Louis," she told me on the first day we met, "I potted Rolf Harris on much less evidence than this," pointing to the highlights brief I'd delivered to her a few days earlier. She had not only read it but consumed and memorised it. And she was used to the libel courts, having won her own libel action against the *Mail*. "I mugged up on libel in the process." Tall, slim and serious is how she comes across in court but in real life she's very funny, cracks jokes and eschews all alcohol except bottled beer.

The team and the two senior *Sun* lawyers met Sasha at chambers. By the end of the meeting, we knew we had got our woman. She was an expert cross examiner with a phenomenal memory. We also added a rising star of the libel bar to the team to help us, Clara Hamer.

We were now ready to go to war.

Descriptions like "trial of the century" get bandied about by over enthusiastic sub editors of newspapers every few years. With the century just two decades in, this description of our case from *The Times* sounded a bit over the top but we were happy to take it. Popular opinion, these days measured by people who spend too much of their lives on Twitter (now X), Facebook and now TikTok, made us the likely losers. An abstainer from all three, I paid it no heed. And I told Enfys, still avidly monitoring social media, not to get downhearted.

Johnny's PR campaign was at full pitch in the weeks leading up to trial. And so were his leaks to the media. The trial, originally due to start in late March was postponed in face of the pandemic and the government's stay at home order.

By then we had got our witness evidence more or less sorted out and statements had been filed at court. Two more transatlantic trips had taken place. One saw Jeff fly to Vancouver where Amber was filming *Aquaman*. Between filming schedules, he was able to get from her some more of the complicated details of the story.

The other trip saw me and Jeff fly to LA to finalise Amber's all-important trial witness statement and persuade some of our witnesses not to pull out in the face of the huge upswell of support for Johnny. And their fears that the Depp propaganda machine would turn on them. Two of our witnesses held firm: Whit, still a rock for her sister, and Kristina Sexton, who had re-located to Australia and recalled Amber's traumatic account of a sexual assault by Johnny. Another witness, Melanie Inglessis, who had applied make-up to Amber's bruised and battered face to cover up her swollen lips and bruises after a Johnny beating just before a long-scheduled appearance on the *Late Show* with Britain's own James Corden, was less willing to testify. For this crucial witness, we had to summons her to compel her attendance at court.

This last trip, a month before the original March trial date, sure had its moments. As we waited in the departure lounge, Jeff got an email that another Depp leak, a recording, had hit DailyMail.com, the US website of the *Mail*. Some of the earlier leaks had found their way to mainstream public attention so using this news outlet was no surprise. This time it was a big leak. It was a recording we had not come across before someone on Johnny's side decided to give it to the media. Was it a coincidence it happened on the day we were flying off to get Amber's statement and nail down the other witness statements? Of course, I told Jeff. It is not as if they know what we are doing or advertising it.

On the plane in the next row sat Robbie Williams and his wife which was entertaining. He spent most of the time watching movies when he wasn't helping himself to fruit snacks in the galley or petting his dog on his lap. Where they kept the dog the rest of the flight was a mystery. Did the Air New Zealand staff look after celeb's dogs as well? I shrugged and wondered once more about the privilege afforded to the rich and famous.

But then something happened after we landed which made us wonder whether our movements were being monitored. Soon after our arrival an email popped into my inbox. It was from Adam Waldman. The last time we had been in touch was when we traded insults about our respective cases after the shortest ever meeting in Mayfair. We had never corresponded before.

The new email was short. And telling.

"When we met last, you said "amber heard would have to be 'gone girl'"
for her abuse allegations to be false…There are more [leaked] tapes to
come. I assumed you were blindsided by these tapes…If you would like to
discuss a way out of the morass for your client, please call me. I'm in Los
Angeles on…"

Waldman's email told us in plain terms there would be further leaks like
the one we got wind of at Heathrow and that he was behind it. He boasted we
were in deep trouble – boasting being a pre-requisite for US entertainment
lawyers, it seemed – and he was in LA for any discussion which suggested to
us that he knew we were there too. Still, I wasn't unduly concerned about this.
If our movements were being monitored it was a sure sign they were worried.
To this day we don't know how they knew we were in LA if our suspicions
were correct.

The Covid rules brought additional problems. International travel was
only just re-starting and our trial judge, recognising the importance of this
most high profile of libel trials took the plunge and ordered a new date in July.

Amber and Whit had to go into isolation for three weeks before the start
of the trial after flying into the UK. On top of everything else I became their
travel consultant, fixing flights, retreats, security and hotels for their stay.

It was the weirdest of times. London was like a vast ghost town.

Because of Covid rules, it was impossible to fill the court to the brim which
happens in big, headline grabbing cases. Uniquely, the judge decided that the
case would occupy five courtrooms within the mostly empty building. The
'live' number 13 court, where the judge sat, would hear the evidence with the
two core legal teams. The rest of the legal teams would be watching on live
TV from the second court which was called the legal overflow court. A third
court was for watching witnesses and other key members of the respective
teams. A fourth housed the journalists and the last one was for the public.
The public court was packed out with the Depp Heads, his unswervingly loyal

band of fans who followed him.

The Strand was unusually traffic free which meant the hundreds of Depp Heads, many in costume, could roam. It was a Depp carnival. Gathering ourselves in the coffee shop over the road and watching the carnival blocking our entrance to court, we laughed and smiled at the *Edward Scissorhands* and *Pirates of the Caribbean* lookalikes. There was even a drive-by van proclaiming Justice for Johnny as well as some abuse for Amber. The Johnny bandwagon was definitely in town and would remain camped there for the next three weeks. Thankfully, there was no libel jury to be influenced by this wave of pro-Johnny support.

We met with Amber on the eve of trial. She was on top form. Engaged, fully appraised of her case and the case against her and was raring to go. I marvelled at her calmness. In their three week long retreat deep in the middle of an English forest, she got down to it like an undergraduate studying for her Finals. She told me her routine was to start work mid-morning and go on until late in the evening with minimal breaks. The paperwork was heavy, and we reminded ourselves of how emotionally difficult it was, re-living memories from the unhappiest years of her turbulent time with Johnny.

She surprised me when she showed me her bedside reading material. It was a book on human rights law written some years back by our trial judge, Andrew Nicol.

"How come?" I asked.

"Oh, you know. So far, I've been impressed with his interim rulings, especially not getting sidetracked by Johnny's team and their tricks. And I'm understanding a lot more about English law by reading this."

Amber's girlfriend joked with me, eyebrows raised, "Yeah and she keeps reading me extracts." Sasha and I laughed, impressed with Amber's seriousness and work ethic. It is usually the exact opposite with celebs.

The other side was now represented by a new and very expensive law firm, Schillings. They weren't exactly new to the case. They had represented JK Rowling in the early skirmishes and we found out that, leaving nothing to chance, they had been marking the homework of their predecessors throughout. This would have vastly inflated their costs expenditure.

Our tight team of three was outgunned in numbers by their team of six, including two partners Jenny Afia and Joelle Rich. Their counsel team, like ours, had grown to three. James Price had retired from practice the year before so they brought in another veteran of the libel bar, Desmond Browne QC. But no sooner had he been appointed he was then replaced. Why, we wondered? Was it because he gave Johnny some sensible advice such as there is a high risk you may lose, so don't do it? We had no idea nor do we still, but it was the shortest QC appointment on a case I have ever experienced.

In his place was David Sherborne, by now well established as the darling of the claimant media bar and well-known individuals seeking redress for breaches of privacy and harm to reputation. We had crossed swords many times before. One occasion was so bitter he was still refusing to speak to me.

Although the teams are up close and personal, there is very little communication between them in a trial. But still, it added even more spice to the mix, especially when Sherborne came into court each day with a lever arch file with a spine labelled in large letters, 'Amber's Lies'. I take my hat off to him for his client-getting abilities, for he is quintessentially a showman as well as a leading barrister in the field.

And taking a leaf out of our book, they added Eleanor Laws QC to their team specially for cross examining Amber. Eleanor is a well-known criminal specialist, like Sasha. The two knew each other well and there was clearly mutual respect.

Our division of labour was relatively straightforward. Adam Wolanski would front up all the libel applications before and during the trial, and do so with his usual brilliance, whilst Sasha Wass would present the case, cross examine the factual witnesses and deliver our closing speech. Team Johnny had Sherborne doing everything except cross examining Amber and our other witnesses. To me this set up smelt of bitter compromise. Were egos in play? And would Adam Waldman make an appearance after we had chosen to disclose his February email to me in open court in a preliminary skirmish a few days earlier? It didn't take long to find out.

Given the pro Depp crowd and patent hostility towards Amber, I negotiated for her to be brought into the yard of the Royal Courts of Justice by car each morning with her American lawyer, Whit, Jen and girlfriend, shielded by her security. Their daily exits from the car would be filmed and circulated on mainstream news and social media within minutes. Theatres were still closed, and people were tired with streaming. It was *the* show in town. Lots of newspaper columns and messages about the case were written, many saying, 'Thank goodness, some non-Covid news we can get stuck into'.

From inside, we saw Johnny make his entrance. He was all smiles, kisses, waves and cheers. He was treated more like a rock star than an actor whose peak was some years back. Finally, we all settled down in our five courts and, like a referee, our judge read out some rules we had to stick to. Quaintly this is called housekeeping. Some of his rules were the usual ones about time management. He gave each side the same length of time to cross examine the other's witnesses. Rightly, he explained that the evidence of Johnny and Amber was far and away the most important in the case and on which he had to reach a decision as to whether the very serious wife beating allegations were true or not.

Or, as David Sherborne said more than once, "Somebody is lying in this case" when he addressed the judge on just how important it was for his client to get a reasoned judgment at the end of the case to vindicate Johnny's reputation. He may well have come to regret these words later on.

Three weeks of trial followed.

We were very happy with the way the case went. Amber and all the witnesses we called gave their evidence without any hiccups. Depp's performance in the box was not so good. His entourage of witnesses weren't compelling either. It was a shame Waldman didn't put in an appearance; instead he watched proceedings from the public gallery.

We felt optimistic.

After the last closing speech everyone went outside for final photo calls. Outside court, Amber delivered her only public statement about the case which was carried live on Sky News and other channels, explaining, above the din of the Depp Heads calling her a liar and worse, she had faith in British justice. The crowds outside had swollen. For the first time I hung around close to the Depp Heads to get a feel for their mood. They were jubilant and thought their hero had won. I just smiled and took my team off to the pub, making sure we weren't too big a group to break Covid rules.

We now had to wait for the judge to let us know his decision.

The days of waiting turned into weeks which turned into months. It was a nerve-racking time. Some judges are faster than others. Mr Justice Nicol was quicker than most but as September turned into October there was still nothing.

But suddenly, late in October, three months on from the trial, we got an email from the judge's clerk. The judge, she told us, was now ready to deliver his decision but each side had to agree that only the counsel team plus one solicitor – four on each side – would be allowed to know what it said. We were to read it for the usual task of 'perfecting', that is proofreading, the factual details to pick up on anything that needed correcting. We had to give solemn promises not to divulge the decision or anything in the judgment in the few days between the draft and publication of the decision. Adam, Sasha, Clara and I quickly gave our promises as did our opponents.

In the old days we used to trudge along to court and listen to decisions being read out. These days the decisions quietly drop into your inbox. We didn't know what time. It came mid-morning. After two years of work almost exclusively on this one case, I suddenly had sweaty hands as I opened the decision.

It was long. Very long. 129 pages. The judge had been thorough.

I went straight to the end to try and find the magic words as I sat alone in my study at home. But the end was an appendix so then I had to go back up the pages until I found the words I had been praying for:

"The Claimant has not succeeded in his action for libel...the Defendants have shown that what they published in the meaning which I have held the words to bear was substantially true."

I let out a scream of victory. It was the libel litigator's equivalent of winning the FA Cup Final. When I went downstairs my daughter, Eva, then six months pregnant, gave me a strange stare and asked, "What's up?" I replied, "Oh, nothing. Just some good news about my football team." I had to let off steam. I went to my local swimming pool for my daily swim and swam faster than I had for years. What a rush. But I couldn't tell anyone except my closed circle who were no doubt feeling the same.

They too were over the moon and for the first few minutes we discussed the contents of the decision. It could not have gone much better – 12 of the 14 assaults proved, the other two not reaching the necessary threshold of proof. Amber was believed ('preferred') to Johnny where their accounts differed. The evidence we had uncovered helped him reach decisions.

Even the much-publicised accusation that Amber had left a turd on the marital bed was swiftly dispensed with by the judge. He devoted a short paragraph to it, saying it was remote from the central issue of whether Depp assaulted Amber, adding:

"For what it is worth, I consider it is unlikely that Ms Heard or one of her friends was responsible. Mr Depp had left that night for his property in Sweetzer. As long as he was away, it was Ms Heard who was likely to suffer from the faeces on the bed, not him. It was, therefore, a singularly ineffective means for Ms Heard or one of her friends to 'get back' at Mr Depp."

But there was work to do. Some of the factual details in the draft judgment needed checking and the knowledge was mostly with Jeff and Enfys. Sombrely I explained I had the decision, couldn't tell them anything but please check out something for me. Both were bursting to know, of course, but knew I wouldn't say. They came through with the information and I curtly thanked them, trying to sound neither triumphant nor miserable. I adopted the same tone with Justin and the other *Sun* lawyers when telling them the handing down date. They and the Editor and Dan Wootton could only be told an hour before it was made public on the judiciary website.

The entire legal team except Sasha, who was in court, trooped early morning into News UK's headquarters in the building known as the Baby Shard, which sits alongside the Shard. For once the Editor was early. I tried to pass the time by talking about anything but the decision. They searched for clues on our faces, but we were sticklers for the rules. Finally, as I watched my iPhone display trip from 8.59am to 9am, I blurted out the words. "We've won!" Huge cheers filled the boardroom. And relief.

I could finally tell Jeff and Enfys what I was forced to hold back for the past few days. They both said I was so grumpy with them in my attempts not to sound happy they were sure the result had gone the other way.

Newspapers rarely win major libel trials. This was my second for *The Sun* in less than seven years. The restrictions on us meant we could not go into detail for another hour, so the champagne came out instead but once it was 10am I left Adam to explain the findings. I had to speak to Amber before the news reached her as she wanted to hear it from me directly.

It was 2am in LA but Amber said she'd wait up for our FaceTime call. She was up alright, surrounded by Whit and her closest friends. They were all outside in her back garden enjoying a balmy night in LA. I could hear the clinking of glasses and chatter in the background which soon fell to a hush as I told Amber the result.

When I explained we'd won convincingly she screamed with joy and Whit held her tight. I had to tell her more than once for it to sink in. The whoops continued as I took the phone into the boardroom so she could say thanks to everyone assembled. The decision was already featuring in breaking news bulletins on everyone's phones and on rolling TV news. The story which went around the world was Johnny Depp held to be a wife beater by High Court judge. It couldn't have been a better outcome and was a moment to savour.

Now the world knew the judge's decision. Depp had gambled in the London libel casino and lost.

Schillings issued a bitter denunciation of the ruling on behalf of their client describing it as "perverse as it is bewildering" and "so flawed it would be ridiculous for him not to appeal".

They applied for permission to appeal from the trial judge who gave them short shrift, so they asked the Court of Appeal. Unusually, rather than decide the merits of their application by reading the paperwork, the court decided to hold a hearing which would last half a day. A few weeks later, in March 2021, we all trooped off to the Court of Appeal for the hearing.

Now Depp brought on a very senior libel silk, Andrew Caldecott QC, who spent most of his address to the judges trying to persuade them the judge had gone wrong in his fact-finding exercise.

My mind raced back to another case which we had won before a High Court judge but then lost in the Court of Appeal. And to all the recent reversals by media defendants in the Court of Appeal. Surely not...

But by the time the judges finished picking up Caldecott on his seven points where he insisted the trial judge had gone wrong, I felt confident enough to turn to the others and whisper that, despite the latest silk's customary eloquence, the judges appeared to concur with us that you cannot make a silk purse from a sow's ear.

And so it proved to be.

Shortly afterwards their decision came down: permission was refused. There was no basis for challenging Mr Justice Nicol's decision. It was a huge blow to Depp. Now three judges had the same view and the door to an appeal was slammed in Johnny's face.

That was the end of Depp's attempt to sue *The Sun* and its journalist for libel in this country.

Two years later in the US, Depp won his libel claim against Amber with several commentators noted drily it was legally safe to call him a wife beater here but not in the United States. I have lost count of the number of people who have asked me; how come she won in London – where the task of proving a libel is much easier for a claimant – and lost in a much more defendant friendly jurisdiction in the States. My answer is always the same: resources. I would also tell them to go and read Nicol J's decision, contrast that with the US jury decision which simply answered yes or no to what happened and then make your mind up which you prefer.

In London we operated on a level playing field. Each side had two specialist teams of lawyers and could deploy broadly similar resources to the case. It was a fair fight, resources-wise.

In the US case where Amber had to rely solely on her very limited resources her team, bravely led by Elaine Bredehoft, was much smaller that Depp's team. And he could also use his resources to fund a wave of online hostility towards Amber which no doubt would have an impact on jurors. Amber was funded through a personal insurer which meant her team could only stretch as far as the insurer deemed it necessary.

There was never a level playing field in Virginia.

And that is how litigation so often goes. And why the rich get disproportionately positive results in court. But that, as they say, is for another day...

Chapter 26

The Birmingham Six and *My Big Fat Gypsy Wedding*

On the face of it there is nothing linking the former Labour minister and investigative journalist Chris Mullin and his groundbreaking investigation into the Birmingham Six with the popular Channel 4 series *My Big Fat Gypsy Wedding*. Except that in each case there was an attempt to seize journalistic material by police forces from West Midlands, in Chris' case, and Essex Police, in Channel 4's case, thus seeking to undermine hugely important principles of journalistic independence from the state and wider issues of freedom of expression.

Applications by the state using the Police and Criminal Evidence Act (PACE) and anti-terrorism legislation have become depressingly familiar when journalists cover certain kinds of stories. Sometimes, as with Chris Mullin, the fundamental and sacrosanct principle that you protect your sources is also in play.

I've acted for journalists suddenly caught up in this quagmire since the mid-nineties. Such cases rarely attract attention.

However, both of these did because of the notoriety of the subject matter: terrorism and mass rioting. Each one raises the critically important dilemma which the law impels a judge to decide, balancing which right should trump the other; freedom for the media to investigate and get stories which may not come to light, or helping the police catch wrongdoers when useful information is in the hands of the media.

* * *

They say never meet your heroes because it will be a let-down. Most of the time this is borne out. Not in the case of Chris Mullin. Chris is the author of *A Very British Coup*, a fine novel about the undermining of a left-wing Labour Prime Minister which hit a chord with many of us in the Thatcher dominated eighties. It was turned into a TV drama and worked brilliantly well. As a wannabe author of political thrillers, it hit all my buttons. More importantly, Chris was the author of *Error of Judgement: The Truth About The Birmingham Bombings*, the culmination of his investigations which began when he was a TV reporter, into the six men wrongly convicted of the pub bombings in 1975 following the atrocity which killed 21 people. The Irish Republican Army (IRA) had been increasing its activity in Britain, and the bombings were quickly attributed to the group. They became known as the Birmingham Six and put behind bars for a crime they did not commit.

Chris' book was published 11 years into their life imprisonment sentences. The documentaries he helped to make for *World in Action* were major milestones in the men's fight for justice. They focused on the weakness of the forensic evidence against the men and their treatment over three days which resulted in them making false confessions. Without Chris' journalism, this appalling miscarriage of justice may never have been established.

Chris went on to become a Labour MP and minister and a renowned political diarist, including *A View from the Foothills*, which remains one of the funniest and most astute diaries a politician has ever published. Part of the reason it became so popular was because of Chris' lack of ego and honesty about the nature of government and the state of politics.

Fast forward 45 years on from 1974, I saw Chris come under fire from the relatives of the pub bombing victims for his steadfast refusal to provide information about a confidential source to a new inquest hearing into the pub bombings. The inquest featured in many news reports and Chris was criticised by the usual suspects in the right-wing media for not helping the victims achieve some belated justice by naming his source.

Not long afterwards the West Midlands Police (WMP) got in touch with him and made a formal written request for his co-operation to identify one of his sources.

By now, Chris was no longer an MP and led a busy life: writing, serving on boards and spending much of the time in his garden. He was still publishing books, both fiction and non-fiction. He needed legal advice urgently about the request, not so much as to what his response might be – that was a given – but where it might end up. I felt I knew him already from having read his diaries when I was asked by his union, the National Union of Journalists (NUJ), to advise him.

Chris' wife Ngoc, who he met in Vietnam, answered the phone.

"Hold on, please. Chris is in the garden."

What seemed like an age later, he picked up their landline. After the usual introductions, I explained I would be happy to help with a response he was about to make to the WMP. He explained his unwavering position which he has since published in the *London Review of Books* just before he gave evidence to the 2019 inquests:

"I know the names of the bombers. Four men were involved: two bomb-makers and two planters. More than 30 years ago two of them described to me what they'd done in some detail…But I have never named names. Journalists do not disclose their sources. I interviewed many of those who were active in the IRA's West Midlands campaign. To gain their co-operation I gave repeated assurances, not only to the guilty, but to innocent intermediaries, that I would not disclose their identities. I cannot go back on that now, just because it would be convenient. My purpose at the time was to help free the six innocent men who had been convicted of the bombing. I was never under the illusion that I could bring the perpetrators to justice. My researches, conducted between 1985 and 1987, formed the final chapters of my book about the case, *Error of Judgement*. In it two of the perpetrators are quoted at length, but not identified. I no longer have any compunction about identifying two of the men involved, who are now dead (I am about to do so), but the man described in my book as the 'Young Planter' is still alive, and I will not name him."

Chris explained to me that although his research into the ill treatment of the Birmingham Six featured shocking police malpractice, he realised it would not be enough to overturn their convictions unlike in many other cases. There was too much at stake here. He was convinced the only way he could do this would be to find who did do it. This was a herculean task. To get admissions from the actual bombers would turn out to be one of the most difficult journalistic tasks ever undertaken as I was soon to find out.

I went online and watched archive material from *Who Bombed Birmingham?*, one of his *World in Action* documentaries showing one of the bombers, wearing a mask, being interviewed by Chris and confessing to his role in the atrocities. This was the Young Planter.

The immediate task at hand was to assist Chris in the response to WMP. In the letter we drafted, he explained the chilling effect on public interest, investigative journalism if he were to reveal a lifelong guarantee of anonymity. He expressed his continuing sympathy for the victims and their relatives and his determination to constructively engage with WMP. But his help would fall short of identifying Young Planter whilst the bomber was still alive.

The correspondence went on for the next few months, back and forth, but essentially the positions were unchanged. The investigators and us were locked into our respective positions. Chris passed over as much information as he could within the limits of his position.

He reflected to me how deeply ironic it would be were he to become the subject of a criminal prosecution and found guilty, or if a production order was made and he refused to comply, to then be found in contempt of court and become the only person to be punished for the bombings other than the wronged six men. But he was adamant; he would not sacrifice the principle to save himself from such an outcome.

Then the Covid pandemic happened. And nothing. Silence. The letter demands petered out.

We heard not a peep out of WMP.

Chris and I took the same position: no news is good news. Then, all of a sudden, not long after the final lockdown, I received an extraordinary letter from WMP. They told me that, unbeknownst to us, the WMP had asked the Attorney General to authorise a prosecution of Chris under the Terrorism Act legislation. There are provisions which criminalise anyone assisting a terrorist act. The definition of assisting is so open to interpretation and potentially contentious that the approval of the Attorney General is, rightly in my view, needed. But to ask for Chris to be prosecuted under this provision was desperate on their part, and a sure sign they were feeling under pressure from the families of the victims. The letter went on to say that the approval had not been given.

I rang Chris straightaway and once again, Ngoc had to call Chris inside from tending his much-loved garden.

He greeted me tentatively. For me to be calling he guessed there was some news. I quickly explained the letter's contents and emailed it to him so he could pore over it. As it happened, he had already been called by WMP to say they weren't prosecuting him.

We talked it over and he agreed with me that whilst their inclination to prosecute was over the top and recognised as such by the Government's most senior law officer, it was a relief that the door had been closed. With that, I added, I think we can happily say this is an end of the case. They had gone for a prosecution (which was refused) rather than a production order route.

Not for the first time, I guessed wrong.

A week later the WMP sent me a production order demand under the Terrorism Act that Chris hands over the material to identify Young Planter. We had previously sent them redacted copies which had blanked out his name. Quite rightly, I too was – and remain – unaware of his identity.

This time, the call from me to Chris was not so cheerful and began, "I'm sorry Chris but they've now gone down the production order route." He wasn't best pleased but at the same time realistic enough to know that if WMP remained under pressure from the victims' families then they had to make sure every route was explored, no stone left unturned.

The next few months were gruelling for Chris, but he never once showed it to me, putting up a phlegmatic appearance whenever we met or spoke. I have represented lots of journalists in his position. Only a few would be willing to go to jail – or pay a massive fine – if found to be in contempt of court by refusing to give up their sources. I was never in any doubt Chris was one of those very few, even though he would have not had a scintilla of sympathy for Young Planter. In addition, he explained, he also remained obligated to the innocent intermediaries who helped him find and contact the bomber.

I advised that if we lost, the likeliest outcome was a financial penalty, potentially unlimited, rather than jail. In his latest memoir, *Didn't You Use to Be Chris Mullin?* Chris records me saying this to him in his diary for 18 August. He goes on to add: "A dark cloud is beginning to cast a shadow over my otherwise golden life."

I had already spoken to Gavin Millar QC, the doyen barrister to defend journalists in such cases. A week later the three of us met up at Gavin's chambers with Chris anxious to hear the QC's advice. London was still half empty after the end of lockdown. Cooped up so long inside, we decided to meet in a socially distanced way in the chamber's gardens.

Gavin was upbeat. He said for all their bluster WMP might not take it all the way or, if they did, a judge would be reluctant to compel production of the documents identifying Young Planter. If he was wrong and Chris, refusing to comply, was fined, then the penalty could be in the region of £20,000. Gavin said some or all of a penalty in this region could be crowdfunded, as Chris reports in the book.

The next few months saw us caught up with the usual twists and turns of a production order case. At the start of December, we finally got their disclosure running to several hundreds of pages. It was a forensic trawl through what happened from the very start with Chris' journalistic comments on TV, articles and extracts from his autobiographies. Their approach was rigorous and, superficially at least, attractive. They sought to undermine Chris at every point.

Chris came to the office and looked through the four bulging lever arch files we had taken possession of. I had pored over them in previous days. Chris records in his diary, "Louis is optimistic. Me less so. This could be ruinous."

He also describes me as both cheerful and optimistic about the eventual out-come of the case. I must admit I wasn't entirely optimistic, omitting to tell Chris I had lost nearly all my previous production order cases, but what made me feel positive was how sympathetic a judge should be towards him in these circumstances.

Lockdown meant I could not travel to meet potential character witnesses. I took statements from several famous alumni of the journalistic world. In the end we decided to limit the number to four so as to not breach that well established legal principle – never over-egg the pudding.

Alan Rusbridger, former editor of *The Guardian* for two decades, drafted an excellent statement to explain the wider context of journalistic principles and the importance of such high public interest journalism. Paul Lashmar, an investigative journalist turned academic and now a Professor in the flag-ship journalism department at City St George's, University of London, added more weight to the argument. Charlie Falconer, a former Lord Chancellor, added his considerable weight to the principles at stake including what was in the New Labour government's mind when he steered the legislation through Parliament. Finally, the General Secretary of the National Union of Journalists (NUJ), Michelle Stanistreet, explained the position on behalf of the union. Their support, both financial and moral, was hugely welcome from start to end in the case.

This evidence, plus Jack Straw's letter to *The Times* declaring that the Terrorism Act 2000 which he had taken through Parliament as Blair's Home Secretary was never intended to be used against journalists, gave us a leg up.

The case was listed for two days in late February 2022. The WMP tried to get an order for it to be heard privately. Not for the first time, the move had a galvanising effect, getting the likes of the *Daily Mail* and *The Times* more interested than they might otherwise have been. Chris records in his diary a change in his legal team's mood. He says that Gavin and I gave him the impression, at our eve of trial meeting, that we were pessimistic about the outcome. I don't recall saying anything negative but pre-trial concentration on strengths and weaknesses makes you more serious. I didn't think WMP's case amounted to much despite the excessive volume.

The case was heard at the Old Bailey, the Central Criminal Court. Chris and I met up early in a local coffee shop and we walked together down Old Bailey, past the entrance for the prison vans. There were photographers and journalists to greet him. NUJ members, with good wishes and banners, were also present and Chris posed for photographs alongside them.

The start of the hearing was taken up with whether the press could be admitted and a sensible compromise was reached; the names of suspects who the WMP wanted Chris to give up were to be identified by random letters of the alphabet like AB.

Finally, the hearing got underway. Our witnesses, apart from Chris, were all agreed; in other words, Lewis had no questions for them so the judge could take their evidence as unchallenged. So this cut down the time.

Gavin cross examined WMP's only witness, a detective called Darren Sutton. He gave him what we like to call a good going over to, as Chris so eloquently describes it, dispose of a few canards in his witness statement in which he suggested that Chris had lied about the existence of his original notebooks. They weren't now saying this, he confirmed, which came as a relief to Chris who has always struck me as scrupulously honest as well as precise. This suggestion had riled him in the run up to the trial. We got from Sutton what we hoped and then, after lunch, it was Chris' turn in the box.

We had warned him to expect a grilling but in the relatively refined atmosphere of Court 4, without an audience of angry relatives, James Lewis kept it short. In a few different ways he asked the central question: was he willing to give up Young Planter's identity and confirm the police suspicion about another individual he had interviewed? No, came the answer, he would not. Again, Chris repeated his reasoning.

Chris had always maintained the police were simply seeking to confirm who they suspected Young Planter to be. Lewis' central thesis was that Young Planter's admission to Chris was going to change everything and turn it into a case which could now be prosecuted. We said this was rubbish and that such an admission would be worth very little in criminal proceedings.

WMP had three tests to overcome in order to get home. The first was the easiest: does the application relate to material which involves serious criminal acts of terrorism? The second, which we hotly disputed, was whether the material sought would add substantial value to the criminal investigation or whether it was simply a fishing expedition. The third was the one we felt should succeed if the others failed: was it, especially in the circumstances of this case, in the public interest to order disclosure given the implications for investigative journalism? This, of course, was a paradigm case where, as one observer put it, Chris lit the fuse for the Six's eventual exoneration by the Court of Appeal.

Common law means that judges can develop the law by interpreting earlier judicial decisions rather than solely relying on statutes passed by legislatures. Here we were able to point to a previous appeal ruling that the threshold for the public interest test was high: there needed to be "clear and compelling" public interest to displace the journalistic source protection right. This came from a case where Gavin had defended a journalist called Shiv Malik a few years earlier. The name rang lots of bells: he was the same journalist a client of mine had sued for libel a few years before his well-known production order case. It was indeed a small world.

Judge Lucraft listened keenly to all the evidence and submissions. He decided to reserve his judgment and deliver it on a future occasion.

"How long?" clients reasonably ask me. A few weeks came my reply, adding a question mark at the end.

It took a month. As I was driving down the A1 one evening I saw Gavin's name pop up on the screen. If he is calling me at this time, it probably means the result has arrived. I pulled over and called back.

"We've won. We got home on the public interest."

Phew, what a relief. I couldn't wait to read the decision which ran to 20 pages. I read it over a couple of times. As the judge described it, the public interest point was the crux of the case. I rang Chris, deliberately not telling him I knew the outcome so he would not try to read my mood or tone of voice as we were prohibited from telling our client until an hour before the judge delivered the decision in court a couple of days later. All I could do was tell Chris to book his train later that week and to meet me in our usual coffee shop rendezvous exactly an hour before court was due to start.

Chris described our meeting concisely in his memoir.

"Judgment Day...I meet up with Louis, my solicitor, at Café Nero next to St Paul's Tube Station. He greets me with a broad smile and a thumbs-up. Unknown to me the judgment had already been circulated to the lawyers – and we have won. We are sworn to secrecy, however, until judgment is formally delivered."

We both wore our most serious, straight faces as we walked past the journalists, photographers and supporters. I wanted to high five the NUJ's General Secretary, Michelle Stanistreet, as I walked past but had to resist the temptation. The judge read out the summary of the decision and then left the waiting media to read the 20-page document in which he explained his findings.

I had already homed in on the key sentence at paragraph 62, right at the end:

"The journalism in issue was of the highest public interest value exposing serious failings on the part of the criminal justice system which resulted in the wrongful conviction and imprisonment of six innocent men."

The judge agreed with our submissions on this, namely that the police's asserted public interest did not override Chris' magnificent investigation and the breach of his Article 10 rights in protecting sources. When I read that sentence, I felt immensely proud of Chris' standout journalism. In three decades, I had fought and lost most of these sorts of cases. This was the most important one, and we had won it, fair and square, on the key public interest issue. Chris' brilliant investigation was the winner.

Chris is not one for indulgent celebration and he remains sensitive to the failure of the police to bring the true perpetrators to justice. Many would argue this is pure bunkum, as he can help them get closer to that whenever he wants as Young Planter, half a century on, is alive and unconvicted of these atrocities. But without the assurances he gave which must hold, the WMP would never have got to this point and would have been content to let the Six rot in jail. And they would be much farther away from the identity of the perpetrators.

The decision made the news that day and the next. I got to be *The Times* Lawyer of the Week for a second time and whilst the decision is not binding, it can be prayed in aid for whenever serious, investigative journalism and source protection is under threat from police seizure through the means of a production order application. Chris sent me a note afterwards thanking me and calling my work "a class act" which I treasure. But really, he is the true class act. Hats off.

* * *

10 years earlier Dale Farm, near Basildon in Essex, was one of the biggest gypsy encampments in Europe and had been the subject of protracted legal proceedings brought by Basildon Council to evict them from land which was owned by one of the travellers.

The Channel 4 team which made the wedding series *My Big Fat Gypsy Wedding* had been sent to Dale Farm to film residents in the run up to the eviction which was about to take place in October 2011. This was the year when the series was at peak popularity with seven million viewers.

Channel 4 were still filming when the bailiffs and the police crashed into Dale Farm to enforce the court ordered eviction. They hadn't filmed the clashes which the police were now investigating, preferring instead to focus on the fears and emotions of the families, holed up in their caravans whilst chaos and confusion took place at the entrances, with police helicopters overhead and orders being shouted over megaphones.

Back in 1995, I had already witnessed Essex Police breaking up an animal rights protest about the export of livestock at the port of Brightlingsea. It was harsh and, at times, quite brutal. This police intervention, the BBC news reporter on the ground stated, was similar.

The police, the travellers were told, would only be there to maintain the peace and prevent criminality. But when the eviction operation started unexpectedly early one morning, it was more of a police operation supported by bailiffs than the other way round. The siege of Dale Farm had started. One report described the beginning of the operation:

> *They came in first light, across a farmer's field, outflanking protesters who had chained themselves to the main gate...Tasers had been deployed, and more than 100 riot police had breached the barricades. It was an impressive show of force, designed to shock the travellers and their supporters...Anyone who stood in their way was knocked aside with riot shields. I saw batons being used, and snatch squads pulling out the ring leaders.*

In late 2011 Channel 4 asked me to defend an application brought by Essex Police for seizure of all material arising from disturbances at Dale Farm under PACE on grounds the material would be of substantial value to their investigations of people who attacked police officers and committed other offences during the eviction of travellers from the site. Channel 4's presence at Dale Farm was not initially known to the police, and they were added to the list of television companies summonsed to Chelmsford Crown Court for a legal fight at a late stage. The story had become national news. We were now set to resist the application all the way once the Essex Police's summons arrived.

My advice to Channel 4 was the same as it was to the BBC's production company, Hardcash, that this was a very widely drawn up order that should be resisted and there was a good chance of winning. Hardcash, which had also made *Undercover Mosque* (see Chapter 14), led by David Henshaw, had made a serious documentary about the lives of the gypsy community for BBC Panorama.

Channel 4 had an extra argument – unlike the news teams from the main broadcasters, Channel 4 was not even on the frontline. Their interest was simply to film the impact of the mass eviction on the families, particularly the young children. I had watched the rushes – the raw material which was yet to be edited – and could see for myself that there was nothing here of evidential value. Surely the police would back down once we explained this?

This was already the view of the various legal teams for the BBC, ITN and Channel 4. It was a classic 'fishing expedition' application – general and sweeping – threatening to turn news reporters and photographers into an arm of the state. If the police are able to obtain the film material from journalists, then their safety is threatened by protesters and their independence is lost. Those arguments have raged in cases such as these since the passing of the Police and Criminal Evidence Act in 1986 which first recognised this right, which lawyers call a qualified privilege, attaching to journalistic material.

Next stop, the Crown Court where Channel 4 and several other broadcasters faced a summons to give up its footage to the police.

The gaggle of lawyers on the train to Chelmsford Crown Court the next month filled half the carriage. The coverage of the evictions had led the news. Opinion was split. Opprobrium was heaped on the gypsy supporters who had turned up to resist the eviction.

I have been in front of lots of judges in the Crown Court. Most are case hardened and sceptical about claims and counter claims of each side. Some are regarded as prosecution minded, others pro-defence. In the run up to any case, especially in the Crown Court, practitioners eagerly await the identity of the judge to see whether the odds of you winning go up or down. The best judges are those who are 'straight down the middle'. In other words, they are fair, and the odds have not shifted.

It appeared to me that this judge, whilst no doubt having read and understood the arguments and evidence we put before him, seemed unimpressed with the media respondent's case. The judge is required to balance the competing rights, both of which are important and fundamental in our society. He looked bored with our counsels' submissions. I was frustrated and felt we were not getting the fairest of hearings. How could he not see this fishing expedition lacked merit? It was then I had a lightbulb moment. Believe me, these don't come often. If you are lucky, you get them every few years.

I opened up the brick size textbook known to criminal practitioners as 'Archbold' to remind myself of the strict procedural requirements of section 9 of PACE.

In essence, when applying for a warrant to seize journalistic material, the police have to show they have tried and failed to obtain the material by voluntary means. This is usually evidence in writing and typically will take the form of a letter or notice, often drafted by the police force's lawyers. It also benefits the police by putting the journalist or media organisation on notice not to alter or destroy the evidence being sought. This effectively starts the clock running. It is mandatory. Something wasn't right here though. I remembered that there hadn't been the usual request. In fact, there hadn't been any communication with Channel 4 at all before the police added the broadcaster to the list of media organisations in their sights.

Channel 4 had simply been tacked on recently to the summons by Essex Police. The cops had skipped a compulsory stage.

I walked to the back of the courtroom and just inside the first set of doors, I quietly rang Dominic Harrison, a relatively new Channel 4 lawyer who had practised criminal law. I explained that we may have a procedural argument, arguing there was a defective process. I pictured Dominic's eyebrows arching upwards and he quickly whispered back, "Yes, let's give it a go."

I tugged at our barrister Adam Wolanski's gown, and he turned to me. I quickly explained that we wanted to take this procedural point and would he please make it. He shrugged his shoulders and smiled, "Happy to, no problem."

The judge screwed up his face when Adam explained that we were additionally submitting there had been no compliance with the regime which governs the rules on journalistic "special procedure material" as it is designated by the Act.

Our objection could not be contradicted by the Essex Police barrister.

It didn't take long for the judge to make his ruling. It was entirely in favour of the police apart from in relation to Channel 4, where the judge accepted they were obliged to write to us first and seek voluntary agreement for obtaining their material. He refused the application against Channel 4 and instead gave the police seven days to write to us. By now they knew the paucity of the footage we held from the evidence we had provided. I was optimistic they would give up and not go through this all over again. And I was right – despite a half-hearted attempt to ask for the material voluntarily they soon gave up once they saw Dominic's witness statement about the contact the Channel had with the police.

As for Sky, ITN, BBC, Hardcash and a freelancer, they all unsurprisingly appealed the order made against them. The appeal goes to specialist administrative law judges sitting in the Divisional Court of the High Court in a judicial review of the original decision. Happily, the Crown Court judge's decision was reversed in the appeal, and no footage was compelled to be provided.

The court ruled that the police had failed to make a strong enough case. Their case fell down on what we had been arguing all along – they could not show there would be substantial value to the police investigation if seizure was ordered.

A rare 100% win for journalism.

Chapter 27

Diana, Bashir and that *Panorama*

All hell broke loose when, in 1995, Princess Diana gave an infamous jaw-dropping interview with Martin Bashir, telling him, "There were three of us in this marriage, so it was a bit crowded." It signalled the final parting of the ways between the heir to the throne and his younger wife, for whom many people had much sympathy.

But the exclusive was obtained in the most underhand way imaginable and at a cost to many, none more so than Matthias 'Matt' Wiessler who was fooled into making up two bank statements and then blew the whistle on Bashir's fraud. I am always attracted to whistle-blowers because they are invariably honest and selfless people of principle who nearly always get damaged in the process.

Cover ups are invariably undone in the end. And sometimes the people engaged in the cover up pay the price. But what would that price be in Matt Wiessler's case in which he received grossly unfair treatment by the BBC? Would the big wigs get it in the neck, or would it be the BBC's reputation and their publicly funded pocket which took the hit, rather than those who ordered the cover up?

I had worked on many cases for the BBC, usually to help people needing separate representation. I got to know their excellent in-house legal team over the years. It was thanks to them that I was asked to represent their Director of News when the investigation into the Jimmy Savile film planned for *Newsnight* didn't take place (see Chapter 16). That episode led to an independent inquiry. So when this latest scandal broke I knew a little of what to expect, only this time I was on the outside looking in.

What many people forget is how the Bashir scandal was finally exposed. It took the determined persistence of one dogged ex-BBC journalist, Andy Webb, to uncover the crucial documents to prove foul play over the cover up of Martin Bashir's dirty tricks in getting his famous *Panorama* interview with Princess Diana. The truth had lain dormant for 25 years whilst accolades, awards and anniversary programmes were made about this world exclusive.

Webb was initially refused his FOI request for access to crucial documents in 2007 by the BBC until, just before broadcast of his Channel 4 documentary, a mere 48 hours before transmission in late 2020, the truth finally came out. He had initially been told the Corporation had 80 relevant emails, all of which were legally protected. Further searches revealed 3,288 relevant emails. The dam had burst, and we had no idea why now, after years of obfuscation which suggested to Webb there was a major cover up.

The documents contained, among other things, minutes of a Board meeting which decided my client, Matt Wiessler, would be made the scapegoat in a rush to cover up and protect the *Panorama* which had won the BBC several awards, including the prestigious Bafta. By the end every single award would be returned.

The BBC's Director-General, Tim Davie, had announced an independent Inquiry to be headed by Lord Dyson, a former Master of the Rolls (nothing to do with cars or baking, the Rolls are what all solicitors' names are written on) and former Justice of the Supreme Court. Lord Dyson was, judicially speaking, a Big Cheese. His remit was to look at the way Tony Hall, the BBC news chief, and management initially dealt with the Bashir allegations.

How I came to represent Matt was rather bizarre. It was late 2020, mid pandemic. My mobile rang with a number I didn't recognise. I don't usually take such calls. But stuck at home for much of the day in one of the lockdowns I was bored and answered it.

"Hello, Louis, it's me – Peter Morgan. You helped me make *The Lost Honour of Christopher Jefferies* for ITV. I hope you don't mind me calling out of the blue, but I've a favour to ask?"

Remember? Of course I do, I told him. Peter used me as an unofficial script consultant as well as casting Peter Polycarpou to play me in the award-winning drama (see Chapter 19). And I had been catching up on *The Crown* also written by Peter which, by coincidence, was due to be covering the breakup of Charles and Diana in the next series.

"Sure, Peter. Fire away."

"There's a chap my sister knows who needs a good media lawyer who has been badly treated by the BBC. He lives in Devon, and his name is Matt Wiessler."

He explained what little he knew about the emergence of the BBC Board minutes thanks to Andy Webb's Freedom of Information endeavours. Straight away I said yes. Peter admitted he did have an interest in the outcome as he was still to write the episode featuring the interview for the next series of *The Crown*. I promised to keep him posted.

The next step was to meet Matt. I rang him and explained who I was and why I was calling. He spent the next 10 minutes downloading his anger and upset on me about the episode which had ruined his life. I was barely getting a word in.

"I think it's best you come and see me and we talk it through," I managed to get in.

"Sure, sorry. I'm just so mad with them and it has affected my life so much. I will come to London on my motorbike."

Matt is a tall and handsome man, brought up in South Africa and, seeking his way in the world of the media, he came to London after graduating from the University of Cape Town. He struck me as a proud man, hugely capable in many disciplines. When we met, he was running a specialist bicycle wheel manufacturing business in the southwest.

Another reason for our meeting was to discuss my letter to the BBC delivered two days earlier. The letter, to Tim Davie personally, expressed surprise there had been no attempt to contact Matt about the Dyson Inquiry given his key role in the affair. It was a 'hello-you-can't-ignore-us' missive.

In the letter I emphasised the need for a public apology to Matt now, before the outcome of the Inquiry which promised, given its ambit, to drag on for many months. The second point was the need for full disclosure of the so-called investigation into the affair by Tony (now Lord) Hall back in the nineties. I also sent another letter which was a Subject Access Request (SAR) letter under data protection laws asking for BBC documents mentioning Matt.

The lawyer representing the BBC was Liz Grace, a lawyer who I had come to know well over the years and who had instructed me in the *Funny Money* case for the BBC reporter and producer, Phillip Wright (see Chapter 16). Liz wanted to see me because I told her I was meeting Matt for the first time. When things like this happen, we put our friendship away and just represent our client's interests. Liz wanted to make some opening friendly gestures from her client towards Matt. Yes, she confirmed, the BBC would fund my representation of Matt to the Inquiry as he was going to be a core participant. And the rest was in Lord Dyson's hands, including control of the documents we so desperately wanted. I stressed again the urgent need for a public apology from the Director-General and that my client should be treated as a whistle-blower by the BBC from now on in.

An hour or so later I began the meeting with Matt. It took him three and a half hours to tell his story which had changed the course of his career and life. He managed to keep his anger in check as the details poured out.

At first, everything was going so well. His talents as a graphic designer were quickly recognised at the BBC which led to him being promoted to working on the *Nine O'Clock News* and then on to the Corporation's overhaul of their General Election coverage. He went on to get a Royal Television Society Programme award for the information graphics in the 1992 General Election, unexpectedly won by John Major. A year later he landed in *Panorama*, working on their visual design needs for their weekly current affairs programme. For designers like him, this was the best gig.

With an assistant, he was in charge of *Panorama* graphics creating filmed sequences and re-constructions every week until just before he left in 1995. He decided to set up his own design business focusing on the TV industry with another rising star at the time, Patrick Bedeau. The business was called

Bedeau Wiessler, trading quite rightly on their good names.

It was during Matt's notice period when Martin Bashir visited his home late one night to ask a favour. Bashir was an outsider, like him. They were both strivers and came from outside the traditional world of BBC journalism. Bashir was ambitious and guarded his own work from prying producers and journalists, sticking to just a few people he trusted. The *Panorama* office at that time was staffed by about half a dozen reporters and a pool of producers, all doing their own thing and ultra-competitive with each other, under the control of an Editor, Steve Hewlett.

Matt had previously created copies of documents which were not good enough to broadcast in their original state. Re-construction was and remains a core graphics feature in news and documentaries. One such re-production Matt made was for a film on Terry Venables, then Tottenham's football manager. It featured a company called Penfolds, a small detail which was to become important later on in the story.

When Bashir called him out of the blue one autumn evening, Matt had no idea his career and the course of his life was going to change forever.

"I need to come and see you, there's a job I need doing in a great hurry," said Bashir.

Bashir arrived at his home within half an hour. They had never met outside work before, and Matt was puzzled by the request but got little from the reporter.

"It's very hush hush." Bashir mentioned that it was going to be the biggest story ever.

This time however there was no document to copy. Instead, Bashir read to him, from a blue notebook he kept close to his chest, details of two bank statements Matt was to reproduce on NatWest headed paper. He kept looking at his notebook before giving him figures and dates as well as names, including one of the names from the Venables documentary. Penfolds.

"Really? Wasn't that in the Venables film?" the designer asked.

"That'll do, put Penfolds," Bashir snapped back impatiently, closing off further discussion. Matt was ordered to add the name Alan Waller and payments by News International to the bank statement.

Bashir then said he needed the document by the morning which meant Matt had to do an 'all-nighter' to get it ready. The only explanation he gave Matt before he left his flat an hour or so later was that the document was about people being paid for surveillance.

Matt puzzled over the brief. No document to copy from, no written brief, no producer involvement but he was not there to interrogate Bashir. By then Matt recalled Bashir was the editor's golden boy but not especially popular amongst the staff. It sounded like he was helping the trusted reporter with a scoop. Bashir also reassured Matt that he had seen this information previously and everything was legitimate.

Matt worked diligently through the night, calling Bashir once over some of the figures not adding up correctly.

A BBC motorcycle courier arrived early the next morning to collect the document Matt had finished off, apparently bound for Heathrow Terminal 2 according to cloak-and-dagger Bashir.

Unknown to him, Matt had just played an unwitting part in the grooming of Earl Spencer, Diana's brother, to get to the Princess.

The Diana interview was kept under wraps even from the BBC Chairman, Marmaduke Hussey, whose wife was a lady-in-waiting for the Queen, until it was broadcast on 20 November 1995.

The penny dropped when Matt sat down to watch Bashir's interview with Diana. Initially he was proud that Bashir had got the scoop, but he soon began to worry. There was no mention of Penfolds or the mock-up he had made of the bank statement in the programme, but nevertheless, he told himself this is what he was doing that night. This was Bashir's scoop, ultra hush hush. Matt was worried that there may have been some impropriety in the commissioning of the statements and he guessed they were connected in some way to the scoop.

He went to see Bashir's usual producer, Mark Killick – who Bashir had not used on this programme – about his concerns. Killick, agreeing something was odd, then went to see Hewlett, complaining that Penfolds' name had somehow been used in a mocked-up document as told to him by Matt. Hewlett's response was blunt, telling the producer to fuck off and it was none of their business. Significantly, there was no denial about the document being used.

Matt decided he would go to see the blunt speaking Hewlett himself, as Killick reported back he had got nowhere; he told him in detail about Bashir's visit and the document he had produced. Thanks, he was told. Hewlett would handle things from here on.

Then things went weird.

Matt's flat was broken into, and two things went missing. The first was his sole copy of the disc he kept of the Bashir-ordered bank statement. The second, bizarrely, was one of Matt's coats. The intruder also left a disgusting calling card: an unflushed number two was sitting there in the toilet. "Sounds like the calling card of the spooks," he was later told when recounting the incident.

Matt wasn't for giving up. In a panic he went to see Tim Gardam, then head of weekly programmes and Hewlett's boss, and Tim Suter, another senior manager. He gave his account for the third time, now adding the details of the burglary and his enhanced concerns he was going to be the fall guy. "Leave it with me, I will speak with the relevant people," he was told. Gardam gave Matt his personal phone number and made him promise only to speak to him and the other Tim "about this".

More time passed and nothing happened until the newspapers began knocking on Matt's door wanting to know all about the fake document. Someone had leaked it. Killick suddenly left the BBC around this time. Was it him? To this day, Matt doesn't know.

He decided to have it out with Bashir. They met at a pizzeria in southwest London. Bashir said little except telling him over and over not to speak to the media: "They are out to get me" and "they are jealous". Matt was not to worry. "None of what you did was ever used." This did not reassure Matt.

He was then doorstepped at his home by the *News of the World* and two other tabloids early one Sunday morning. One of the journalists asked him to explain himself, calling him the "master forger". By now Matt was in a rage and, when he had calmed down, took advice: tell the story in full to a sympathetic journalist. Get on the front foot before the BBC get their version out first.

Nick Fielding, the *Mail on Sunday* journalist, stood out as the only one who wanted to hear his version of events. In return Nick told Matt some of the missing detail in the story which was haunting the graphic designer: about how Bashir had used the document to convince Diana's brother, Earl Spencer, to give him access to her. The document was meant to be proof of some wrongdoing by Alan Waller, a *bête noir* of Spencer after a fall out from when he was the Earl's head of security, and a payment made to him by a newspaper and Penfolds, showing a leak in the Spencer set-up. The statement was false and a massive bait to get Spencer onside, to help Bashir get to Diana in suggesting Waller was leaking the Princess's secrets.

It was a despicable fabrication by Bashir, who also produced false statements of others close to Diana, to induce her to speak to him. As Dyson was to find, "Bashir also produced to Earl Spencer other bank statements which, he said, showed payments into the account of Commander Patrick Jephson (Princess Diana's Private Secretary) and Commander Richard Aylard (the Prince of Wales' Private Secretary). It is likely that these statements were created by Mr Bashir and contained information that he had fabricated." Dyson then found that by showing Earl Spencer the fake Waller and Jephson/Aylard statements and informing him of their contents, Bashir had induced Spencer to arrange a meeting with Diana. Matt and others appeared to be no more than collateral damage.

If ever there was an object lesson in never using fabrication to get a story at all costs, this was it.

The Board minutes of April 1996 obtained by Andy Webb helped Matt understand the full extent of Bashir's scapegoating of him contrasted with the incredibly generous treatment of Bashir. Matt had become haunted by these 18 words from the report which was duly endorsed by the Board:

"We are taking steps to ensure that the graphic designer involved will not work for the BBC again…."

The ostensible reason for this blacklisting was that he had been identified as a leaker to the media against BBC interests even though the truth was very different. He had only turned to Nick Fielding at the *Mail on Sunday* as a last resort, on the advice of a top criminal QC.

Bashir, on the other hand, was to get the kid gloves treatment. The investigation report's author, Tony Hall, said he was satisfied "the graphic had no part whatsoever in gaining the interview with the Princess of Wales" but nonetheless, to produce such a graphic was "unwise" and having talked to Bashir about his reasons for compiling the graphic his response was he had no reasons and he "wasn't thinking". Hall concluded this was a "lapse" on Bashir's part. It was a classic understatement. He nonetheless found Bashir to be an honest and an honourable man. And contrite. So Matt was blacklisted, and Bashir was whitewashed.

At the heart of Bashir's account was his insistence that Earl Spencer had previously given him some figures which he used when ordering the false statement from Matt, which was somehow swallowed as credible by the BBC. I wondered how Dyson would treat this canard, given Earl Spencer's claim to have taken detailed notes of his Bashir encounters.

Meanwhile Matt felt a cold shoulder from his former BBC colleagues whenever he pitched for work in his new business. One producer literally whispered into his ear that she'd love to work with him, but the word was out on the street he was "to be avoided". It was Hewlett who had apparently put out the word. The new business didn't prosper. His anticipated BBC commissions failed to materialise. He concluded that the whisper from the producer must be what lay behind this lack of commissions, but Matt was clueless about the Tony Hall blacklisting which spread around the TV industry. The two directors changed the business name to Elephant Hide and ran everything through Patrick in a desperate attempt to avoid trading on their names but still business was slow.

Matt grew more and more disillusioned that his part of the business hadn't worked, and he was letting his partner down. Fed up with it all, Matt gave up working in the media which had promised so much and with his life partner Lucy left London, a bitter man. The accusation he was a forger and a leaker cut deep. Unrectified by the BBC, it spelled the end of his brilliant career. His name was mud.

One event he told me about before leaving London really stood out as truly bizarre. Matt lived in a house situated on a tiny island in the middle of the Thames, in Twickenham, which meant rowing to one of the banks to go anywhere. One day in the late nineties, whilst rowing with his wife and mother-in-law, he saw an elderly suited Asian man walking into the Thames fully dressed. It looked like a ritualistic religious suicide attempt. He quickly changed course and jumped overboard as the man's head was now submerged beneath the water. He dragged him out and shook him to clear his lungs until he came round. The man was in tears and pulled out a photo of Martin Bashir from his sodden wallet.

"It's my son, he is famous. He doesn't talk to me." Matt was flabbergasted and speechless. The emergency services quickly arrived and took over. Apparently, the man was a known self-harm risk and a porter at a nearby hospital.

Matt sent Bashir a message to say he could apologise for his stance in their pizza house meeting and also thank him for saving his father's life.

He got no reply.

Matt never got over the feeling of being scapegoated but couldn't prove a thing. Life was full of 'what ifs'. He felt cursed by the evening visit of Bashir and the subsequent fall out. What hurt him the most was a feeling of guilt. Guilt that he played a pivotal (albeit unwitting) role in the Diana interview and her increasing paranoia which ended with her tragic sudden death in a Paris road tunnel whilst being chased by paparazzi in 1997.

With the new Inquiry Matt was determined his voice would be heard and when, in December 2020, Lord Dyson, through his Inquiry team, wrote to us inviting a witness statement we quickly replied with our answer: yes, willingly.

We were hearing Bashir was too sick to participate.

Written submissions were then followed by a live video interview with Lord Dyson; me in North London and Matt in Devon. I sat at my desk at home in suit jacket, shirt and tie up top, and jeans and trainers down below, marvelling at the new work-from-home technology which was changing the face of litigation practice.

The questions were probing but easy for Matt to answer. He kept his cool and avoided making extravagant claims. We knew there were several more people for Dyson to speak to. We had heard that Martin Bashir was no longer so sick that he could now participate in the Inquiry. We were still missing many documents, but we were provided some – where accounts differed – but not Bashir's; we had to presume he had still not given his to the Inquiry.

Three months on we were told the Inquiry had been completed and the report was ready for publication. As usual, the core participants and their representatives were allowed to see the report on the morning of its publication on a confidential basis. I arrived at the swanky offices of the law firm which oversaw the Inquiry and was shown to a large, empty room.

On the desk was the 127-page report plus appendices which I had to speed read and summarise in my notebook as quickly as possible. Laptops and mobiles were not permitted in case anyone was minded to leak anything ahead of publication.

On the first page I saw in the Executive Summary a passage which brought a wide grin to my face.

Mr Wiessler is an entirely reputable graphic designer who did freelance work for the BBC. Nobody has criticised him for accepting the commission.

In blowing the whistle so soon after the Diana interview, Dyson found he acted responsibly and appropriately. He made a further finding that Bashir used the statement to deceive and induce Earl Spencer to arrange a meeting with Diana. This then allowed him to obtain the interview with her by deception.

At last, recognition for Matt. A quarter of a century too late but still something.

It also meant Dyson had found against Bashir who had tried to explain away his conduct. My suspicions were now confirmed as to why, seven days before the report's release, the BBC announced Martin Bashir had already resigned as the BBC's religious affairs correspondent on grounds of ill health. It was, I was sure, no coincidence. If he hadn't resigned the BBC would have been forced to sack him immediately on publication of the report.

The report set out in detail the contrasting accounts of Bashir and Earl Spencer and explained for the first time why the bank statement was rushed by Bashir. On 31 August he had met Earl Spencer who complained about his former head of security, Alan Waller, who he had dismissed for stealing and leaking to the media stories about him. Earl Spencer told Lord Dyson he thought it most likely he was shown the Waller bank statement on 2 September in a further meeting with Bashir at Heathrow airport. Finally, the penny dropped. Bashir, having heard evidence of Spencer's antagonism towards Waller, needed to show some hard proof to the Earl to curry favour. Hence the urgency, the all-night job and the courier's arrival at 6am to get to Heathrow before Spencer took off.

The fake bank statement was the first part of the inducement, as the report termed it, of Earl Spencer and his sister. It made false references of payments to Waller by News International for stories on Spencer.

Lord Dyson then made a finding that Bashir lied three times to the BBC about never showing the Waller bank statements to anyone, concluding he had "real reservations about Mr Bashir's credibility and reliability...and I treat his evidence with caution" which is judge speak for 'I can't trust this individual who I suspect has told me lies'. Later, he went even further, "... there were significant parts of Mr Bashir's account that I reject as incredible, unreliable and, in some cases, dishonest." The 'd' word from a former Head of Civil Justice is about as bad as it gets.

At every point where Bashir disagreed with the account of another witness – historically, in his witness statement to the Inquiry and in his interview with

Lord Dyson – his evidence was not preferred.

It was the judicial equivalent of a demolition job.

Another important piece of evidence – at the heart of Matt's angst on his role in the obtaining of the interview and the wider issue of Diana's feelings of surveillance and intrusion – came when Dyson asked Earl Spencer what part he thought the showing of the fake Waller bank statements played in his decision to make the introduction to his sister, he gave the judge this answer:

I think Waller was a very easy in to me and I was effectively groomed for the second hit...it hooked me in. I mean, I was duped. So that was clearly their purpose...He very cleverly came to me on my number one bugbear: the bad behaviour of the press... When he had hooked me in on that by showing me a bank statement which seemed to prove what he was saying, then he played his ace.

Dyson was unimpressed with Tony Hall's investigation in April 1996. He described the management moves and thinking in detail and with clarity. As I read it, I realised the depth of the cover up. They were out to scapegoat Matt as a leaker and put the falsities of Bashir down to youthful exuberance.

It was shocking.

The best Hall could come up with about why he was prepared to believe Bashir was that he was "contrite" that he and another senior manager, Anne Sloman, had "got to the bottom of it, that he was telling us the truth about what happened".

Hall had no satisfactory answer as to why he didn't contact Earl Spencer despite accepting Bashir had given him an unsatisfactory explanation for commissioning fake bank statements, something he had lied about three times in the past. Dyson failed to get any better answers from ex Director-General Lord Birt (Bashir was "foolish") or Anne Sloman (Bashir was "out of his depth").

Dyson concluded that the BBC should have been much more sceptical of Bashir's account and their investigation much more effective. He lamented their failure to seek out Earl Spencer for his account saying it was "incumbent on [them] to take all reasonable steps necessary to obtain it". He found it to be a serious flaw in their investigation putting them at a grave disadvantage.

Too right, I muttered. It was a cover up in any other name. And Matt was the scapegoat, the fall guy as he had been telling everyone all along.

The judge also disagreed with Lord Birt's defence of their failure to interview Earl Spencer and then, in a devastating aside, said, "It may simply be that [Bashir] successfully worked his charm on Lord Hall and Mrs Sloman" during their interview with him, calling it "woefully ineffective".

Hall, he opined, "could not reasonably have concluded that [Bashir] was an honest and honourable man who had told the truth and he should not have done so".

This was judge speak to these three bigwigs to pull the other one with their explanations; it's got bells on.

It was no better than Tim Gardam's and Tim Suter's investigations, relying as they did on Bashir's uncorroborated assertions.

There was, of course, nothing in it for the Board to find against Bashir as it would ruin their great exclusive which had been watched by 23 million people. They had to stand behind the liar. And now the judge was gently poking fun as well as his ire at them.

His final finding was that the BBC covered up in its press logs about how Bashir secured the interview and failed to mention it in any of its news programmes; "...the BBC fell short of the high standards of integrity and transparency which are its hallmark."

Game, set and match.

Later that day the report was published and dominated the news headlines. There was then a round of press calls for Matt. He deserved to have his day in the sun. I kept a low profile, saying little other than confirming the report "makes absolutely clear that Mr Wiessler acted responsibly and appropriately throughout...Lord Dyson's findings are a welcome relief to him".

Matt put out a statement, which I drafted, saying:

After a quarter of a century of cover ups and smears, it's good to know the truth is finally out that I acted with integrity and responsibly from day one.

Lord Dyson correctly found the investigation carried out after I raised the alarm was seriously flawed and a smokescreen to protect Bashir. The order from BBC management to make sure I never got any more work was despicable. It had a devastating effect on my career and professional reputation.

It ended by asking those who were responsible for the cover up to apologise to him and lamented the damage done not just to him but Princess Diana and her family. He signed off by thanking the tenacious journalists whose dogged pursuit of the truth brought this to light.

He was suddenly the number one news item for a couple of days, with the BBC in the doghouse.

When I sat down with Matt to tell him the fine detail, he was rightly angry.

"But no one has touched them with their gold-plated pensions and positions," he replied in a raised voice. "Whereas me, the outsider, gets shafted."

I know, I nodded. Time to get even, at least as much as compensation and apologies go, was my reply.

Matt never did get any kind of apology from Lords Hall, Birt *et al* but he did get one from Tim Davie. He told me they met, just the two of them plus his wife Lucy, in his office. And I expect it was Davie's decision to allow the release of the 'lost minutes' to Webb back in 2020, which he would have known would set the ball rolling, so well done on that score.

Now it was also time to call in some heavyweight counsel.

Enter stage left barristers Gavin Millar and William Chapman, the latter who I knew to be an expert on the value of lost careers. Gordon from my office joined the team and for the next few months we prepared the claim for Matt.

The cause of action was not straightforward. After a meeting at the office, we settled on public misfeasance by the BBC as the vehicle to claim damages. It was an unprecedented allegation.

The lengthy letter of claim was sent off. The reply which came in was not unexpected. Could we meet to try and mediate a settlement, please?

I discussed the pros and cons with Matt. He agreed to give it a try. I could tell the Dyson findings had churned him up as the full extent of the cover up sunk in. The next few days were an emotional time for him with Lucy keeping him calm.

Not long afterwards I was sat face to face with Liz Grace and the head of BBC litigation, Nick Wilcox. Confidentiality restraints prevent me from going into any detail about the mediation other than to say we started in the morning and ended at midnight. When it finished, we had secured for Matt a very substantial sum in compensation and a public apology to him by the BBC.

It was something.

But money and sorry can't buy you back the career you should have had.

Chapter 28

Coming back for more helpings

After I announced I was now concentrating on writing over practising as a lawyer lots of people told me, "You can't just leave the stage like that!" "I'm now practising writing fiction" was scoffed at. Some wags asked, "So what's different to what you've been doing for years in your letters?"

And they were right. I couldn't let it go that easily.

Some cases you can't say no to and in the five years after I stopped being the go-to for *The Sun*, happily passing it on to my number two, Jeffrey Smele, I still got dragged back in when he was not around.

All these cases made massive headlines.

Two, Matt Wiessler and James Dyson and his companies (more of him later), I did from start to end which led to taunts from friends that my claim of Depp being my last big case was an outright fib (I pleaded guilty). Two others, for *The Sun*, were just cover for the absent Mr Smele, either because Jeff wasn't answering his phone (Matt Hancock) or he was jetting off to Vegas to attend a wedding (Huw Edwards). Both were to cause widespread public shock and dismay for all concerned.

* * *

I was at my writing desk, tapping out the storyline of my second novel *Cracking Hubris* (about a Cabinet Minister who indecently assaults his SPAD – shorthand for special advisor – and then injuncts the newspaper writing the story about it) when the call came in.

"We can't get hold of Jeff and it's an emergency. You need to come back in." It was an anxious sounding internal lawyer at *The Sun* calling early on a fine, midsummer evening in 2021, less than a year after I had stepped down from full time lawyering.

"Who and what?" I asked, my curiosity piqued.

"It's Matt Hancock," the slightly breathless lawyer blurted out.

Boris Johnson's bumptious Secretary of State for Health and Social Care, made famous by his appearances on TV and other media by his po-faced pronouncements during the pandemic, had been caught kissing and groping a senior official in his department.

I put my writing pen down and rubbed my eyes. Sometimes truth is stranger than fiction. As recent history has shown, politicians are notorious risk takers. This time it was one of Boris Johnson's most senior ministers; the Health Secretary no less had been caught breaking his own Covid rules, snogging someone else's wife.

And who was Gina Coladangelo? As everyone was soon to discover, she was Hancock's friend from their Oxford University days. And he had made her a non-executive director of the Department of Health and Social Care the previous autumn. Both parties had spouses unaware of their workplace affair. They also both had three children.

Alerted to the story earlier that day and asked for comment, the ball was firmly in the Health Secretary's court.

By mid-evening there was no word from Hancock. It was likely he was telling his family about the affair and trying to save his job, instead of fighting it out in court. The injunction team could be stood down as soon as the story went live. Metaphorically caught with his pants down by his own Department's CCTV images, he was a goner from that moment onwards despite initial attempts by him and his boss to resist the inevitable resignation letter. The double page spread headline in *The Sun* summed it up neatly: 'Steamy clinches in office as Covid raged on' with a photo of their embrace complete with Hancock's hand on Coladangelo's left buttock. Like Johnson not long afterwards, it was the rule breaking which broke him.

Undeterred by public opprobrium, especially after he went to his lover straight after breaking the news to his wife and children, Hancock went on to feature in but (thankfully) not win *I'm a Celebrity...Get Me Out of Here!*. It was shameless and his jovial demeanour must have stuck in the throat of so many victims of Covid and the millions who stuck by the rules. It spoke volumes about the integrity of the disgraced politician.

As I remarked later on to colleagues, satire was now well and truly dead.

* * *

I had agreed to be Jeff's holiday cover for three weeks. His last words to me before jetting off were, "I don't think anything much will happen whilst I'm away." This is the legal equivalent of football's commentators' curse, when a pundit exclaims the brilliance of a defender all game and seconds later said defender needlessly gives away a penalty.

Just as Jeff's plane was taking off for Vegas in July 2023, the newspaper decided to publish on its front page a story about Huw Edwards without naming or identifying him other than to say he was a prominent BBC personality. They had already written to him and asked for comment about his relationship with a teenager following a complaint by the teen's parents to *The Sun*.

He responded in the usual way. Letters came in from his high-powered law firm, threatening litigation.

I took the first call just after arriving to stay with friends for a blissful weekend by the sea.

I kept going off to remote corners to take the calls and coming back with a serious look, abandoning my Friday evening beer. "I thought you were giving up?" I was asked by my enquiring wife with a raised eyebrow.

I said, "Yeah but, no but..." And then the phone would ring again.

When I got back our hosts, one of whom is a communications expert, quizzed me on what and who the story was about. I had to stay schtum knowing that I was one of only a handful of people who knew at that point who it was about.

Every article about the story in *The Sun* made it clear that the newspaper was not going to identify the teen's gender or Edwards' identity (other than as a prominent BBC presenter) and set out the story of his grooming of the young person straight, including details of the financial payments. This aspect was both important and commendable.

The downside of not naming Edwards was that several days of frenzied speculation inevitably followed. The young person, through his lawyer, then claimed *The Sun*'s allegations were "rubbish" which heaped more attacks on the newspaper. Another pile-on, I thought. Little do they know the real picture.

Two days later, after various BBC individuals said, "Not me", Edwards' wife identified him, explaining he was suffering from mental health issues.

The newspaper based its story on interviews with the young person's mother and stepfather. It focused on the mother's concerns about the presenter's behaviour and funding a drug habit as several *Sun* articles explained. Despite reporting that the funding ran into tens of thousands of pounds, unfair criticism rained down on the paper. We gritted our teeth and quietly got on with gathering evidence.

Meanwhile the BBC was in full defensive mode, launching enquiries into what happened when the teen's parents complained to the BBC and were brushed away. Lots of judgement calls on what to present in the newspaper's defence were needed and taken. The problem was that we could not use the material we had at our disposal; instead, we hoped the BBC investigation would do its job properly to get to the bottom of it. Meanwhile several other media organisations and prominent journalists were intent on trashing *The Sun* for making it a story, ignoring the obvious public interest.

Later in July, I sent the BBC a dossier of witness statements from other people Edwards tried to get embroiled with. One was a bedazzled 17-year-old schoolboy, writing to the star who took a shine to the boy's photograph. Edwards then engaged in sending the youth love heart emojis and kisses at the end of messages. From what I could see, it was clear to me that Edwards favoured young people he liked the look of and ignored the rest.

In the end what brought him down was something unrelated: the receipt of indecent photographs of children, taken by sex abusers. Was it all part of his emotional make-up? I wondered whether Edwards' problems went back to his strict upbringing.

He escaped going to prison after pleading guilty. *The Sun* campaigned that the sentence was too lenient but the principle of parity of sentencing held sway. The man who had sent him the material had already been sentenced to 12 months imprisonment suspended for two years which meant, as a matter of consistency, Edwards as the lesser offender should not get more. His sentence was six months imprisonment suspended for 12 months.

The fall in his reputation and the loss of career was enough, argued many people, and he should therefore escape prison. What pleased me most was the young person who had claimed *The Sun*'s allegations were rubbish recanted and agreed he had been groomed by Edwards, confirming he was paid to send sexually explicit pictures of himself when he was a vulnerable teenager.

The journalism was sound and groundbreaking. It was total vindication of the newspaper's journalism. None of its critics were to be found regretting their words of support for the news presenter when he was convicted. None apologised for getting it wrong.

It was an important story and although the BBC apologised to the young person's parents for its treatment of them, the other whistle-blowers who came forward heard nothing about the outcome of that aspect of the Corporation's investigation.

My month back in the saddle came to an end when Jeff got back. I was happy to hand the reins back to him and get back to fiction. It had been an adrenaline rush, but I was fine with giving it up. My addiction was almost cured.

* * *

The case of James Dyson and the Dyson companies against ITN and Channel 4, defending Channel 4 News about the making of Dyson products in Malaysia, was to see me immersed back in the job, this time for two and a half years. I had to do it, I told my nearest and dearest as they gave me a puzzled look when I said, "Just one more case". "Look," I explained, "lose this and it's the end of serious documentaries and investigative reporting on TV for good. I can't pass it on." I felt I owed it to the brilliant news journalists I had worked with over the years as well as the ones in this case.

So, what was it that drew me back in, against all my inclinations – excuse the pun – not to get sucked back in? It was outrage, pure and simple. The idea that Sir James Dyson and his companies could successfully sue for what was a balanced news report about a set of allegations by workers who claimed poor working and living conditions in Malaysian factories working to the Dyson schedule. If Dyson could succeed with such a tenuous claim, then it was the end of times for me. News reporting would have to be so cautious it would be not only neutered but boring. It also felt like a form of SLAPP.

The workers who were suing through a well-known London law firm, Leigh Day, were entitled to have a news report explaining their allegations together with their solicitor who articulated what their recently launched High Court case was about. Channel 4 News and ITN, who make Channel 4's news output, did the responsible thing and allowed a lengthy interview by Dyson's spokesperson in Singapore to strongly deny any wrongdoing on the part of the Dyson entities.

Worse still, after the broadcast which went out on my birthday, 10 February, the solicitors – Schillings – also weighed in with a claim for the boss, Sir James Dyson.

I watched the 12-minute package on catch up and called John Battle, the indefatigable legal head of editorial at ITN. Dyson's primary complaint was that Channel 4 News had sided with the claimants in alleging Dyson were responsible for the conditions complained of. Bias, in other words, which harmed their reputation.

"This case must not be allowed to succeed," I told John and said I would gladly put together a legal team. "I'm sure we can see them off in a few weeks," I predicted. Wrongly.

Soon enough there were four of us – two solicitors and two counsel (later joined by a third) – working flat out with the three journalists who were responsible for the well-researched package which had taken months to put together.

I had worked with the head of the investigations team, Job Rabkin, before when John asked me to be on standby in case Cambridge Analytica tried to injunct another Channel 4 news report exposing their tactics. The now notorious company didn't try to (and eventually folded because of the exposé) and the team quietly stood down.

Initially Emma Linch was my number two who worked tirelessly on the case and later I was joined by Gordon Clough after Emma went on maternity leave. Both deserve huge credit for their work on this complex and difficult case. Together we battled against Schillings who were their usual verbose selves with hourly rates of up to a gob smacking £765.

The case featured a trip to the Court of Appeal after the High Court judge agreed with our application to strike out the English-based Dyson companies for lack of reference in the broadcast which was about Dyson operations in Asia. However, the Court of Appeal allowed the companies to stay in and progress the case.

'Reference' is an obscure but important aspect of libel law. For an individual (or company) to bring a claim they must be able to establish that the defamatory statement, directly or indirectly, identified or referred to them.

One part of our initial win was confirmed: Sir James Dyson had not been personally defamed in the broadcast so he could go away and just let his two companies battle it out with us.

In our preparations for the case we had seen he was keen on sending aggressive lawyers' letters to other publications to stop or reduce the impact of their reporting. His pre-action letters hadn't stopped Channel 4 News, and we found we were not alone. Dyson had also sued the *Daily Mirror* for an article which called him "the vacuum-cleaner tycoon who championed Vote Leave due to economic opportunities it would bring to British industry before moving his global head office to Singapore". The journalist continued: "Kids, talk the talk but then screw your country and if anyone complains, tell them to suck it up." The newspaper at trial defended the article as honest opinion and the judge found that not only did the opinion defence succeed but also the libel claim failed because it had not caused the entrepreneur any serious harm.

We quietly toasted the *Mirror*'s win over Christmas drinks and got down to the enormous task of defending the case now the reference point had been settled.

The next few months saw an enormous amount of work done by the solicitor, counsel and journalist team with a hugely important trip to Malaysia by one of the journalists to get evidence.

In the spring of 2024, we were finally ready. The defence was necessarily long: 180 pages and featured three main prongs; truth, responsible journalism and an attack on the notion that the two companies had been caused serious financial harm.

It was an exhausting exercise with the third counsel and Gordon working on it non-stop with the three tireless journalists.

The other side unsurprisingly asked, as they were entitled, for the supporting evidence referred to in the defence which we supplied. They then got a couple of time extensions to formulate their Reply, which invariably follows after a defence is filed in libel cases.

The Reply was due on the Friday before the August bank holiday. Just about every litigation lawyer is on holiday that weekend, including me. It was a baking hot afternoon in Cyprus and I was waiting to receive a massive tome in response on my laptop when instead I heard the ping of a text message. It was from a colleague who was 'babysitting' the case for me and Gordon back at the office.

'SCHILLINGS LETTER JUST IN – THEY'VE DISCONTINUED.'

I let out a "WHAT?!" and rang my colleague back. He explained the letter was in my inbox and I quickly read it. They had caved in completely, telling the court of their two clients' discontinuance ostensibly to focus on the Leigh Day claimants. I rang John and we laughed a lot before getting down to any serious talk. Afterwards I went for a long swim and drank an ouzo or two to toast absent friends: the team had won it. Not one single individual: everyone had played their part including heroic confidential sources back in Malaysia who had provided us with the gold dust including revelatory documents and crucial information to help fill gaps in our knowledge.

Victory was sweet but the addiction was over.

It was to be my very last litigation case. I never expected it to last two and a half years.

Job and his colleagues Lee Sorrell and Ed Howker were entirely vindicated, and TV News and current affairs were no longer in jeopardy. I could resume what little legal advice work I was doing and go back to writing. Nowadays I stick to advice work for clients although when I get a call about a new case, the buzz is still there.

Chapter 29

Media law: where are we now?

This book isn't intended to throw light on the contemporary scene and gaze into the future. There are plenty of commentators around voicing their views about whether the balance between claimants and defendants is well struck. In reputation terms, libel is no longer on its own. Nowadays privacy and data protection claims are the latest weapons being deployed by claimants either in a pre-emptory sense before publication/transmission or afterwards, to salvage a damaged reputation. A good example of the latter is Cliff Richards' privacy case against the BBC. This is because the reforms in the 2013 Defamation Act rightly tightened up the areas which concerned defendants, especially around cases which were relatively trivial, many years old or unworthy of being heard here because the claimant's reputation was not in this country.

Privacy is still a growth area, and I expect that to continue.

I have two bugbears which I am always happy to sound off about, albeit briefly.

The first is about cost. You only need to look at reports about the exorbitant costs generated in the *Rebecca Vardy v Colleen Rooney* spat to see a case straight out of *Footballer's Wives* featuring WhatsApp messages and tabloid stories. The costs bill of just under £2 million for the winning defendant was obscene. Even if a costs judge takes an axe to it there will still be more than a million to pay. The case is about tittle tattle between a group of friends, not a complex history of political intrigue or police corruption.

Some media lawyers have got greedy. And they are driving up the costs.

If I was Secretary of State for Justice, I would impose a costs ceiling which would allow lots more trials to be fought without the fear of bankruptcy and financial ruin for the losing claimant and, on the defendant side, allow the publisher to fight cases without a costs risk which amounts to a form of financial blackmail.

My second beef is the freedom of journalists to do their work without fear of harassment, imprisonment and attack. Every year the Committee to Protect Journalists publishes an annual report. The figures get worse year by year. The recent killing of journalists in Gaza has resulted in the highest ever number of fatalities. Journalism is vital which is why journalists are targeted so often, and freedom of expression is under attack.

At the very least, it should be a war crime to target journalists. There are many brave journalists all around the world which is increasingly being taken over by oligarchs and tyrants.

I will leave it there, step off my soap box and get back to writing fiction.

Acknowledgements

I wish to acknowledge and thank several people in helping me with this book.

First and foremost are my former clients who generously agreed to allow their stories to be told and encouraged me to complete it. In particular I want to thank Michael Gillard, Hikmet Tabak and Helen Boaden for their support and continuing friendship. Thanks too go to Chris Atkins for the original spark to write this memoir.

I want to thank my editor, Helen Lacey, for her support, expertise and dedication to bringing this to print. I also want to thank David Chaplin at Bath Publishing and my agent, Sonia Land, for taking me on. Thanks also go to Clare Hoban, Katie Read, Lucy Fawcett and Hannah-Louise Shergold.

My friends Kevin Sutcliffe, Gem Stafford, Martin Soames, Anna Savva, Don Eachells and Adam Szreter have all been a huge source of encouragement in my writing endeavours now and in the past, generously giving their time. Author Richard T Kelly and the Faber writing gang of 2020 as well as the 2003 St Cere writers' group have been sources of inspiration and help.

Lastly, I want to express my gratitude to wonderful colleagues at Simons Muirhead Burton especially Mel Matheson and Chloe Gunn, the best PAs any lawyer could wish for. The partnership, led by Razi Mireskandari, gave me the freedom to develop and put together the great media disputes team, especially Jeffrey Smele, Gordon Clough, Emma Linch and Enfys Jenkins. Special mention goes to Simon Goldberg for his support and the initial introduction to Bath Publishing through their joint struggles for the Post Office subpostmasters to get justice.

The art of storytelling comes from the tradition of the spoken word. I learnt it from my dear mum and have her to thank. Always.

Index